TYPOGRAPHY NOW TWO

imfhfnginr

# TYPOGRAPHY NOW TWO

EDITED BY RICK POYNOR

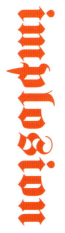

implosion

First published in 1996
First published in paperback in 1998
by Booth-Clibborn Editions
12 Percy Street, London W1P 9FB

Copyright © 1996 Rick Poynor

ISBN 1 86154 023 X

Published and distributed in the United Kingdom

Worldwide direct mail rights:
Internos Books
12 Percy Street
London W1P 9FB
England

Trade distributors for the rest of the world:
Hearst Books International

Trade distributors in the USA:
F & W Publications Inc.

Printed and bound in Hong Kong by Dai Nippon Printing Co.

EDITOR, COMPILER AND WRITER     RICK POYNOR

ASSISTANT EDITOR     EMILY KING

ART DIRECTORS     JONATHAN BARNBROOK

STEPHEN COATES

COVER, INTRODUCTION AND

DIVIDER PAGE DESIGN     JONATHAN BARNBROOK

PAGE DESIGN     JASON BEARD

## Sources for divider page quotations

### PAGES 16/17

John Plunkett
"Plugged in"
*Metropolis*, October 1994

Joshua Berger
"Regarding the design, typography
and legibility of this publication"
*Plazm* no. 6, 1994

Tobias Frere-Jones
"Towards the cause of grunge"
*Zed* no. 1, 1994

Rudy VanderLans
"Radical commodities"
*Emigre* no. 34, Spring 1995

Jan van Toorn
*Thinking design: issues
in culture and values*
Western Carolina University, 1993

### PAGES 78/79

P. Scott Makela
quoted in Michael Rock
"P. Scott Makela is wired"
*Eye* no. 12 vol. 3, 1994

Katherine McCoy
interviewed by Rick Poynor
*Eye* no. 16 vol. 4, 1995

Jonathan Barnbrook
interviewed by Rick Poynor
*Eye* no. 15 vol. 4, 1994

### PAGES 106/107

Edward Fella
letter to Rick Poynor, 1995

Lorraine Wild
quoted in Anne Burdick
"A sense of rupture"
*Eye* no. 14 vol. 4, 1994

Louise Sandhaus
"An introduction from the
designer of this journal"
*Errant Bodies*, Winter 1994

J. Abbott Miller,
"Must books be ugly, too?"
*AIGA Journal of Graphic Design*
vol. 11 no. 2, 1993

### PAGES 182/183

Brian Schorn
letter to Rick Poynor, 1995

Michael Worthington
*Hypertype*, featured on California
Institute of the Arts' 25th
Anniversary CD-ROM, 1995

Jeffery Keedy
*Fast Forward*
California Institute of the Arts, 1993

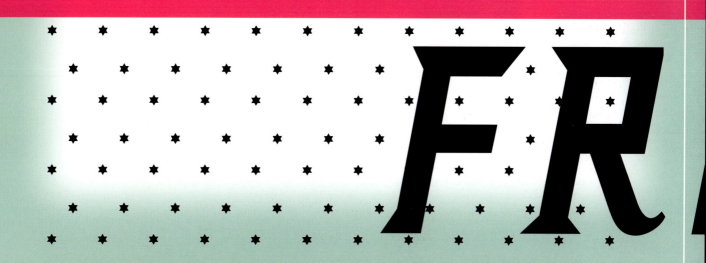

**The five years that have passed since first publication of this book's predecessor,** *Typography Now: The Next Wave,*

**have seen the mainstreaming of experimental approaches to typography**

that were until quite recently much more likely to be identified with "hothouse" design schools, or obscure arts journals with tiny circulations, than with the contents of the commercial break or the newsstand magazine. In 1991, when *Typography Now* was in preparation, such work, even within the design community, seemed to be a minority taste. Interesting as it was to observers like myself, it still came as a genuine surprise that a publisher was prepared to put out a book that concentrated – to the exclusion of all other forms of typography – on what many regarded as a wholly ignorable lunatic fringe.

**BY RICK POYNOR**

# EEZING

¶*Typography Now Two*'s purpose is therefore both different from the first book's, and the same. It is different in the sense that, while I hope the book contains many unfamiliar examples, work of this kind is by now sufficiently familiar as a genre, even to those who still don't like it, not to require any special introduction (explanation is another matter). Whether it is seen as a regrettable fad that will eventually pass when the deluded finally see sense, or as an established and legitimate design method with plenty of remaining potential, **the "new typography" can no longer be said to be especially shocking – within the design profession, at least – or even particularly new. And, like any cultural form that sets out to kick over the traces, only to find itself applauded for the effort, its less thoughtful manifestations are subject to the law of diminishing returns.**

¶What *Typography Now Two* does share with its predecessor is a documentary intention. Enough time has elapsed for significant developments to have occurred and this book attempts to chart them. One of the most immediate differences in putting it together was the sheer volume of material to choose from five years on. The first wave of experimentally inclined typographers, whose careers began in the 1980s or earlier, have been joined in the 1990s by countless others inspired by their example. Designers who were undergraduates in 1991 now have work experience or second degrees behind them. The effect of earlier influences is noticeable at an institution such as London's Royal College of Art. It wasn't until the college's 1995 degree show that a marked sense of engagement with typographic concerns dating back anything from five to ten years in the United States surfaced across the body of student work. To give a sense of where typography may be heading in the next few years, this book looks at postgraduate work from the Royal College of Art, Cranbrook Academy of Art and, perhaps the most significant centre of new typography in the 1990s, California Institute of the Arts.

Press advertisement
Designer: Geof McFetridge
Client: California Institute of the Arts
USA, 1994-95

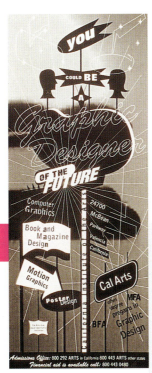

Student project on the
Kennedy assassination
Designer: Carlo Tartaglia
Royal College of Art
Great Britain, 1995

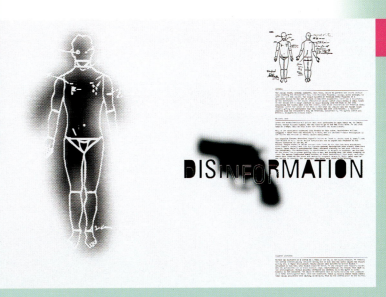

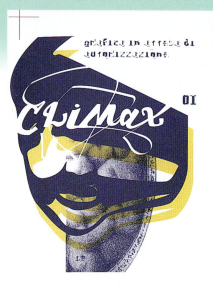

¶Given the international dimension and scale of these developments (which are still under way) no claims to definitiveness can be made for a collection of this size. *Typography Now Two* aims instead to give a selective but representative account of the experimental typography that characterised the period and a picture of some of the key ideas that accompanied it. The book shows significant minor projects that have a particular story to tell, or simply deserve to be better known, alongside more familiar examples, such as *Emigre* or *Raygun*, which must, by any reckoning, be regarded as central to typographic change in the 1990s.

¶**These changes have not been accomplished without loud cries of pain from some sections of the design community.**

Even as the first *Typography Now* was going to press, Massimo Vignelli was publicly blasting *Emigre* as a "factory of garbage". "That is a national calamity. It's not a freedom of culture, it's an aberration of culture . . . They show no responsibility. It's just like freaking out, in a sense. The kind of expansion of the mind that they're doing is totally uncultural."[1] Two years later, Paul Rand pitched in against "indecipherable, zany typography; tiny type with miles of leading; text in all caps (despite indisputable proof that lowercase letters are more readable, less formal, and friendlier); ubiquitous letterspacing; visually annotated typography; revivalist caps and small caps; pseudo Dada and Futurist collages; and whatever 'special effects' a computer makes possible."[2]

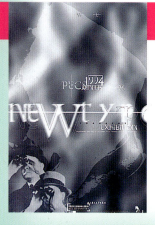

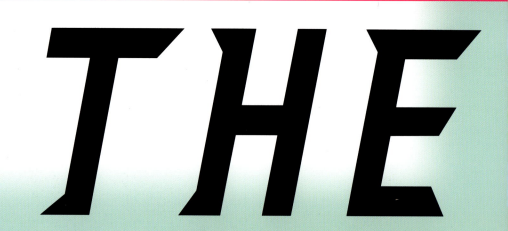

THE

¶If that didn't seem to leave many options open to the would-be typographic rebel, New York art director Henry Wolf was even more specific. He singled out a particular offender for detailed stylistic rebuttal, P. Scott Makela's *Living Surfaces* poster (reproduced on page 97), doubting "that history will repeat itself here".[3] But the most sustained and incisive attack on the perceived excesses of the new typography came from Steven Heller in his now notorious essay "Cult of the ugly". Heller's polemic triggered a fusillade of angry letters from supporters of typographic experimentation on both sides of the Atlantic and inspired an issue of *Emigre* (taken to task in the essay) devoted to probing Heller, eliciting the responses of some of those he had criticised, and clearing up what the magazine believed to be a misunderstanding of the purpose and context of the new design.[4]

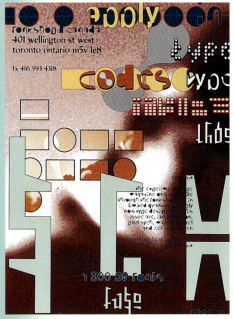

Advertisement in *Blur* magazine
Designer: Scott Clum
Client: FontShop Canada
USA, 1993

**¶The irony of these attacks was that it was already too late. While conservative critics focused on work produced within the insulated sanctum of the academy, or aimed at other designers, hotly contesting its relevance to the "real world", the genie of typographic inspiration (or vandalism, depending on your point of view) was already at large in the culture.** The first issue of *Raygun*, art directed by David Carson, appeared in November 1992 and the magazine's immediate North American impact and rapport with its young readership helped to confirm and consolidate advertising and communication trends that had been gathering momentum since the 1980s. *Raygun*'s pyrotechnic type treatments, much like those of *The Face* ten years earlier, appeared to offer a fail-safe set of graphic codes for reaching a generation – "Generation X", as the novelist Douglas Coupland dubbed it – increasingly unmotivated by conventional means of address.

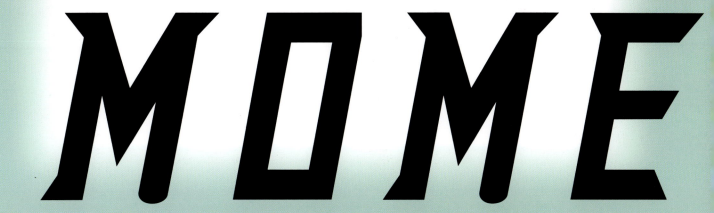

MOME

¶The difference, this time round, was that the advertising agencies did not dilute the message by making their own pale copies, as they had with Neville Brody's work in the mid-1980s. They bought the product straight from source. Nike's US agency, Wieden & Kennedy, was one of the first to set a premium on fashionable type by calling in Brody himself to help sell training shoes in 1988. In Europe, in the 1990s, Nike has commissioned type-led campaigns by Why Not Associates, David Carson and the London-based multidisciplinary team Tomato. Robert Nakata, a Cranbrook Academy of Art-educated typographer known for boldly experimental projects at Studio Dumbar, left the Hague-based company to join Wieden & Kennedy's Amsterdam office, where he has created print campaigns for Nike and Microsoft. **At the same time, designers of high-impact type effects have forged an emotive new genre of ambient typography in their contributions to television commercials, pop promos and other moving-image projects, initially as typographers, but increasingly as directors, too.**

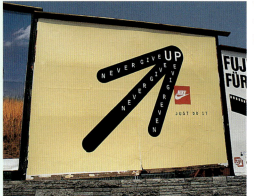

Outdoor brand campaign
Designer: Robert Nakata
Agency: Wieden & Kennedy
Client: Nike Europe
The Netherlands, 1992

Video for the song "Cowgirl"
Directors: Graham Wood, Robert Shackleton
Design company: Tomato
Client: Underworld
Great Britain, 1993

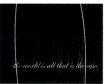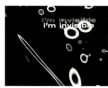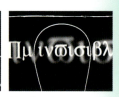

In Britain, Tomato, Why Not Associates and Jonathan Barnbrook probably have the highest profile; David Carson, Barry Deck and P. Scott Makela are perhaps the most strongly identified with the movement in the United States.

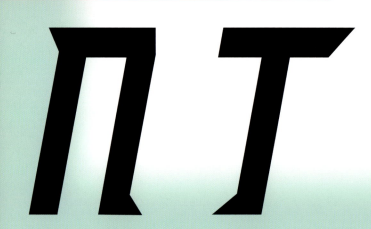

**¶Type and typography are receiving more public attention in 1996 than at any previous time.** The worldwide explosion, in the wake of Emigre Fonts, of small independent type foundries firing off little catalogues offering faces made with Fontographer that run the gamut from sublime to ridiculous has helped to put typographic design on the media map. David Carson is probably the only graphic designer at this point whose celebrity can command television coverage or a profile in *Newsweek*, but it is still not uncommon in the 1990s for *Esquire* to run an article on the grunge font phenomenon, for *Wired* to profile type designers Barry Deck and Jonathan Hoefler, or for a newspaper such as the *Chicago Tribune* to take a long, hard look at local goings-on in the typographic undergrowth – which led it to conclude, with laudable balance, that "New fonts have something to say, even if you can't always read them."[5]

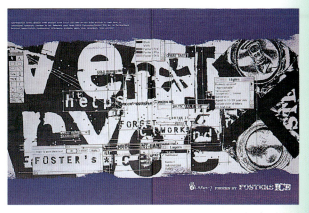

Press advertisement for Foster's Ice beer
Designer: Cornel Windlin
Creative director: Ian Swift
Client: Scottish Courage
Great Britain, 1996

¶A telling instance of the emerging media belief that typography and the people who produce it are interesting to non-designers (or ought to be) came in a recent advertisement designed by Cornel Windlin for Foster's Ice beer. The double-page ad, a fractured collage of broken type and Macintosh screen commands, appears to mock its own claim to offer – in its own words – a "subversive appeal to 18-24 year olds". The ironic foregrounding of the usually hidden marketing and design thinking that underpins the ad is reinforced by the panel of copy at the top: "Typo-anarchist Cornel Windlin comes straight outta Zurich with some serious Swiss attitude to wreak havoc on conventional typography wherever he can." This is followed by a list of the materials and technology used by Windlin to create the image.

¶There is something quite poignant about an ad which employs the typographic signifiers of "subversion" to acknowledge its own complicity in the commercial process. But the ad's very knowingness poses larger questions about the purpose, within the commercial arena, of "experimental" or "radical" design. If the aim of the new typographers working within advertising (apart from making some money) is to enlarge the available repertoire of visual languages and shake off the design profession's last few remaining rules and constraints, then the battle appears to have been won.

# Aesthetically, almost anything is possible now.

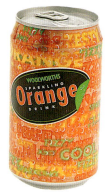

Soft drink can
Design company: Reed Design
Client: Woolworths
Great Britain, 1995

*But the question remains:* **what exactly, in broader communication terms, is the new typography for?**

Advertisers might reply that the new advertising is open-ended, that viewers are free to pursue their own private associations and make of it what they like. But this apparent openness is merely a means to an end, and this end, not unreasonably, is the same as it ever was: *buy our product.* The Foster's ad tries to achieve it with a double bluff: "Look, we're being 'subversive' and we know you know it's a pose – we're OK." But the only small option for subversion, however original the design, is also the same as it ever was:

## savour the aesthetics by all means, but don't buy the product.

¶If radical typography's purpose amounts to nothing more challenging than a new way to shift the goods – and amuse the designer in the process – it is destined to last only as long as it continues to intrigue the consumer. Within the cultural arena, too, experimental typography faces similar pressing questions of purpose. In hard communication terms, leaving aside the deconstructionist theory, which few typographers can be said truly to understand, what is it for? Exciting as it may be to look at, does it represent a functional improvement on more conventional ways of delivering the same essential message? It is easy to justify extreme manipulations of small quantities of text in a poster or a television commercial when the emotion of the message is as important as what the words have to say and, historically, designers have always sought to achieve a balance between typographic legibility and the need for expression.

¶But longer texts for continuous reading pose more demanding problems of interpretation for the typographer. In 30 issues of *Raygun*, David Carson and his design assistants pulled text typography as far from convention as it has ever been taken in a mass-market publication. Carson argued that his intention was to encourage reluctant MTV-generation readers to read, and they wrote to the magazine in droves to say that they liked the approach. Other American designers advanced similar arguments. "Television has conditioned everyone at being very good at discerning what an image is and 'getting' it within a few frames," explained Rick Valicenti. "If you don't like it, you hit the remote control. So print, quite often, does the same thing: it freezes a moment where a lot of things are happening to provide an impression. People can either stay there and engage the interesting aspects, or turn the page."[6]

Spread from *Raygun* no. 14
Designer: Rodney Shelden Fehsenfeld
Art director: David Carson
Client: Ray Gun Publishing
USA, 1994

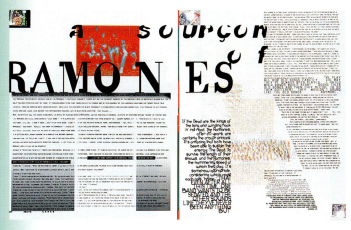

¶While such claims rapidly became almost axiomatic in some sections of the design world, they remain entirely untested in any rigorous sense of the word. What impact do such typographic strategies have on reading speed and comprehension?

# Is it really the case that a text that is typographically demanding to read is more memorable once deciphered?

And how much previous commitment to the subject matter do you need to even want to begin to decipher it?

¶There are certainly many who question the need for designers to intervene so deterministically in the reading process. **Reading, argues British information designer Paul Stiff, is a highly complex, far from passive set of activities, operating on many levels. "When people read," he notes, "they make strategic choices, constantly generating inferences and hypotheses – about intention, relevance, tone of voice, and so on."[7]**

American critic Marc Treib points out that an over-activated text is "like getting a book that is already underlined, and if you have some idiot who is marking phrases that are unimportant in terms of your reading of the book, it's something you have to overcome to get back to the original message."[8] In an issue of the *American Center for Design Journal*, published in 1994, the designers' typographic interpretation of an article, based on footprint shapes, became a source of public bad feeling expressed in a special note tacked on to the article itself by the writers: "As authors, we feel compelled to state our objections to the layout . . . First, we believe that setting the text in the shape of footprints compromises legibility and discourages people from reading . . . Second, while our article compares dancing to interdisciplinary collaboration, dance is a metaphor and not the true subject of the article."[9]

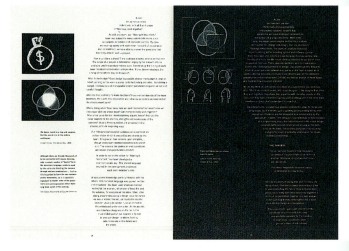

Spread from *American Center for Design Journal* vol. 8 no. 1
Design company: Tanagram
Client: American Center for Design
USA, 1994

Project from *Zed* no. 2
"Selected notes to ZeitGuys"
Designer: Bob Aufuldish
Writer: Mark Bartlett
Client: Virginia Commonwealth University
USA, 1995

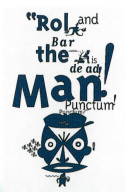

¶If a clash such as this, within a journal publicly committed to design as a "form of authorship", suggests there is some way to go before designers and writers routinely coexist in a state of happy interaction, *Typography Now Two* shows that such collaboration can sometimes be achieved. *Emigre*, though it has the self-referential advantage of being a publication about design, continues to offer a model for a typographic articulation of text achieved in a way that is engagingly expressive, genuinely functional and a lasting contribution to practical research. The design journals *Form + Zweck* and *Zed*, publications very much in the *Emigre* tradition, also exhibit a high degree of thoughtfulness in their exploration of the experimental interface of writing and design.

¶In publishing's mainstream, such approaches are still not as common as their academic and advertising impact might lead one to expect, perhaps because the traditional hierarchies and divisions of responsibility are much slower to shift than in small independent publications. *Raygun* aside, *Wired* is perhaps the most striking example of a newsstand publication which attempts to meld typography and image in the service of an editorial vision. *Wired*'s pre-contents introductory pages are "advertisements", inspired by the books of Marshall McLuhan and Quentin Fiore, for key techno-cultural ideas from the heart of the magazine, conceived and realised at journalistic speed in scintillating verbal and visual metaphors for the fluid information transfers of the digital realm.

¶It is too early to say whether the liquid condition of the emerging screen-based typography – see Michael Worthington's *Hypertype* project on page 218 – will have a lasting reciprocal influence on the typography of the paper realm. Print will continue to exist for the foreseeable future, though, and it seems likely that many of the experimental approaches gathered here will become permanent features of typographic practice. More than anything, the picture that emerges from *Typography Now Two* is one of flux and transition. **The implosion of traditional typography may, like a sloughed skin, be a sign of renewal, or it may prove to have been a marker of millennial anxiety, profound uncertainty in an accelerating culture, perhaps even long-term decline.** That is for future historians to decide. What can be said with some certainty is that the mutations of typography in the 1990s reflect a deep scepticism about received wisdom and a questioning of established authorities, traditional practices and fixed cultural identities, which has parallels throughout society. They tell us a great deal about the increasing value we place, as a culture, in the mediating power of typography as an interpreter of the reality we inhabit. They encapsulate the moment while also, in the largest sense, being wholly of their time.

Spread from *Wired* no. 2.08
Creative director: John Plunkett
Designers: John Plunkett, Eric Adigard
Design company: Plunkett + Kuhr
Client: Wired Ventures
USA, 1994

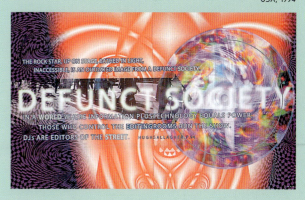

THE ROCK STAR, UP ON STAGE, BATHED IN LIGHT, INACCESSIBLE, IS AN OUTDATED IMAGE FROM A DEFUNCT SOCIETY.

DEFUNCT SOCIETY

IN A WORLD WHERE INFORMATION PLUS TECHNOLOGY EQUALS POWER, THOSE WHO CONTROL THE EDITINGROOMS RUN THE SHOW. DJs ARE EDITORS OF THE STREET. HUGH GALLAGHER '94

Subscription card for *Now Time* magazine
Designer: Edward Fella
Client: A.R.T. Press
USA, 1993

1  "Massimo Vignelli vs. Ed Benguiat (sort of)", *Print* XLV:V, September/October 1991.

2  Paul Rand, "From Cassandre to chaos" in *Design, Form and Chaos*, Yale University Press, New Haven and London, 1993.

3  Henry Wolf, "The view of a curmudgeon, junior grade", *AIGA Journal of Graphic Design*, vol. 11 no. 4, 1993.

4  Steven Heller, "Cult of the ugly", *Eye* no. 9 vol. 3, 1993. *Emigre* no. 30, "Fallout", Spring 1994. The "fallout" continued up to the time of writing. In 1996, a digital type foundry, Beaufonts, based in Manchester, England, published a brochure, *Beaufonts 1, Excess Baggage*, containing a text that wittily mangles the words of Heller's original essay to make a perverse kind of (non)sense.

5  Hugh Hart, "It takes all types", *Chicago Tribune*, 2 June 1995.

6  Quoted in Hugh Hart, *Chicago Tribune*.

7  Paul Stiff, "Stop sitting around and start reading", *Eye* no. 11 vol. 3, 1993.

8  Quoted in Michael Dooley, "Kicking up a little dust" in Michael Bierut, William Drenttel, Steven Heller & D. K. Holland (eds.), *Looking Closer: Critical Writings on Graphic Design*, Allworth Press, New York, 1994.

9  Lauralee Alben and Jim Faris, "The interdisciplinary dance (shall we?)", *American Center for Design Journal*, "Interact", vol. 8 no. 1, 1994.

We're page malleable the tech,

trying to nature eerie hand-

to represent of "perfection" made

create its the of imagery

visual opposite: Net. computer- ...

metaphors the We're generated high

on a electronic, equally images tech/

static, nonlinear, interested and high

printed infinitely in low- touch".

John Plunkett

SOME READERS MAY CHOOSE TO INTERPRET A LAYOUT AS BEING UNREADABLE; AS HAVING CROSSED THAT LINE BETWEEN FORM AND FUNCTION. THE QUESTION IS: IF WE DIDN'T EXPERIMENT, IF WE SET ALL OUR TYPE IN A THREE COLUMN GRID, WOULD YOU EVEN BE INTERESTED? PROBABLY NOT. THE CLEAN GRID OF MODERNITY HAS BEEN FORMALLY REJECTED BY THE NIHILISM OF INDUSTRIAL YOUTH CULTURE. Joshua Berger

SALES

The new ability has become the new aesthetic ... Like the arabesques of the 1880s and the swashes of the 1970s, the contortions of the 1990s will fall out of favour, but not before showing us what the new tools can do.

Tobias Frere-Jones

CLEAN GRID OF MODERNITY

Massimo Vignelli

commercial

Instead of always looking at it from the point of view that mass consumption is a bad thing, and anything assisting it is guilty by association, perhaps a bit of credit is due to the mainstream for taking some risks, and to the avant-garde for infiltrating mainstream culture ... I'm not saying that the avant-garde exists simply to supply the commercial world with the means to sell more products, but I do think it can be beneficial for both to occasionally share ideologies.

Rudy VanderLans

THE POWER OF CAPITALIST CULTURE TO COMMODIFY AND CONTROL HAS DISPERSED THE DESIGNER'S FORMS AND INSTRUMENTS OF CRITICISM AND MADE THEM HARMLESS IN THE DAZZLING SPECTACLE ...

JAN VAN TOORN

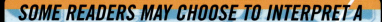

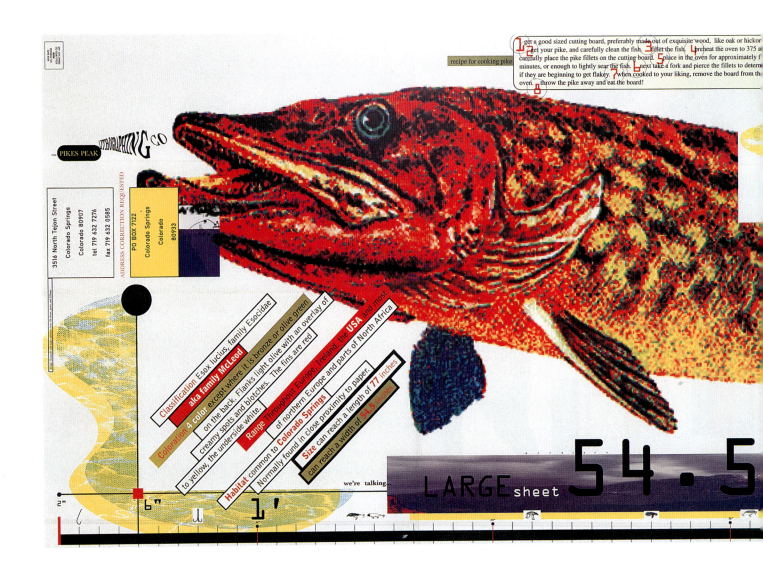

recipe for cooking pike

1. get a good sized cutting board, preferably made out of exquisite wood, like oak or hickory. 2. get your pike, and carefully clean the fish. 3. fillet the fish. 4. preheat the oven to 375 a... carefully place the pike fillets on the cutting board. 5. place in the oven for approximately f... minutes, or enough to lightly sear the fish. 6. next take a fork and pierce the fillets to determ... if they are beginning to get flakey. 7. when cooked to your liking, remove the board from th... oven. 8. throw the pike away and eat the board!

THE PIKES PEAK LITHOGRAPHING CO

3516 North Tejon Street
Colorado Springs
Colorado 80907
tel 719 632 7276
fax 719 632 0585

ADDRESS CORRECTION REQUESTED

PO BOX 7122
Colorado Springs
Colorado
80933

Classification Esox lucius, family Esocidae
aka family McLeod
Coloration 4 color except where it is bronze or olive green on the back. Flanks light olive with an overlay of creamy spots and blotches. The fins are red to yellow, the underside white.
Range Throughout Europe, Ireland, the USA and most of northern Europe and parts of North Africa
Habitat common to Colorado Springs. Normally found in close proximity to paper.
Size can reach a length of 77 inches can reach a width of 54.5 inches

we're talking...

LARGE sheet 54.5

2"    6"    1'

Promotional poster for a large-sheet printer
*DESIGNER/ILLUSTRATOR* April Greiman
*PRINCIPAL TYPEFACES* Baskerville, DIN Mittelschrift, OCRA, Bell Gothic
*CLIENT* Pikes Peak Lithographing

*USA, 1994*

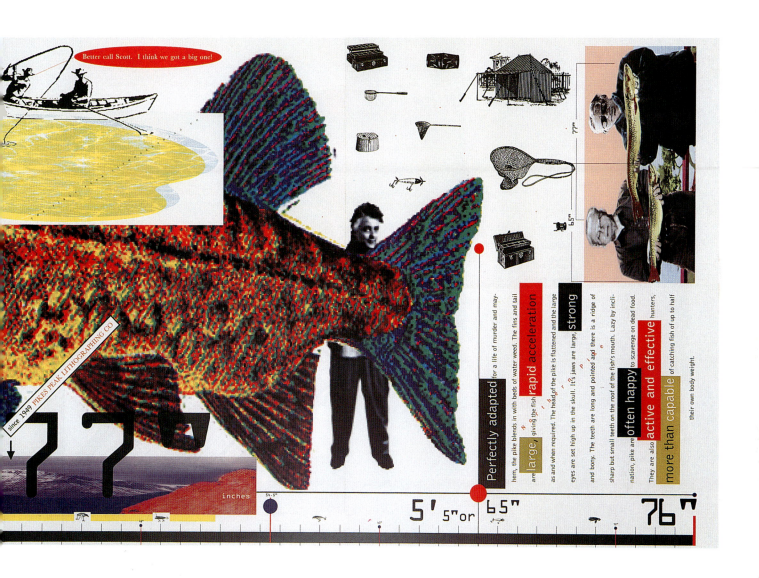

Better call Scott.  I think we got a big one!

since 1949 PIKES PEAK LITHOGRAPHING CO

**Perfectly adapted** for a life of murder and may-hem, the pike blends in with beds of water weed. The fins and tail are **large**, giving the fish **rapid acceleration** as and when required. The head of the pike is flattened and the large eyes are set high up in the skull. It's jaws are large, **strong** and bony. The teeth are long and pointed and there is a ridge of sharp but small teeth on the roof of the fish's mouth. Lazy by incli-nation, pike are **often happy** to scavenge on dead food. They are also **active and effective** hunters, **more than capable** of catching fish of up to half their own body weight.

inches    54.5"    5' 5"or 65"    76"

77"    65"

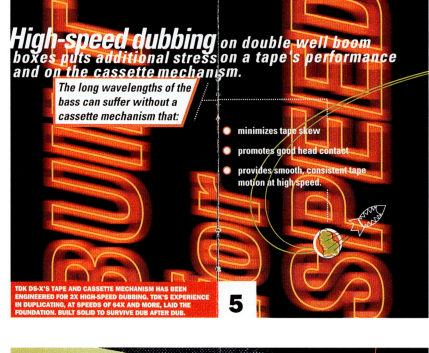

**High-speed dubbing** *on double well boom boxes puts additional stress on a tape's performance and on the cassette mechanism.*

The long wavelengths of the bass can suffer without a cassette mechanism that:

- minimizes tape skew
- promotes good head contact
- provides smooth, consistent tape motion at high speed.

TDK DS-X'S TAPE AND CASSETTE MECHANISM HAS BEEN ENGINEERED FOR 2X HIGH-SPEED DUBBING. TDK'S EXPERIENCE IN DUPLICATING, AT SPEEDS OF 64X AND MORE, LAID THE FOUNDATION. BUILT SOLID TO SURVIVE DUB AFTER DUB.

**5**

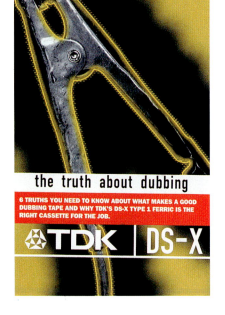

**the truth about dubbing**

6 TRUTHS YOU NEED TO KNOW ABOUT WHAT MAKES A GOOD DUBBING TAPE AND WHY TDK'S DS-X TYPE 1 FERRIC IS THE RIGHT CASSETTE FOR THE JOB.

**◈TDK | DS-X**

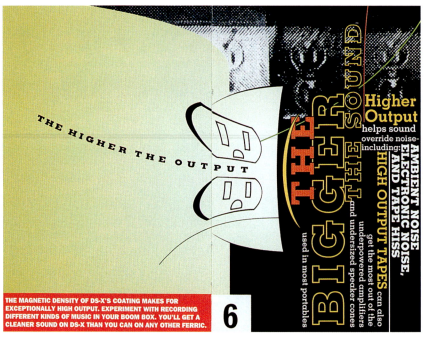

THE HIGHER THE OUTPUT

**THE BIGGER THE SOUND**

**Higher Output** helps sound override noise-including:

**AMBIENT NOISE ELECTRONIC NOISE, AND TAPE HISS**

**HIGH OUTPUT TAPES** can also get the most out of the underpowered amplifiers and undersized speaker cones used in most portables

THE MAGNETIC DENSITY OF DS-X'S COATING MAKES FOR EXCEPTIONALLY HIGH OUTPUT. EXPERIMENT WITH RECORDING DIFFERENT KINDS OF MUSIC IN YOUR BOOM BOX. YOU'LL GET A CLEANER SOUND ON DS-X THAN YOU CAN ON ANY OTHER FERRIC.

**6**

**The Truth Series**

Promotional mailers

ART DIRECTOR / Steve Farrar
DESIGNERS / Kirk James, Andrew Szurley, Richard Curren
DESIGN COMPANY / Jager Di Paola Kemp Design
PRINCIPAL TYPEFACES / Franklin Gothic, DIN
CLIENT / TDK

USA, 1993-94

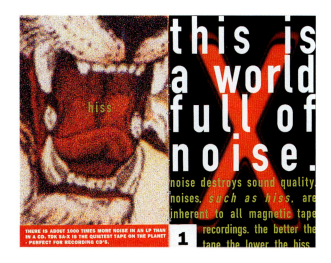

**this is a world full of noise.**

noise destroys sound quality. noises, *such as hiss,* are inherent to all magnetic tape recordings. the better the tape the lower the hiss.

hiss

THERE IS ABOUT 1000 TIMES MORE NOISE IN AN LP THAN IN A CD. TDK SA-X IS THE QUIETEST TAPE ON THE PLANET - PERFECT FOR RECORDING CD'S.

**1**

Team TDK is a progamme developed to deliver product information, services and merchandising tools to the sales forces of music and audio stores. Each of the three mailers contained a blank cassette and a cassette-sized educational booklet aimed at design-aware retail managers and sales people. By keeping copy short and direct and reinforcing it with dynamic conceptual imagery, the designers hoped to make information easier to absorb and recall.

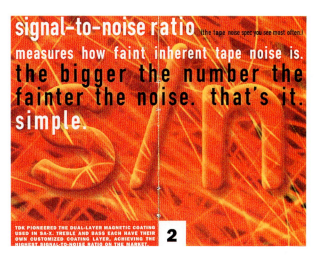

**signal-to-noise ratio** (the tape noise spec you see most often.) measures how faint inherent tape noise is. **the bigger the number the fainter the noise. that's it. simple.**

s/n

TDK PIONEERED THE DUAL-LAYER MAGNETIC COATING USED IN SA-X. TREBLE AND BASS EACH HAVE THEIR OWN CUSTOMIZED COATING LAYER, ACHIEVING THE HIGHEST SIGNAL-TO-NOISE RATIO ON THE MARKET.

**2**

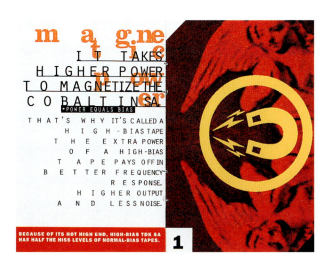

**magnetize**

IT TAKES HIGHER POWER TO MAGNETIZE THE COBALT IN SA
*POWER EQUALS BIAS*
THAT'S WHY IT'S CALLED A HIGH-BIAS TAPE THE EXTRA POWER OF A HIGH-BIAS TAPE PAYS OFF IN BETTER FREQUENCY RESPONSE, HIGHER OUTPUT AND LESS NOISE.

BECAUSE OF ITS HOT HIGH END, HIGH-BIAS TDK SA HAS HALF THE HISS LEVELS OF NORMAL-BIAS TAPES.

**1**

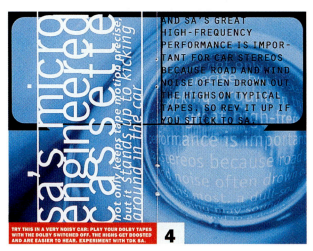

**sa's micro engineered cassette** not only keeps tape motion precise, but it stands up to kicking around in the car

AND SA'S GREAT HIGH-FREQUENCY PERFORMANCE IS IMPORTANT FOR CAR STEREOS BECAUSE ROAD AND WIND NOISE OFTEN DROWN OUT THE HIGHS ON TYPICAL TAPES. SO REV IT UP IF YOU STICK TO SA.

TRY THIS IN A VERY NOISY CAR: PLAY YOUR DOLBY TAPES WITH THE DOLBY SWITCHED OFF. THE HIGHS GET BOOSTED AND ARE EASIER TO HEAR. EXPERIMENT WITH TDK SA.

**4**

Electronic Telegraph

Information sheet for online newspaper
DESIGNER Carlo Tartaglia
PRINCIPAL TYPEFACE Helvetica
CLIENT The Telegraph

Great Britain, 1995

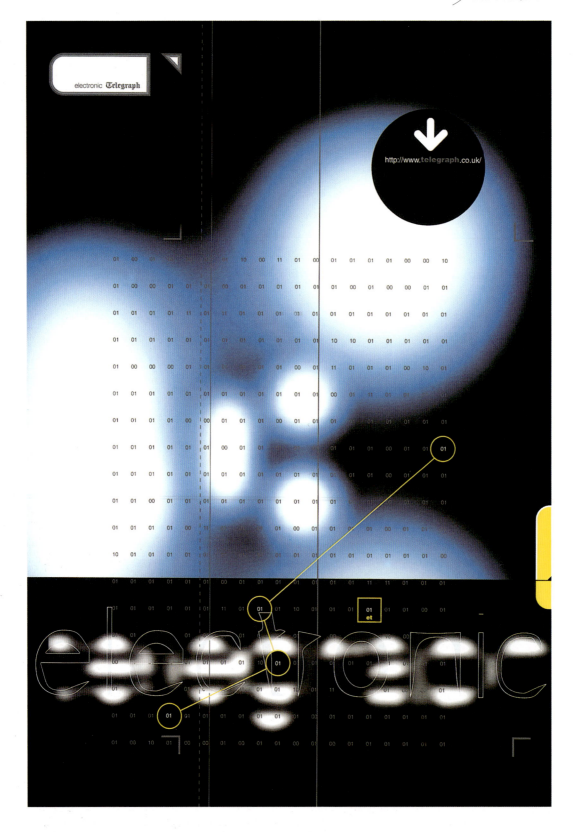

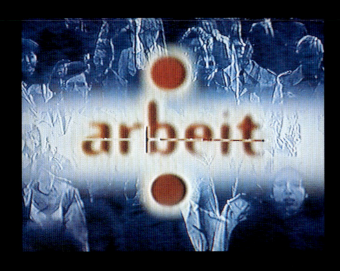

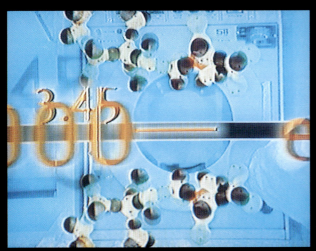

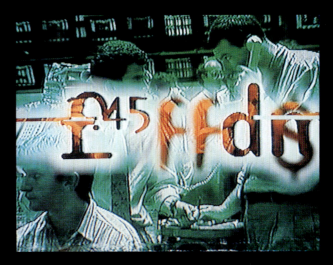

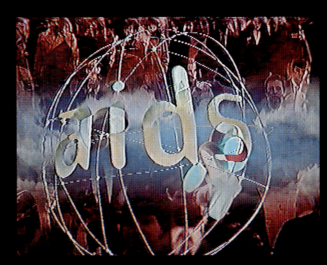

Punctvox

Graphic stings for a German news channel
DESIGNERS | Andy Altmann, David Ellis
DESIGN COMPANY | Why Not Associates
PHOTOGRAPHER | Rocco Redondo
PRINCIPAL TYPEFACE | Template Gothic
CLIENT | Vox TV

*Great Britain, 1994*

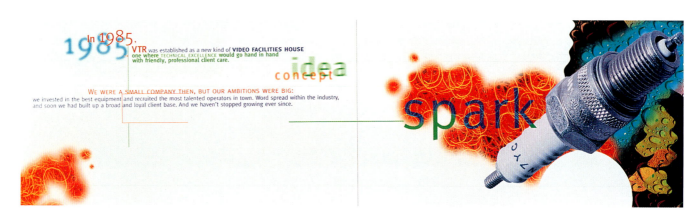

In 1985, **1985** VTR was established as a new kind of **VIDEO FACILITIES HOUSE** – one where TECHNICAL EXCELLENCE would go hand in hand with friendly, professional client care.

idea

concept

spark

WE WERE A SMALL COMPANY THEN, BUT OUR AMBITIONS WERE BIG: we invested in the best equipment and recruited the most talented operators in town. Word spread within the industry, and soon we had built up a broad and loyal client base. And we haven't stopped growing ever since.

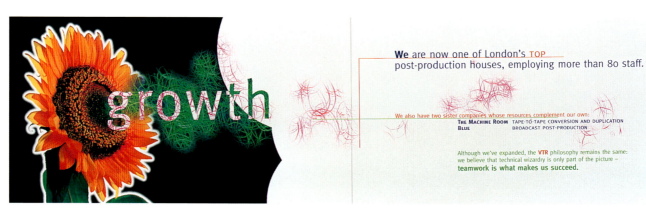

growth

**We** are now one of London's TOP post-production houses, employing more than 80 staff.

We also have two sister companies whose resources complement our own:
**THE MACHINE ROOM**   TAPE-TO-TAPE CONVERSION AND DUPLICATION
**BLUE**   BROADCAST POST-PRODUCTION

Although we've expanded, the **VTR** philosophy remains the same: we believe that technical wizardry is only part of the picture – **teamwork is what makes us succeed.**

Promotional brochure for a TV and video facilities house

DESIGNERS / Andy Altmann, David Ellis, Patrick Morrissey
DESIGN COMPANY / Why Not Associates
PHOTOGRAPHERS / Photonica, PhotoDisc
PRINCIPAL TYPEFACE | Meta
CLIENT | VTR

*Great Britain, 1995*

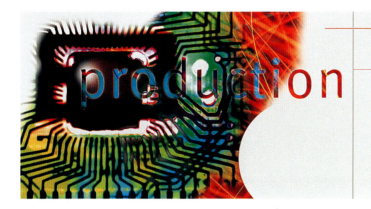

**We** want every job to be as
worry-free
AS POSSIBLE, FROM **concept** meeting
right through to completion.

THAT'S WHERE THE
**VTR** PRODUCTION TEAM
COMES IN:
they are there to provide clients with
PROFESSIONAL ADVICE and friendly support from start
to finish, and to keep a close eye on bookings and costs.

WE ALSO HAVE A TRAINED ENGINEERING DEPARTMENT ON HAND AT
ALL TIMES TO ENSURE THE smooth RUNNING OF OUR EQUIPMENT.

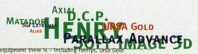

AXIAL
D.C.P.
MATADOR
SGI EXTREME
URSA GOLD
ALIAS
HENRY
PARALLAX ADVANCE
SOFTIMAGE 3D

With a broad range of the best equipment there is – including Henrys, Ursa Gold
telecines, Axial edit suites, Parallax Advance, Alias and Softimage 3D–we can find
the solution for even the most demanding project, whether it's multi-layering,
morphing or any other special effect. But although we're at the forefront of
technological innovation, we put the emphasis firmly on user-friendliness:
we want to dazzle you with the results,
not blind you with science.

equipment

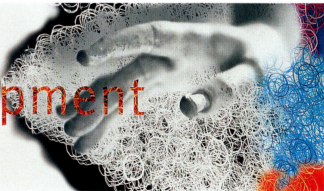

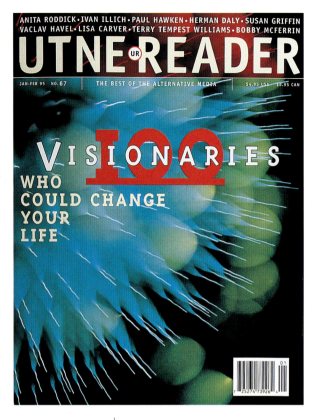

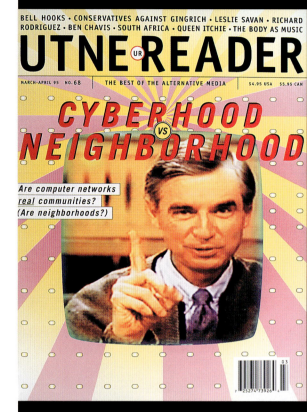

Utne Reader no. 67

Magazine cover

DESIGNER DIRECTORS | Jan Jancourt, Andrew Henderson
ASSOCIATE ART DIRECTOR | Andrew Henderson
DESIGN COMPANY | Jancourt & Associates
PRINCIPAL TYPEFACE | Officina
CLIENT | LENS Publishing

*USA, 1995*

Utne Reader no. 68

Magazine cover and spreads

DESIGN DIRECTORS | Jan Jancourt, Andrew Henderson
ASSOCIATE ART DIRECTOR | Andrew Henderson
DESIGN COMPANY | Jancourt & Associates
PRINCIPAL TYPEFACE | Officina
CLIENT | LENS Publishing

*USA, 1995*

*Utne Reader* is an independently published
digest of new writing and articles of
interest selected from other publications,
both marginal and mainstream. In 1994,
eleven years after it was founded by Eric
Utne, the magazine's editorial philosophy
was rethought and a redesign was
commissioned to embody its new vision. The
*Reader*'s new format is both livelier than
before and more rigorous in mood, while
transmitting the urgency of its socially and
culturally attuned content.

CYBERHOOD VS NEIGHBORHOOD

# Is There a There in Cyberspace?

SPECIAL TO UTNE READER | John Perry Barlow

I am often asked how I went from pushing cows around a remote Wyoming ranch to my present occupation (which *Wall Street Journal* recently described as "cyberspace cadet"). I haven't got a short answer, but I suppose I came to the virtual world looking for community.

Unlike most modern Americans, I grew up in an actual place, an entirely nonintentional community called Pinedale, Wyoming. As I struggled for nearly a generation to keep my ranch in the family, I was motivated by the belief that such places were the spiritual home of humanity. But I knew their future was not promising.

At the dawn of the 20th century, over 40 percent of the American workforce lived off the land. The majority of us lived in towns like Pinedale. Now fewer than 1 percent of us extract a living from the soil. We just became too productive for our own good.

Of course, the population followed the jobs. Farming and ranching communities are now home to a demographically insignificant percentage of Americans, the vast majority of whom live not in ranch houses but in more or less identical split-level "ranch homes" in more or less identical suburban "communities." Generica.

In my view, these are neither communities nor homes. I believe the combination of television and suburban population patterns is simply toxic to the soul. I see much evidence in contemporary America to support this view.

Meanwhile, back at the ranch, doom impended. And, as I watched community in Pinedale growing ill from the same economic forces that were killing my family's ranch, the Bar Cross, satellite dishes brought the cultural infection of television. I started looking around for evidence that community in America would not perish altogether.

I took some heart in the mysterious nomadic City of the Deadheads, the virtually physical town that follows the Grateful Dead around the country. The Deadheads lacked place, touching down briefly wherever the band happened to be playing, and they lacked continuity in time, since they had to suffer a new diaspora every time the band moved on or went home. But they had many of the other necessary elements of community, including a culture, a religion of sorts (which, though it lacked dogma, had most of the other, more nurturing aspects of spiritual practice), a sense of necessity, and, most importantly, shared adversity.

I wanted to know more about the flavor of their interaction, what they thought and felt, and since I wrote Dead songs (including "Estimated Prophet" and "Cassidy"), I was a minor icon to the Deadheads, and was thus inhibited, in some socially Heisenbergian way, from getting a clear view of what really went on among them.

Then, in 1987, I heard about a "place" where Deadheads gathered where I could move among them without distorting too much the field of observation. Better, this was a place I could visit without leaving Wyoming. It was a shared computer in Sausalito, California, called the Whole Earth 'Lectronic Link, or WELL. After a lot of struggling with modems, serial cables, init strings, and other computer arcana that seemed utterly out of phase with such notions as Deadheads and small towns, I found myself looking at the glowing yellow word "Login:" beyond which lay my future.

"Inside" the WELL were Deadheads in community. There were thousands of them there, gossiping, complaining (mostly about the Grateful Dead), comforting and harassing each other, bartering, engaging in religion (or at least exchanging their totemic set lists), beginning and ending love affairs, praying for one another's sick kids. There was, it seemed, everything one might find going on in a small town, save dragging Main Street and making out on the back roads.

I was delighted. I felt I had found the new locale of

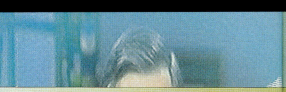

> *Computer networking can help bring community
back to the center of modern life*

CYBERHOOD VS NEIGHBORHOOD

# The Virtual Community

Howard Rheingold

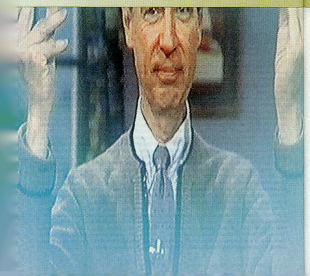

In the summer of 1986, my then-2-year-old daughter picked up a tick. There was this blood-bloated *thing* sucking on our baby's scalp, and we weren't quite sure how to go about getting it off. My wife, Judy, called the pediatrician. It was 11 o'clock in the evening. I logged onto the WELL, the big Bay Area infonet, and contacted the Parenting conference (a conference is an on-line conversation about a specific subject). I got my answer on-line within minutes from a fellow with the improbable but genuine name of Flash Gordon, M.D. I had removed the tick by the time Judy got the callback from the pediatrician's office.

What amazed me wasn't just the speed with which we obtained precisely the information we needed to know, right when we needed to know it. It was also the immense inner sense of security that comes with discovering that real people—most of them parents, some of them nurses, doctors, and midwives—are available, around the clock, if you need them. There is a magic protective circle around the atmosphere of the Parenting conference. We're talking about our sons and daughters in this forum, not about our computers or our opinions about philosophy, and many of us feel that this tacit understanding sanctifies the virtual space.

The atmosphere of this particular conference—the attitudes people exhibit to each other in the tone of what they say in public—is part of what continues to attract me. People who never have much to contribute in political debate, technical argument, or intellectual gamesmanship turn out to have a lot to say about raising children. People you knew as fierce, even nasty, intellectual opponents in other contexts give you emotional support on a deeper level, parent to parent, within the boundaries of this small but warmly human corner of cyberspace.

In most cases, people who talk about a shared interest don't disclose enough about themselves as whole individuals on-line to inspire real trust in others. But in the case of the subcommunity called the Parenting conference, a few dozen of us, scattered across the country, few of whom rarely if ever saw the others face to face, have a few years of minor crises to knit us together and prepare us for serious business when it comes our way. Another several dozen read the conference regularly but contribute only when they have something important to add. Hundreds more read the conference every week without comment, except when something extraordinary happens.

Jay Allison and his family live in Massachusetts. He and his wife are public-radio producers. I've never met them face to face, although I feel I know something powerful and intimate about the Allisons and have strong emotional ties to them. What follows are some of Jay's postings on the WELL:

*"Woods Hole. Midnight. I am sitting in the dark of my daughter's room. Her monitor lights blink at me. The lights used to blink too brightly so I covered them with bits of bandage adhesive and now they flash faintly underneath, a persistent red and green, Lillie's heart and lungs.*

*"Above the monitor is her portable suction unit. In the glow of the flashlight I'm writing by, it looks like the plastic guts of a science-class human model, the tubes coiled around the power supply, the reservoir, the pump.*

*"Tina is upstairs trying to get some sleep. A baby monitor links our bedroom to Lillie's. It links our sleep to Lillie's too, and because our souls are linked to hers, we do not sleep well.*

*"I am naked. My stomach is full of beer. The flashlight rests on it, and the beam rises and falls with my breath. My daughter breathes through a white plastic tube inserted into a hole in her throat. She's 14 months old."*

Sitting in front of our computers with our hearts racing and tears in our eyes, in Tokyo and Sacramento and Austin, we read about Lillie's croup, her tracheostomy, the

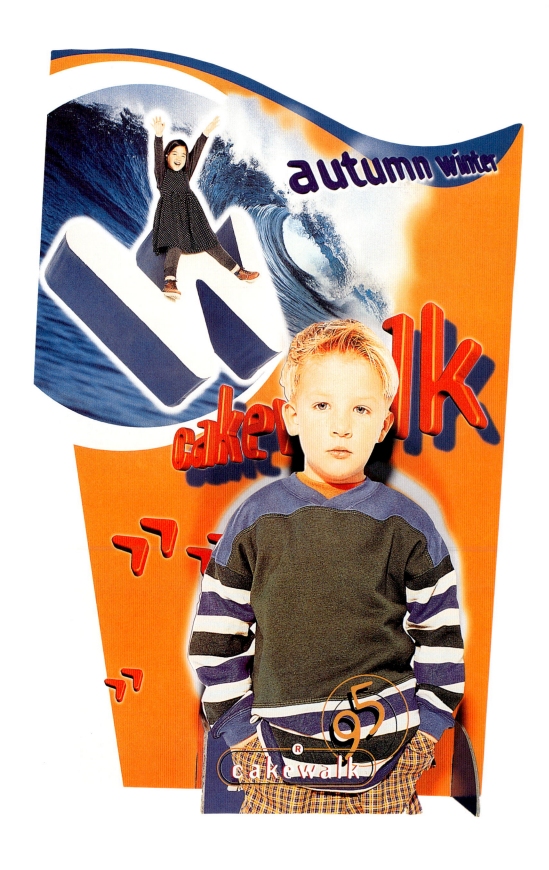

Double-sided point-of-sale promotion
for a children's clothing manufacturer
DESIGNERS / Andy Altmann, David Ellis, Patrick Morrissey
DESIGN COMPANY / Why Not Associates
PRINCIPAL TYPEFACE / Template Gothic
CLIENT / Cakewalk

Great Britain, 1995

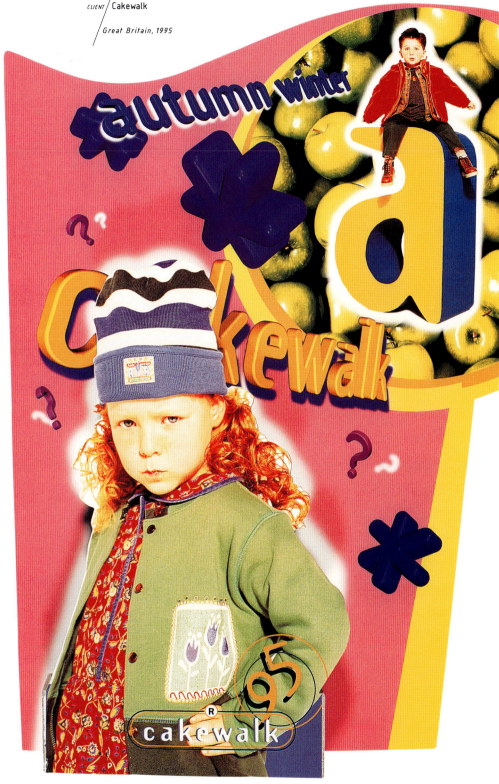

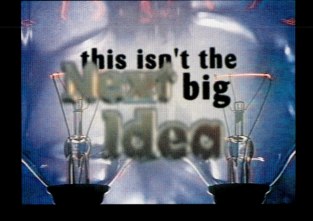

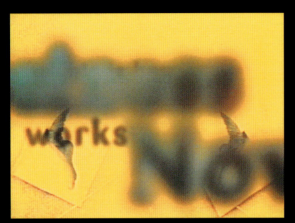

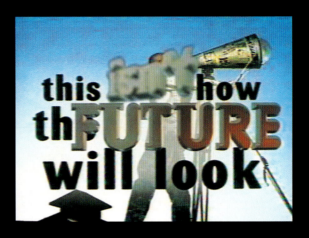

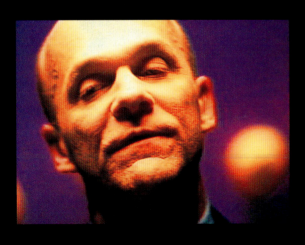

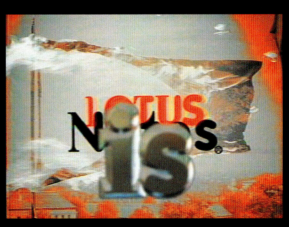

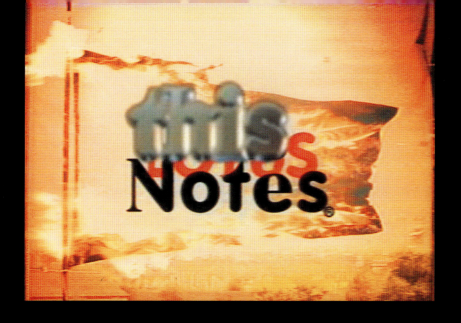

**Lotus: This is Notes**

Television commercial

| | |
|---|---|
| *DIRECTOR* | Jeffrey Plansker |
| *ART DIRECTOR* | Steve Sumne |
| *DESIGN DIRECTOR* | P. Scott Makela |
| *DESIGN COMPANY* | Words and Pictures for Business and Culture |
| *SPECIAL PHOTOGRAPHY* | Laura Plansker |
| *PRINCIPAL TYPEFACES* | Dead History, Barmeno |
| *CLIENT* | Lotus Software Corporation |

*USA, 1994*

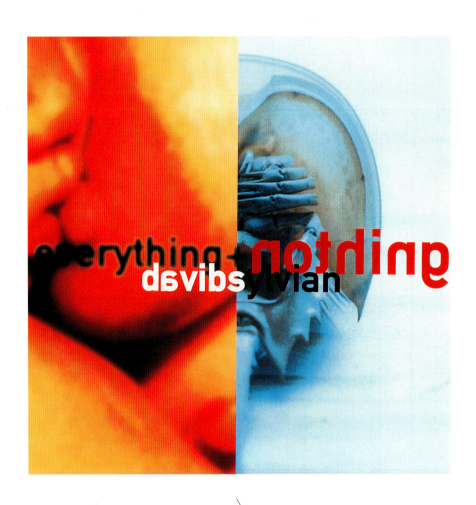

**Everything + Nothing**

|  | Audio CD cover for David Sylvian |
| DESIGNER | P. Scott Makela |
| DESIGN COMPANY | Words and Pictures for Business and Culture |
| PHOTOGRAPHER | Billy Phelps |
| PRINCIPAL TYPEFACE | WAC Mittelschrift |
| CLIENT | Virgin Records |
|  | USA, 1994 |

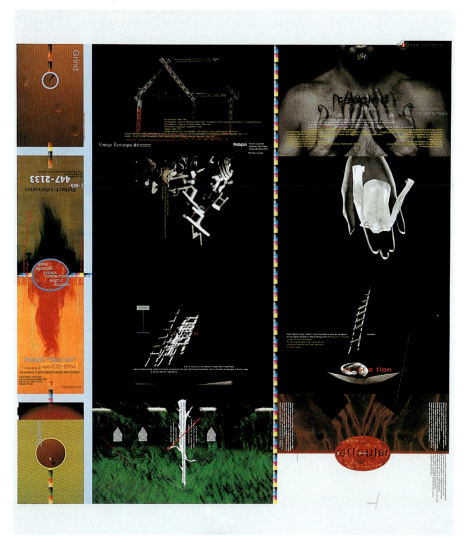

**The Rescinded Muse**

Poster/brochure for a paper company

DESIGNERS | Allen Hori, Charlie Becker, Rob Eberhardt
DESIGN COMPANY | Bates Hori
WRITER | Augustine Hope
PHOTOGRAPHERS | Gaye Chan, Allen Hori
PRINCIPAL TYPEFACES | Helvetica, News Gothic, Bell Gothic
CLIENT | Potlatch Corporation

*USA, 1994*

Allen Hori's paper promotion is a complex "ode to music" which equates the poetic discoveries of the design process with the intuitive explorations of music-making. The recycled paper's character is reflected in the way the press sheet is structured to eliminate trimming and unnecessary wastage. The viewer can treat the piece as a double-sided poster, or use its perforations to take it apart and reassemble it as a brochure.

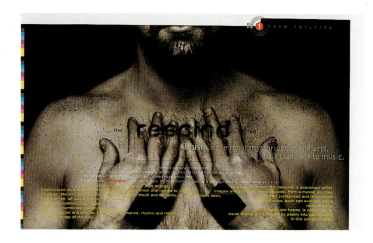

*Wired*'s pre-contents introductory pages are a rare example of structural innovation within a commercial newsstand magazine. Each issue, a quotation from a main editorial feature embodying a key cultural or technological idea becomes the designers' starting point for a McLuhanesque four-page visual essay. Often the typography is woven into the image so tightly that the two become almost indivisible – a new style of journalistic communication that is simultaneously both highly suggestive and editorially specific.

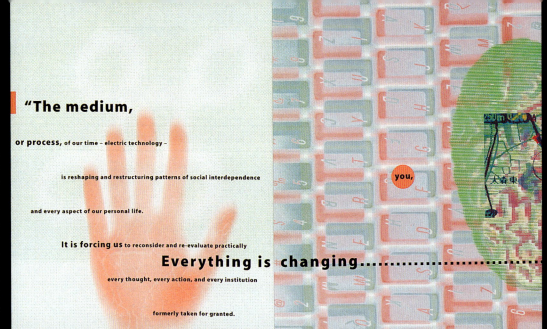

"The medium,

or process, of our time – electric technology –

is reshaping and restructuring patterns of social interdependence

and every aspect of our personal life.

It is forcing us to reconsider and re-evaluate practically

Everything is changing...........................

every thought, every action, and every institution

formerly taken for granted.

you,

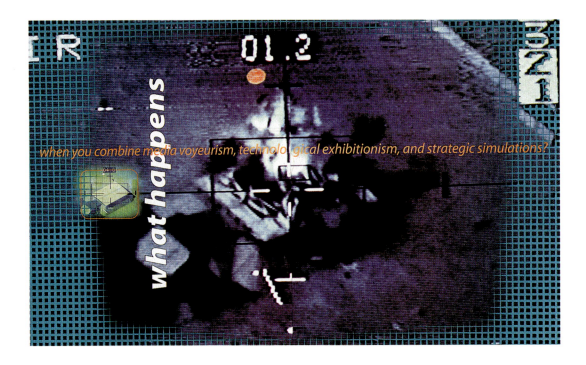

IR    01.2    321

what happens

when you combine media voyeurism, technological exhibitionism, and strategic simulations?

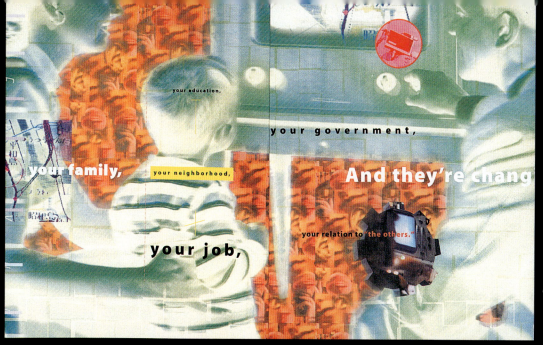

your education,

your government,

your family,

your neighborhood,

And they're chang

your relation to "the others."

your job,

Wired no. 1.1

Magazine spreads
CREATIVE DIRECTOR | John Plunkett
DESIGNERS | John Plunkett,
Eric Adigard
DESIGN COMPANY | Plunkett + Kuhr
ILLUSTRATOR | Eric Adigard
PRINCIPAL TYPEFACE | Myriad
CLIENT | Wired USA

USA, 1993

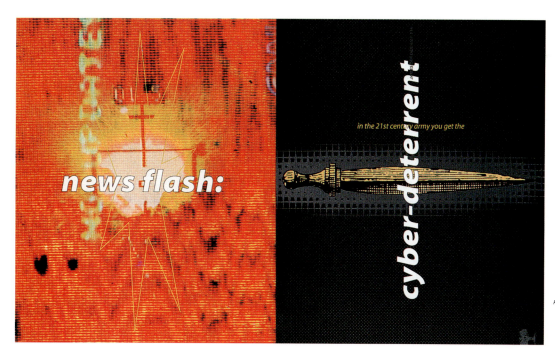

news flash:

in the 21st century army you get the

cyber-deterent

Wired no. 2.09

Magazine spreads
CREATIVE DIRECTOR | John Plunkett
DESIGNERS | John Plunkett,
Thomas Schneider
DESIGN COMPANY | Plunkett + Kuhr
ILLUSTRATOR | Eric Adigard
PRINCIPAL TYPEFACE | Myriad
CLIENT | Wired Ventures

USA, 1994

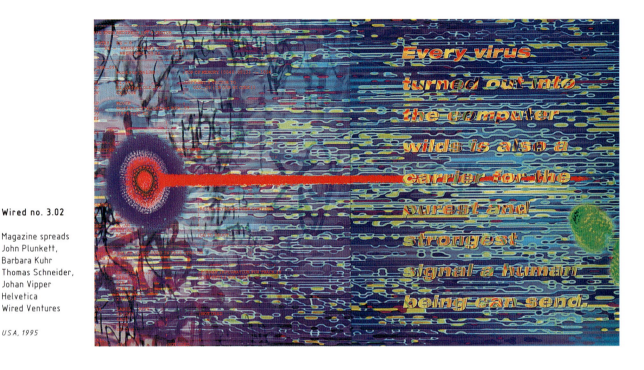

Every virus turned out into the computer wilds is also a carrier for the purest and strongest signal a human being can send.

**Wired no. 3.02**

Magazine spreads
CREATIVE DIRECTORS | John Plunkett, Barbara Kuhr
DESIGNERS | Thomas Schneider, Johan Vipper
PRINCIPAL TYPEFACE | Helvetica
CLIENT | Wired Ventures

*USA, 1995*

The literary culture was fashionable discourse. and ideology empirical testing of ideas

an establishment that dictated It favored opinions over commentary spiraling upon commentary.

**Wired no. 3.08**

Magazine spreads
CREATIVE DIRECTORS | John Plunkett, Barbara Kuhr
DESIGNERS | John Plunkett, Thomas Schneider, Eric Adigard
ILLUSTRATOR | Eric Adigard
PRINCIPAL TYPEFACE | Akzidenz Grotesk
CLIENT | Wired Ventures

*USA, 1995*

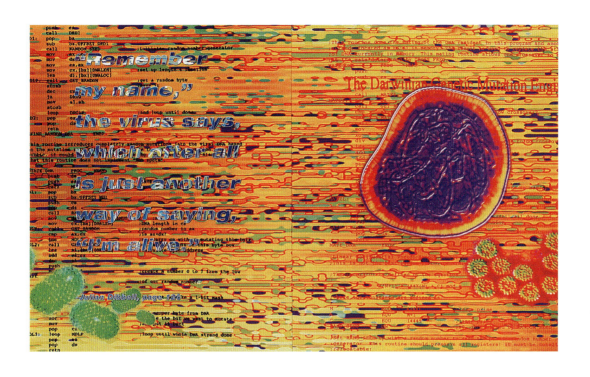

"Remember my name," the virus says, which after all is just another way of saying, "I'm alive."

—Julian Dibbell, page 126

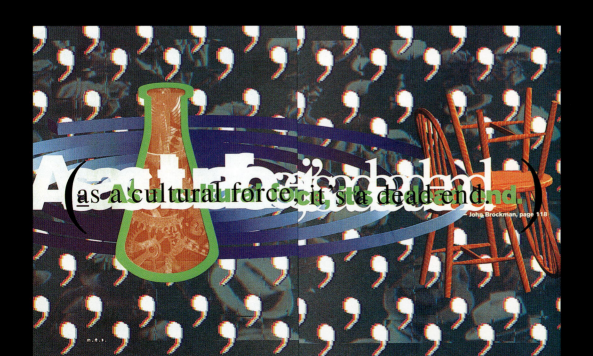

(as a cultural force, it's a dead end.

John Brockman, page 118

## The Future's Paper

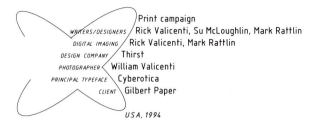

| | |
|---|---|
| | Print campaign |
| WRITERS/DESIGNERS | Rick Valicenti, Su McLoughlin, Mark Rattlin |
| DIGITAL IMAGING | Rick Valicenti, Mark Rattlin |
| DESIGN COMPANY | Thirst |
| PHOTOGRAPHER | William Valicenti |
| PRINCIPAL TYPEFACE | Cyberotica |
| CLIENT | Gilbert Paper |

*USA, 1994*

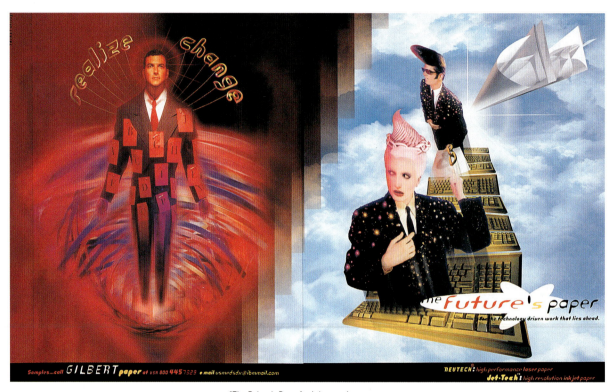

"The Future's Paper" print campaign authored by Thirst consisted of two trilogies and each of the double-page ads ran just once in *Wired*. For the more "human" second series, "Realize Change", familiar iconography – Clark Kent, Betty Crocker, Elvis – was futuristically recast. In a non-typographic extension of the project, Rick Valicenti's photographer brother took life-sized enlargements of the figures to a Midwestern shopping mall, where he invited shoppers to pose with their preferred character – a "twisted look", Valicenti claims, at contemporary confusions between fantasy and reality.

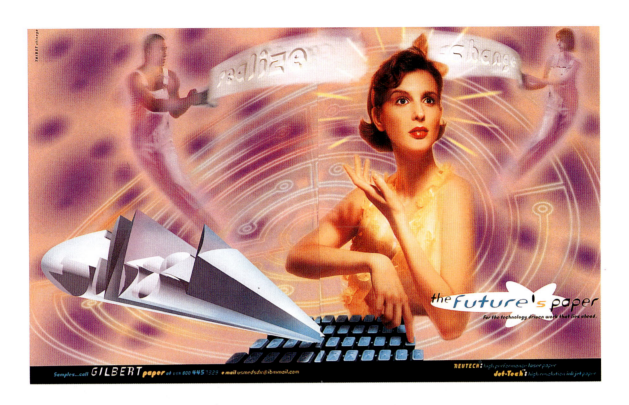

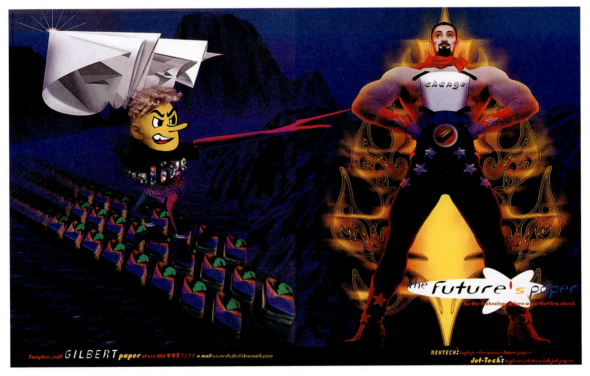

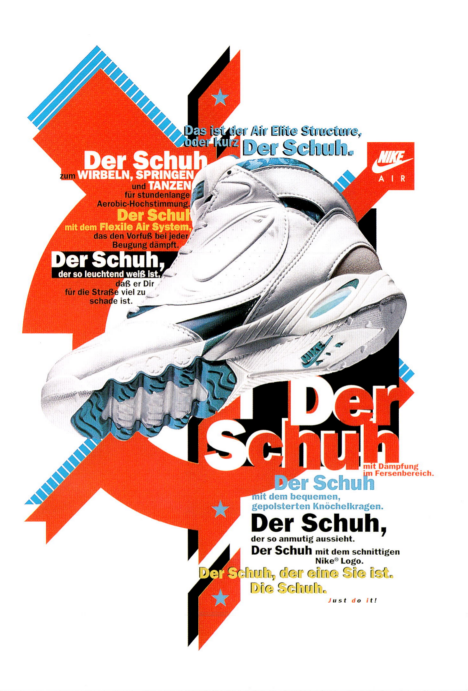

Nike: The Shoe

Print campaign

DESIGNERS   Chris Priest, Andy Altmann, David Ellis
DESIGN COMPANY   Why Not Associates
AGENCY   Wieden Kennedy
PHOTOGRAPHER   Hans Pieterse
CIPAL TYPEFACE   Franklin Gothic
CLIENT   Nike

Great Britain, 1992

Tant qu'il y aura des dunks

Poster/brochure to promote a

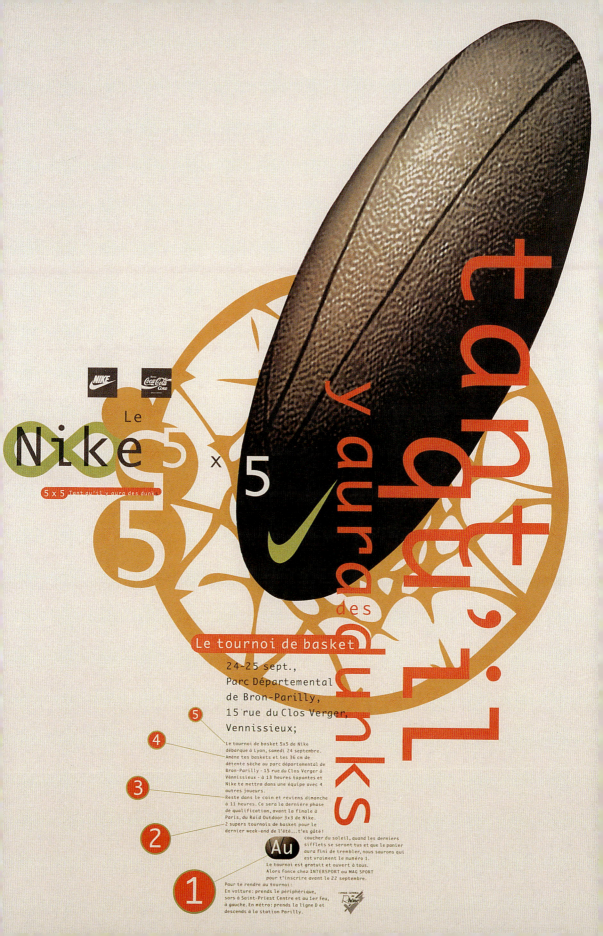

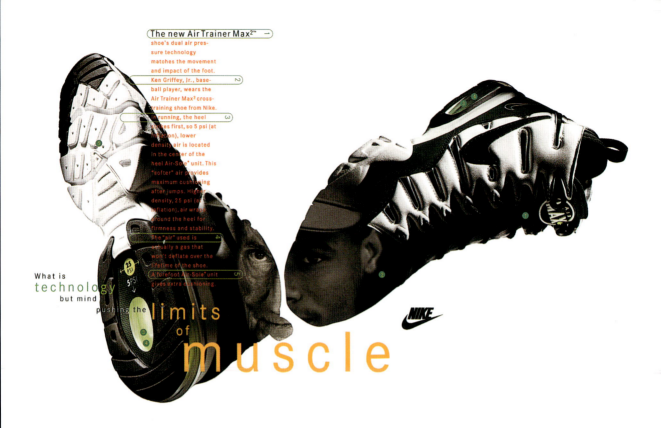

The new Air Trainer Max² →

shoe's dual air pressure technology
matches the movement
and impact of the foot.

Ken Griffey, Jr., baseball player, wears the
Air Trainer Max² cross-training shoe from Nike.

In running, the heel strikes first, so 5 psi (at inflation), lower density air is located in the center of the heel Air-Sole® unit. This "softer" air provides maximum cushioning after jumps. Higher density, 25 psi (at inflation), air wraps around the heel for firmness and stability. The "air" used is usually a gas that won't deflate over the lifetime of the shoe. A forefoot Air-Sole® unit gives extra cushioning

What is
technology
but mind
pushing the limits
of
muscle

NIKE

Air Max 2 Technical

Print campaign
DESIGNER Robert Nakata
AGENCY Wieden & Kennedy
WRITER Jean Rhode
PHOTOGRAPHER Hans Pieterse (shoes)
PRINCIPAL TYPEFACE Corporate S
CLIENT Nike USA

The Netherlands, 1994

**Nike Running**

Print campaign
DESIGNER   Robert Nakata
AGENCY   Wieden & Kennedy
WRITER   Evelyn Monroe
PRINCIPAL TYPEFACE   DIN Mittelschrift
CLIENT   Nike Europe

*The Netherlands, 1994*

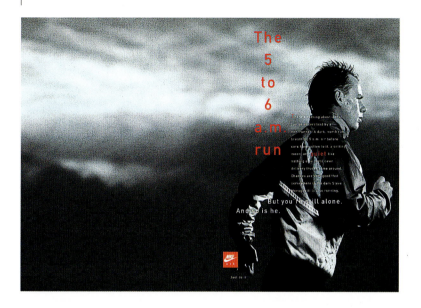

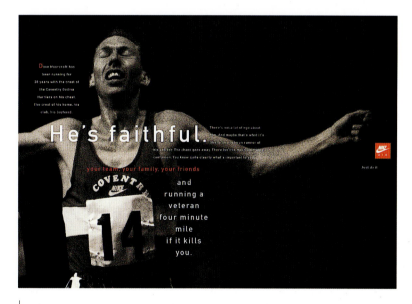

**Nike Running**

Print campaign
DESIGNER   Robert Nakata
AGENCY   Wieden & Kennedy
WRITERS   Ernest Lupinacci, Giles Montgomery, Bob Moore
PHOTOGRAPHER   John Huet
PRINCIPAL TYPEFACES   Argos, DIN Mittelschrift
CLIENT   Nike Europe

*The Netherlands, 1995*

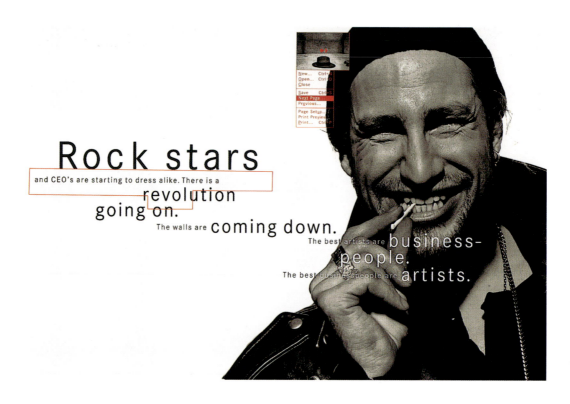

# Rock stars

and CEO's are starting to dress alike. There is a revolution going on. The walls are coming down. The best artists are business-people. The best businesspeople are artists.

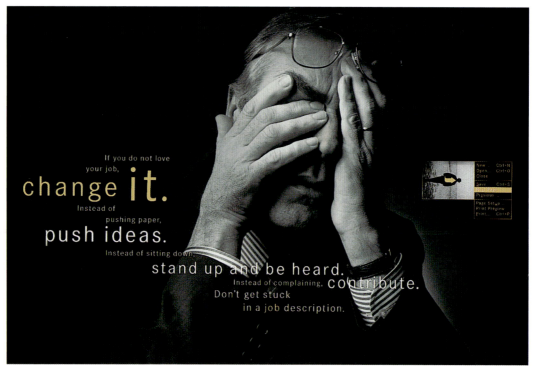

If you do not love your job, change it. Instead of pushing paper, push ideas. Instead of sitting down, stand up and be heard. Instead of complaining, contribute. Don't get stuck in a job description.

**Microsoft Office**

|  | |
|---|---|
| | Print campaign |
| DESIGNER | Robert Nakata |
| AGENCY | Wieden & Kennedy |
| WRITER | Bob Moore |
| PHOTOGRAPHER | Dieter Eikelpoth |
| PRINCIPAL TYPEFACE | Corporate S |
| CLIENT | Microsoft |

*The Netherlands, 1994-95*

44

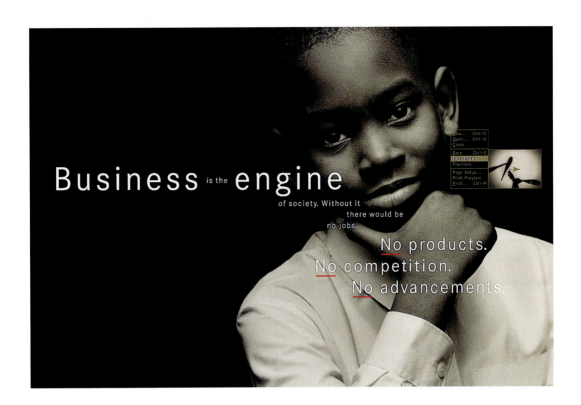

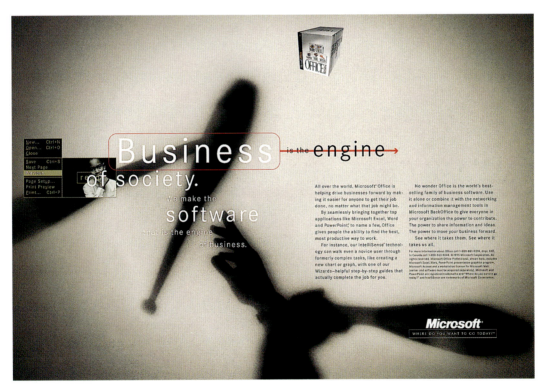

Each of the three portraits – rock star, businessman, young boy – is followed by an "image" spread and, through the copy's emphasis and lack of visible computer, it is hoped the viewer will understand that Microsoft makes software and not hardware. The typography suggests the ease and fluidity with which information can be manipulated in the digital realm, as well as its personal dimension, without resorting to an obviously "computer" look in the choice of typeface.

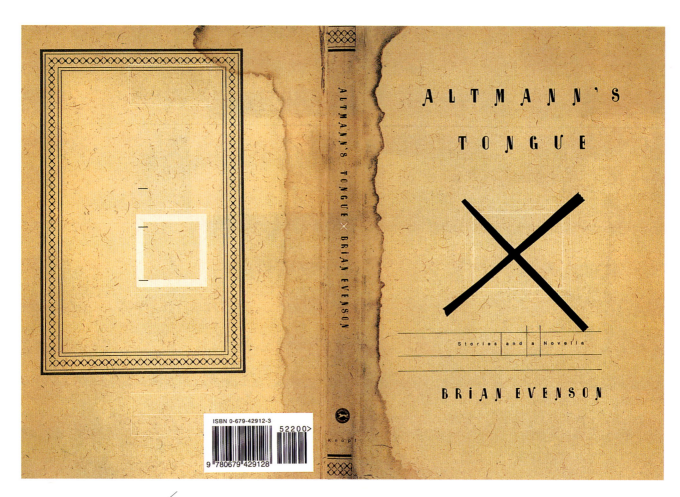

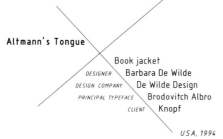

**Altmann's Tongue**

Book jacket
DESIGNER Barbara De Wilde
DESIGN COMPANY De Wilde Design
PRINCIPAL TYPEFACE Brodovitch Albro
CLIENT Knopf

USA, 1994

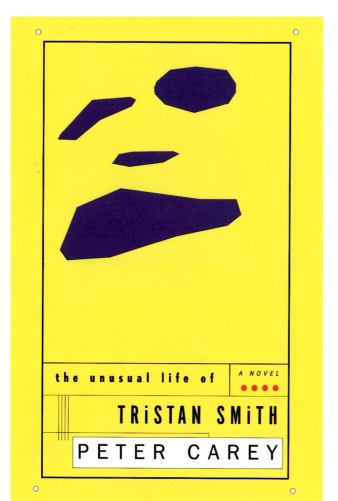

the unusual life of   *A NOVEL*

**TRiSTAN SMiTH**

**PETER CAREY**

The Unusual Life of Tristan Smith

Book jacket
DESIGNER / Chip Kidd
DESIGN COMPANY / Chip Kidd Design
PRINCIPAL TYPEFACE / Univers
CLIENT / Knopf

USA, 1994

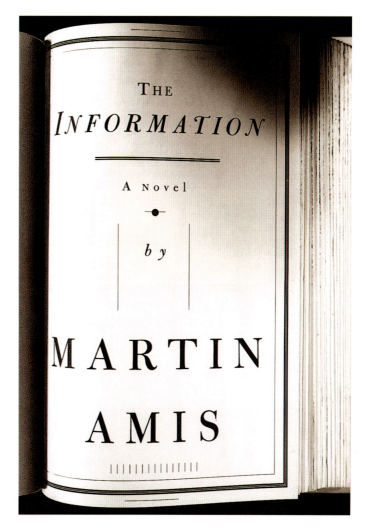

The Information

Book jacket
DESIGNER / Chip Kidd
DESIGN COMPANY / Chip Kidd Design
PRINCIPAL TYPEFACE / Bulmer
CLIENT / Harmony Books

USA, 1995

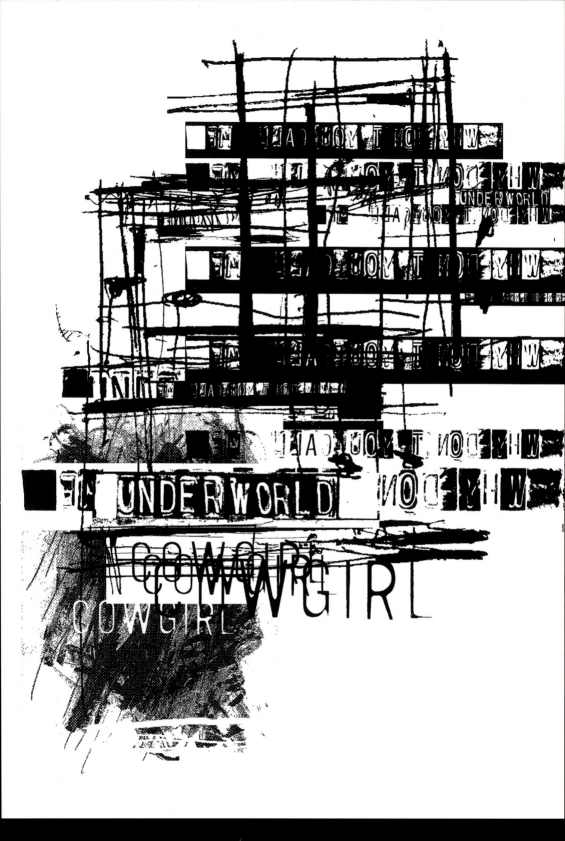

Cowgirl

Promotional poster for a single by Underworld

DESIGNER John Warwicker
DESIGN COMPANY Tomato

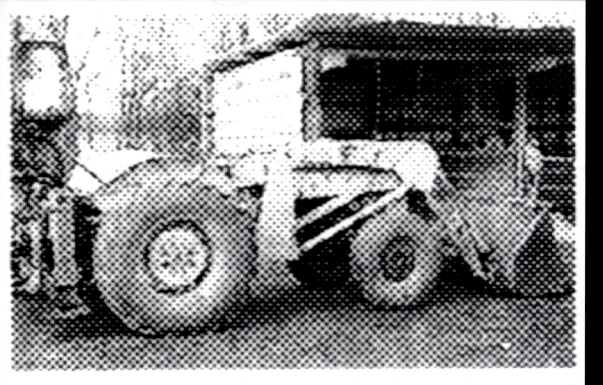

# underw orld : born s lippy . ,

underw orld : born s lippy .TEL EMATIC ; cowg irl; ( W INJER MIX .)

a side, born slippy; ~~TELEMATIC~~. b side, cowgirl (WINJER MIX). written/produced/mixed by UNDERWORLD (smith/hyde/emerson). ℗ + © junior boys own, 1995. junior recordings ltd, the saga centre, 326 kensal road, london w10 5bz, tel 0181 960 4495, fax 0181 960 3256. published by underworld/sherlock holmes music. management: jukes productions, tel 0171 286 9532. manufactured and distributed by rtm/pinnacle. made in england.

jbo29R **JUNIOR** BOY'S OWN

5 026734 002900

Born Slippy

Record sleeve for a 12-inch single by Under
DESIGNERS Jason Kedgley, Graham Wood
DESIGN COMPANY Tomato
PRINCIPAL TYPEFACE Bureau Grotesque
CLIENT Junior Boys Own

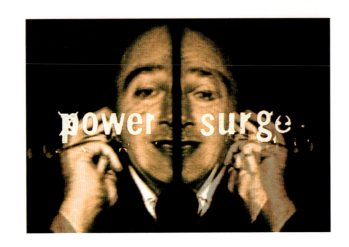

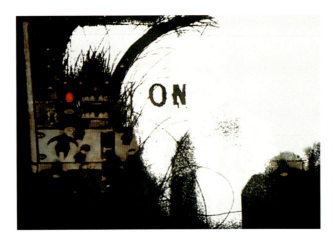

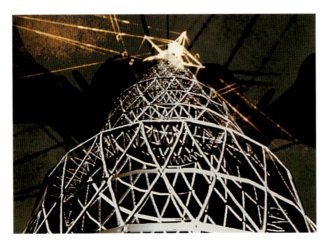

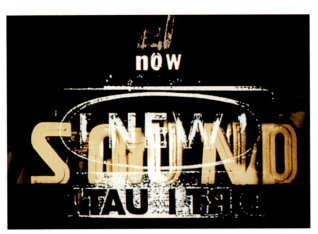

Revolution Radio

Television commercial
DIRECTOR | Walter Pitt
ANIMATOR/EDITOR/PHOTOGRAPHER | Alexei Tylevich
PRINCIPAL TYPEFACES | Custom-made for the project
CLIENT | Rev 105

USA, 1994

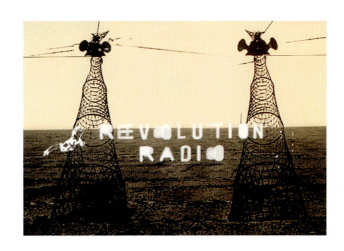

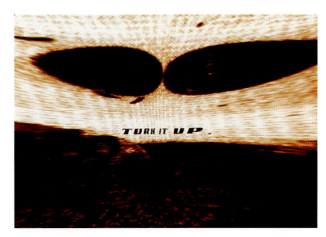

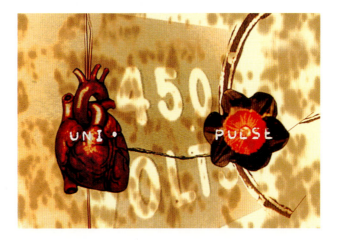

Revolution Radio, an alternative music station based in Minneapolis, gave Alexei Tylevich complete freedom in his choice of imagery and use of editing for a TV commercial. Tylevich's animation was one of a number of segments assigned to different designers. The segments were then spliced together in a televisual version of Exquisite Corpse, the Surrealist game in which each player contributes a section of a drawing without seeing what the other players have drawn.

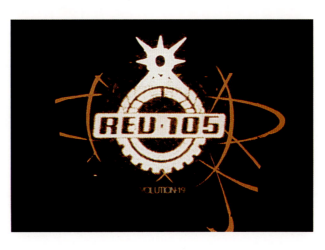

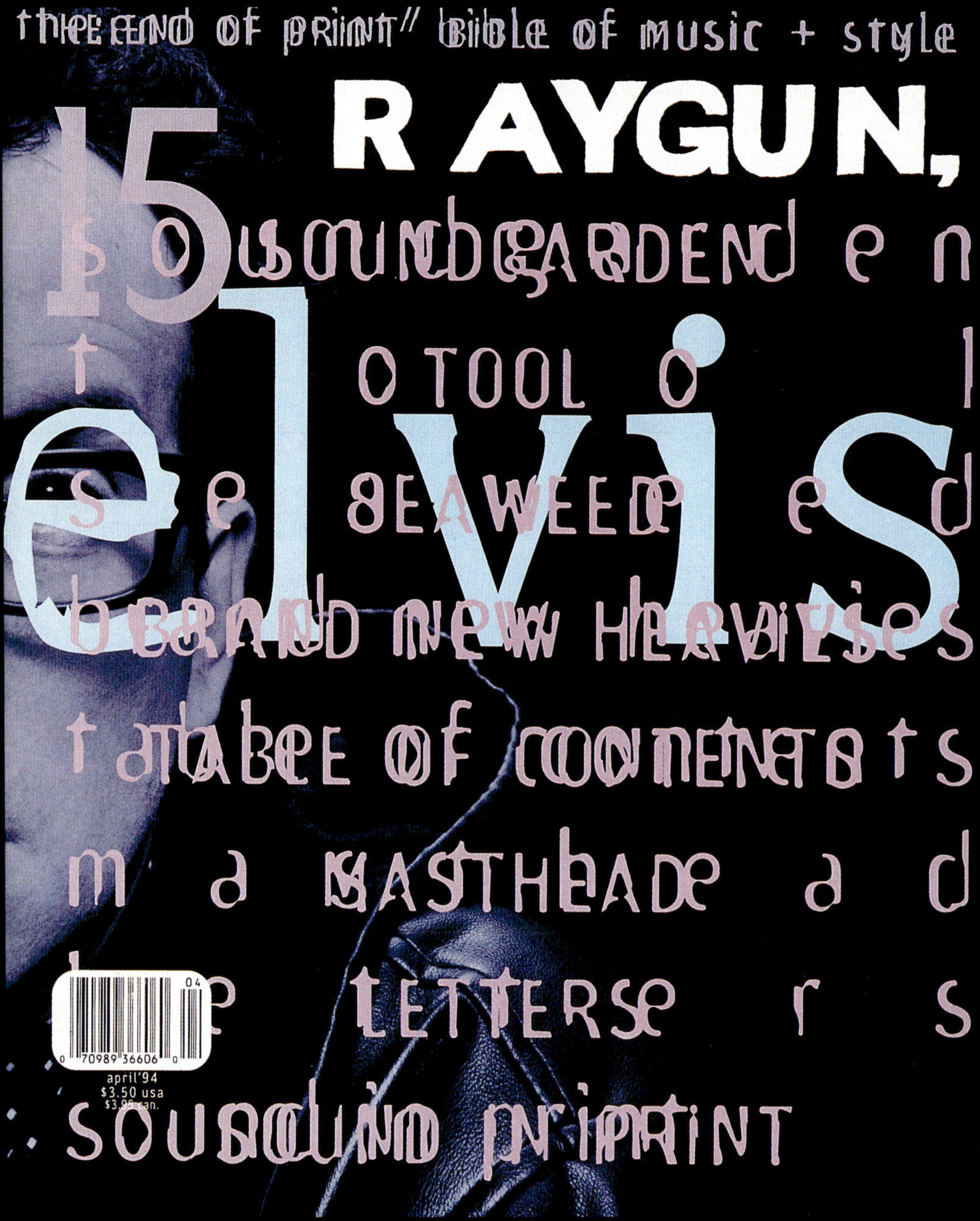

the end of print "bible of music + style

**R AYGUN,**

15 soundgarden en

o TOOL o

**elvis**

seaweed

brand new heavies

table of contents

masthead ad

letters r s

sound in print

Raygun no. 15

Magazine cover
*ART DIRECTOR/DESIGNER* David Carson
*PHOTOGRAPHERS* Davies and Starr
*CLIENT* Ray Gun Publishing

*USA, 1994*

april '94
$3.50 usa
$3.95 can.

Raygun no. 5

Magazine cover
ART DIRECTOR/DESIGNER  David Carson
ILLUSTRATOR  Jim Sherraden
PHOTOGRAPHER  Merlyn Rosenberg
CLIENT  Ray Gun Publishing

USA, 1993

Raygun no. 19

Magazine cover
ART DIRECTOR/DESIGNER  David Carson
PHOTOGRAPHER  Colin Bell
PRINCIPAL TYPEFACE  Teenager
CLIENT  Ray Gun Publishing

USA, 1994

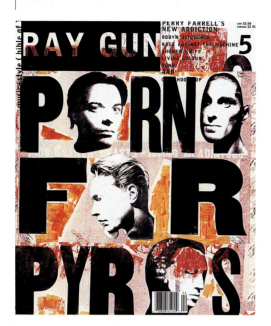

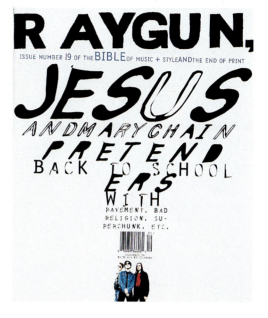

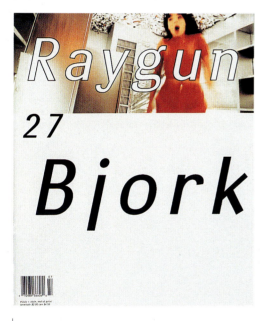

Raygun no. 31

Magazine cover
ART DIRECTORS/DESIGNERS  Hal Wolverton, Alicia Johnson
DESIGN COMPANY  Johnson & Wolverton
PHOTOGRAPHER  Doug Aitken
PRINCIPAL TYPEFACE  Interstate
CLIENT  Ray Gun Publishing

USA, 1995

Raygun no. 27

Magazine cover
ART DIRECTION/DESIGNER  David Carson
PHOTOGRAPHER  David Stewart
PRINCIPAL TYPEFACE  Neulin Sans
CLIENT  Ray Gun Publishing

USA, 1995

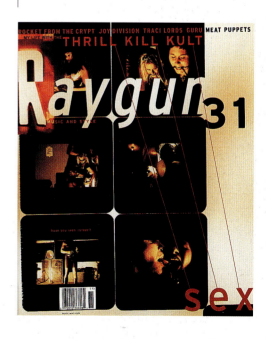

Raygun no. 19

Magazine spread
*ART DIRECTOR/DESIGNER* David Carson
*ILLUSTRATOR* Christian Northeast
*PRINCIPAL TYPEFACE* Teenager
*CLIENT* Ray Gun Publishing

*USA, 1994*

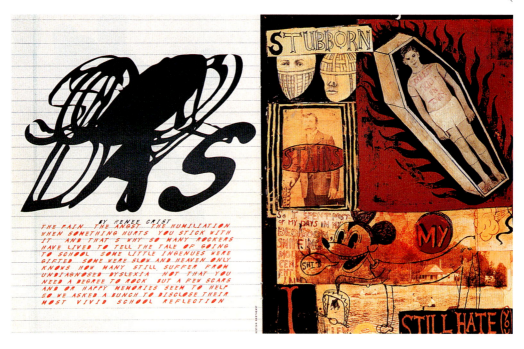

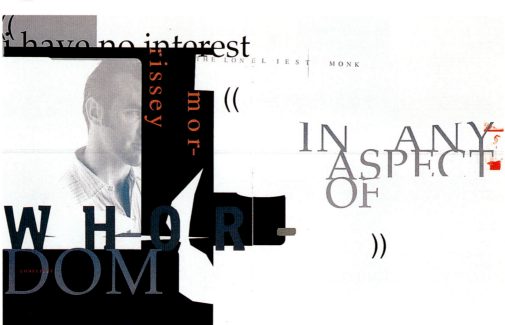

Raygun no. 14

Magazine spread
*ART DIRECTOR/DESIGNER* David Carson
*PHOTOGRAPHER* Chris Cuffaro
*CLIENT* Ray Gun Publishing

*USA, 1994*

Raygun no. 15

Magazine spread
ART DIRECTOR/DESIGNER / David Carson
ILLUSTRATOR / Malcolm Tarlofsky
CLIENT / Ray Gun Publishing

USA, 1994

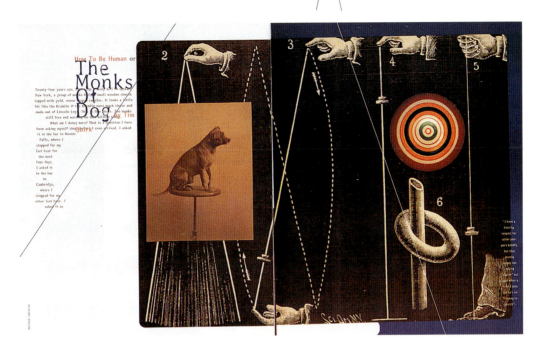

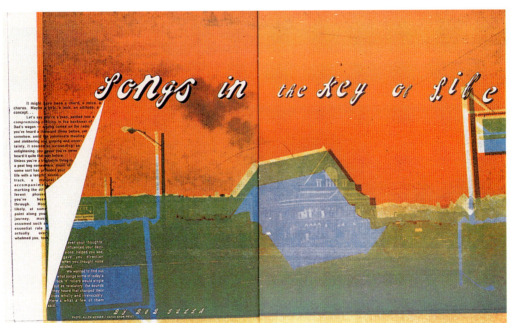

Raygun no. 18

Magazine spread
ART DIRECTOR/DESIGNER / David Carson
PHOTOGRAPHER / Allen Messer
CLIENT / Ray Gun Publishing

USA, 1994

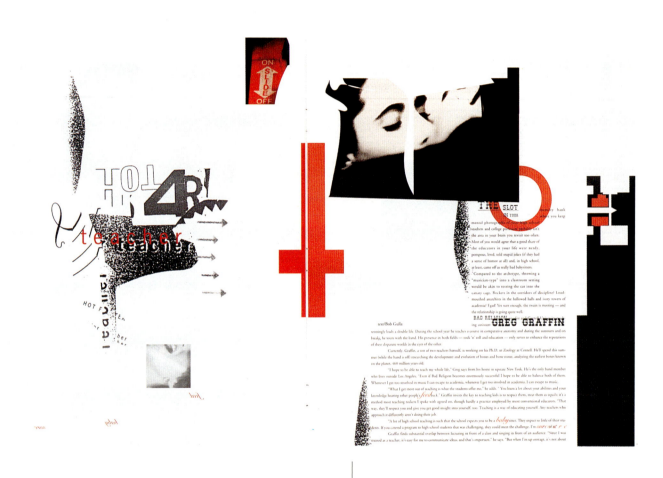

**Raygun no. 19**

Magazine Spreads

ART DIRECTOR David Carson
DESIGNER Martin Venezky
CLIENT Ray Gun Publishing

*USA, 1994*

**Raygun no. 29**

Magazine spread
ART DIRECTOR/DESIGNER David Carson
ILLUSTRATORS Vera Daucher,
Sarah Cromwell,
Nick Whiting
PRINCIPAL TYPEFACE Neulin Sans
CLIENT Ray Gun Publishing

USA, 1995

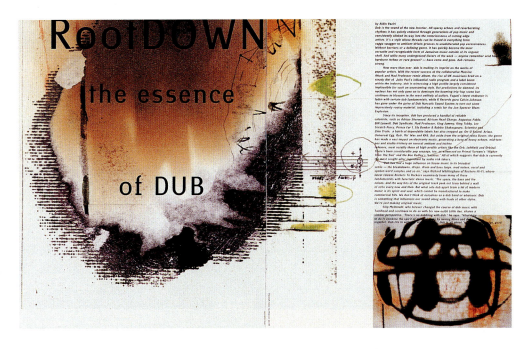

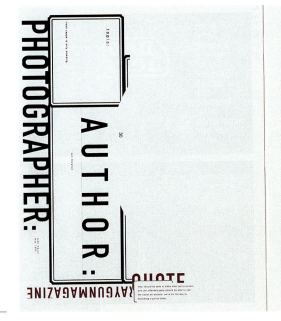

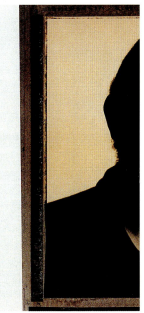

ART DIRECTOR/DESIGNER David Carson
PHOTOGRAPHER Aldo Mauro
CLIENT Ray Gun Publishing

Raygun no. 30

Magazine spread

USA, 1995

In the issues leading up to David Carson's departure from *Raygun*, there was already evidence of a move towards a much quieter typography described by the magazine's publisher, Marvin Scott Jarrett, as "a new simplicity". This was most starkly apparent in issue 30, Carson's swansong, where in place of his customary fractured headline treatments he devised a label-like credit box that emphasised the contributors' functions rather than their bylines.

Bikini no. 3

Magazine spread

| | |
|---|---|
| DESIGN DIRECTOR | Scott Clum |
| DESIGN COMPANY | Ride Design |
| PHOTOGRAPHER | Cynthia Levine |
| ILLUSTRATOR | Scott Clum |
| PRINCIPAL TYPEFACES | Matrix, Osprey |
| CLIENT | Ray Gun Publishing |

*USA, 1994*

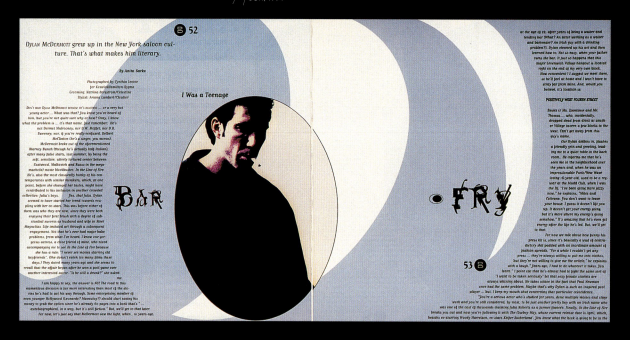

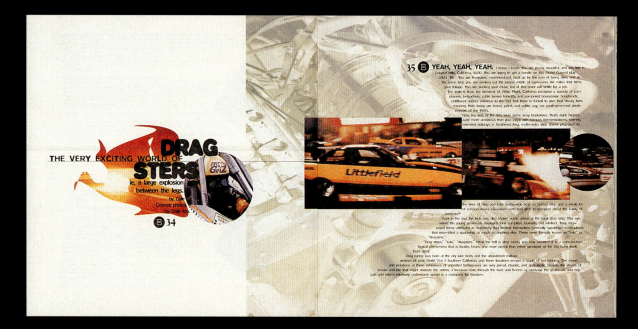

Bikini no. 11

Magazine spread

| | |
|---|---|
| DESIGN DIRECTOR | Scott Clum |
| DESIGN COMPANY | Ride Design |
| PHOTOGRAPHER | Cole Coonce |
| PRINCIPAL TYPEFACE | Blur |
| CLIENT | Ray Gun Publishing |

*USA, 1995*

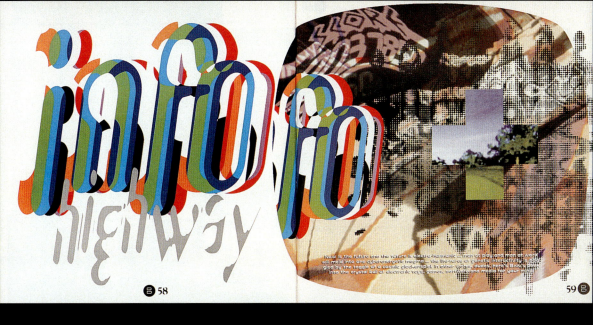

info highway

Now is the future and the future is electro-harmonic ... men at play and men at work will meld into one cyber-energetic imaging ... the life-force of genetic interactivity is boggled by the toggle of a cosmic gladiengold. In other words, dude, lean back and jack into the crystal ball of electronic teletraumas, stertutra and media for your mind.

Bikini no. 2

Magazine spread

| DESIGN DIRECTOR | Scott Clum |
| DESIGNERS | Rey International |
| DESIGN COMPANY | Ride Design |
| CLIENT | Ray Gun Publishing |

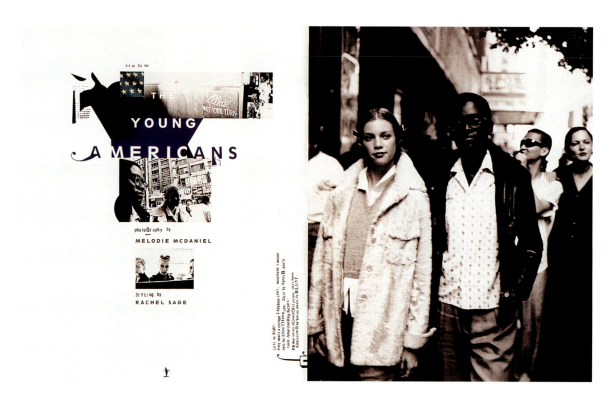

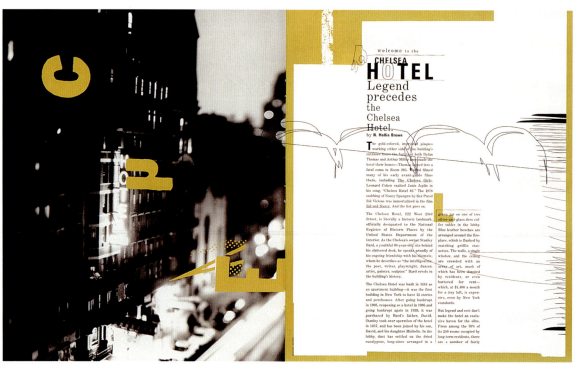

Speak, preview issue

Magazine spreads

ART DIRECTOR/DESIGNER Martin Venezky

CONTRIBUTING DESIGNERS Bob Aufuldish, Fred Bower, Bill Bowers, Elliott Peter Earls, Geoff Kaplan

PHOTOGRAPHERS Melodie McDaniel, Michael Darter, Paige Stuart

PRINCIPAL TYPEFACES Univers, Bodoni, Franklin Gothic, Spartan Classified, Century Expanded, custom-made for the project

PUBLISHER Dan Rolleri

USA, 1995

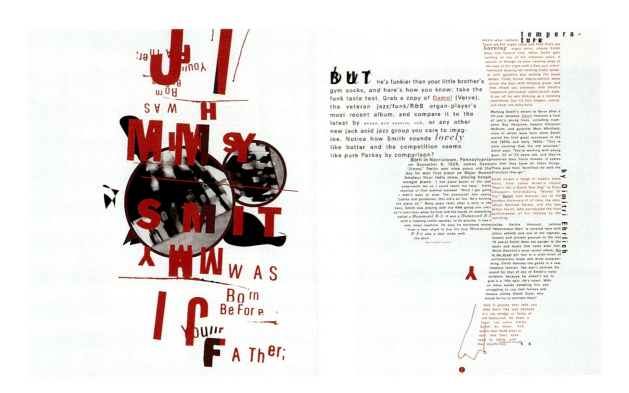

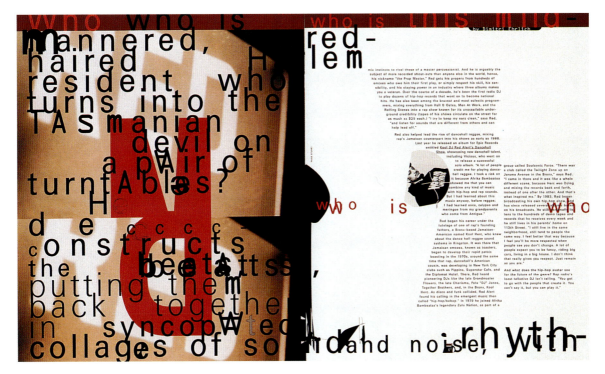

Raygun's impact with readers, advertisers and the design community made it inevitable that others would attempt to apply its lessons. Speak magazine, published in San Francisco, is a quarterly review of fashion, lifestyle and the arts. Martin Venezky, art director for the preview issue, had created a number of pages for Raygun and his design for Speak achieves a balance between readability in the main copy and expression in its display typography and other visual devices. David Carson was appointed art director from the second issue.

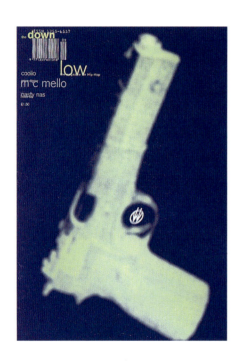

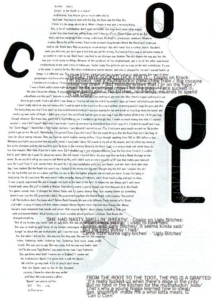

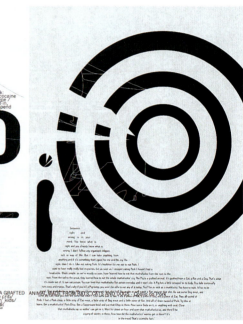

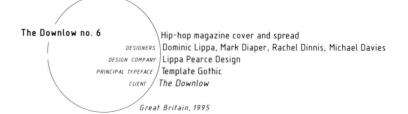

The Downlow no. 6                    Hip-hop magazine cover and spread

DESIGNERS                  Dominic Lippa, Mark Diaper, Rachel Dinnis, Michael Davies

DESIGN COMPANY             Lippa Pearce Design

PRINCIPAL TYPEFACE         Template Gothic

CLIENT                     The Downlow

Great Britain, 1995

**The Downlow no. 9**

Hip-hop magazine cover and spread
DESIGNERS | Michael Davies, Mark Diaper, Birgit Eggers
PRINCIPAL TYPEFACES | Triplex, Citizen, OCRB, News Gothic
CLIENT | *The Downlow*

*Great Britain, 1995*

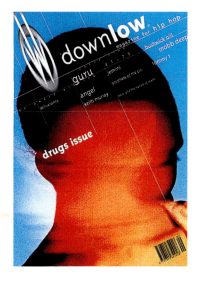

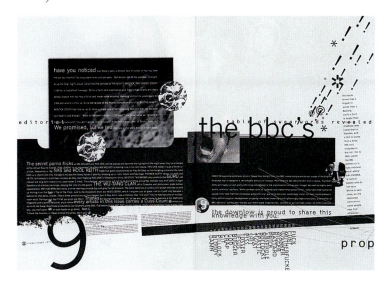

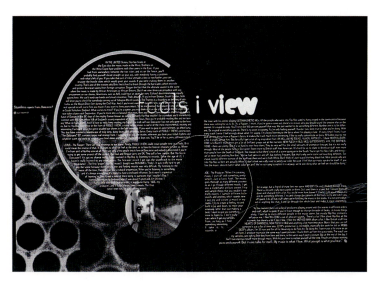

**The Downlow no. 10**

Hip-hop magazine spread
DESIGNERS | Michael Davies, Mark Diaper, Birgit Eggers,
MC Colosseum, Shaun O'Mara, Glen Thornley, Alan King
PRINCIPAL TYPEFACE | Template Gothic
CLIENT | *The Downlow*

*Great Britain, 1996*

Blah Blah Blah no. 1

Magazine cover and spread
*ART DIRECTORS/DESIGNERS* Chris Ashworth, Neil Fletcher, Amanda Sissons
*DESIGN COMPANY* Substance
*PHOTOGRAPHER* Alison Dyer
*PRINCIPAL TYPEFACE* DIN
*CLIENT* Ray Gun Publishing

*Great Britain, 1996*

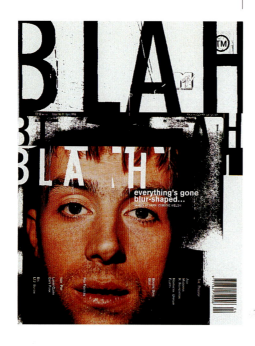

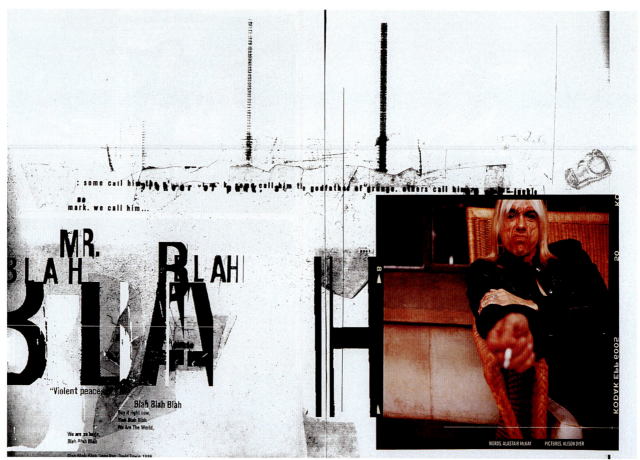

Blah Blah Blah no. 2

Magazine spread

ART DIRECTORS/DESIGNERS | Chris Ashworth, Neil Fletcher, Amanda Sissons
DESIGN COMPANY | Substance
PHOTOGRAPHER | Joseph Cultice
PRINCIPAL TYPEFACE | Compacta
CLIENT | Ray Gun Publishing

*Great Britain, 1996*

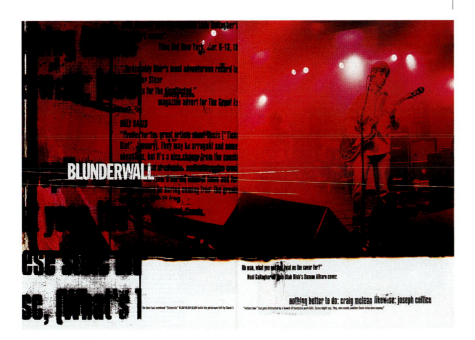

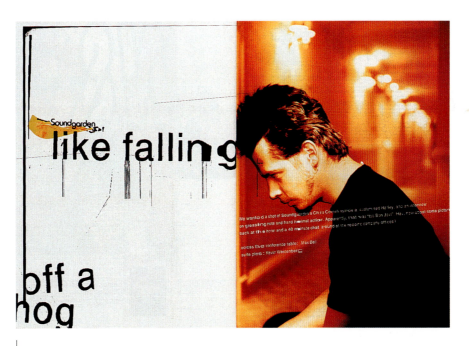

Blah Blah Blah no. 3

Magazine spread

ART DIRECTORS/DESIGNERS | Chris Ashworth, Neil Fletcher, Amanda Sissons
DESIGN COMPANY | Substance
PHOTOGRAPHER | Kevin Westenberg
PRINCIPAL TYPEFACE | Univers
CLIENT | Ray Gun Publishing

*Great Britain, 1996*

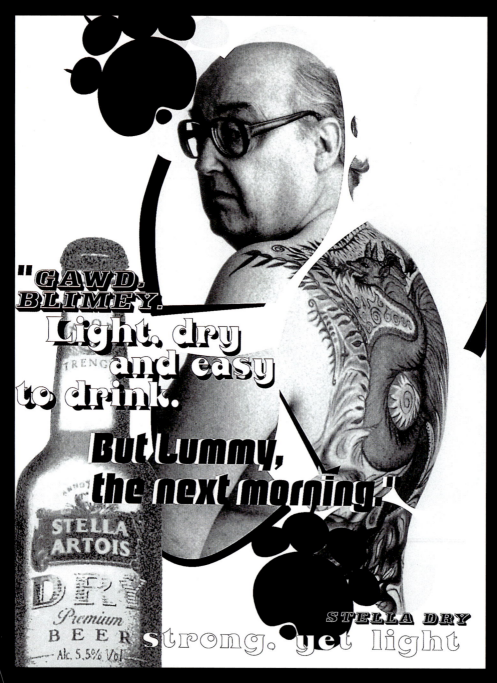

Stella Artois Dry

Print campaign
ART DIRECTOR | Simon Butler
DESIGNERS/ILLUSTRATORS | Whitney Lowe, Somi Kim, Lisa Nugent, James Moore
DESIGN COMPANY | ReVerb
PHOTOGRAPHER | Tim O. Sullivan (tattoo)
PRINCIPAL TYPEFACES | Abbess, Altoona, Acropilis, Dolmen Decorated, Egbert, Enlivan, Falstaff, Siena, Garage Gothic, Helvetica, Melody, Monster, Narly, Pinwheel, Phrastic,
AGENCY | Lowe Howard-Spink
CLIENT | Whitbread

*Great Britain, 1995*

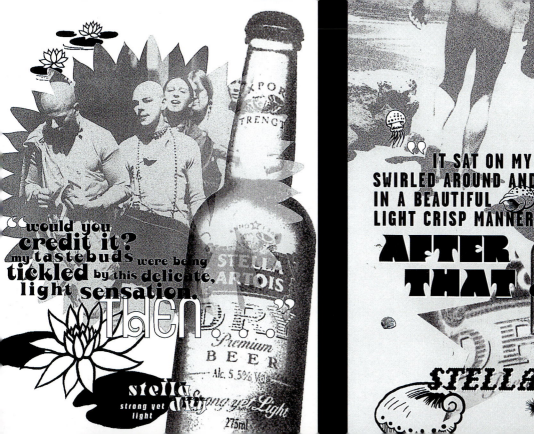

"would you **credit it?** my **tastebuds** were being **tickled** by this **delicate, light sensation.** THEN...

STELLA ARTOIS
EXPORT STRENGTH
Premium BEER
Alc. 5.5% Vol
strong yet Light
275ml

stella dry
strong yet light

"IT SAT ON MY TONGUE, SWIRLED AROUND AND DISAPPEARED IN A BEAUTIFUL LIGHT CRISP MANNER, **AFTER THAT**..."

STELLA ARTOIS
DRY
Premium
Alc. 5.5% Vol
Strong yet light

STELLA DRY

STRONG yet light

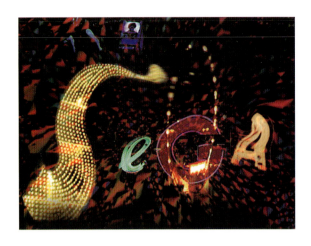

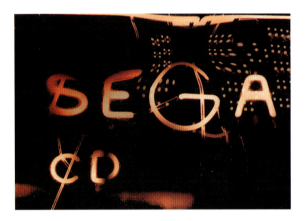

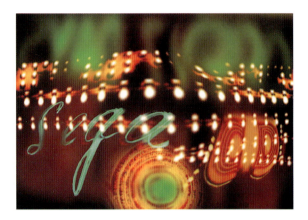

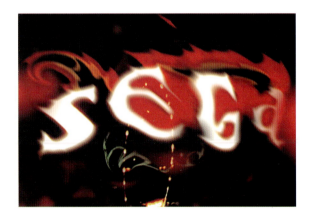

**The Bearded Lady**

Television commercial
DIRECTOR / Kinka Usher
ART DIRECTOR / Todd Grant
CREATIVE DIRECTOR / Bo Coyner
DESIGNER/ANIMATOR / Alexei Tylevich
AGENCY / Goodby, Silverstein & Partners
PRINCIPAL TYPEFACES / Custom-made for the project
CLIENT / Sega

USA, 1994

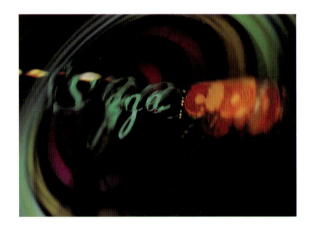

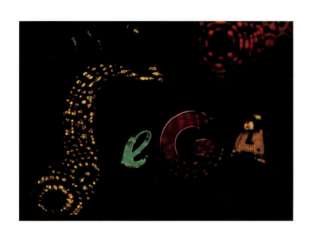

The bizarre narrative of Sega's
commercial for a 32-bit game system
was set in an amusement park freak show.
Alexei Tylevich's animated typographic
segments for both 30 and 60 second
versions reflect the hallucinatory theme
of the commercial's live action.

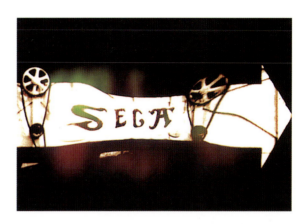

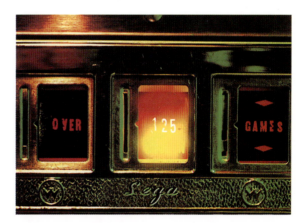

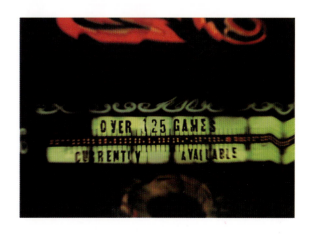

Print campaign

DESIGNER | Simon Taylor
DESIGN COMPANY | Tomato
AGENCY | Bates Dorland
PHOTOGRAPHER | Simon Taylor
PRINCIPAL TYPEFACES | DIN Engschrift, Aachen
CLIENT | Grolsch

*Great Britain, 1995*

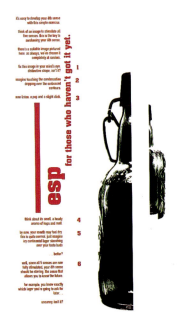

it's easy to develop your 4th sense
with this simple exercise.

think of an image to stimulate all
five senses. this is the key to
awakening your 6th sense.

there's a suitable image pictured
here. as always, we've chosen it
completely at random.

fix this image in your mind's eye.
distinctive shape, isn't it?                    1

imagine touching the condensation
dripping over the embossed                      2
contours.

now listen. a pop and a slight clink.           3

**esp** for those who haven't got it yet.

think about its smell. a heady
aroma of hops and malt.                          4

by now, your mouth may feel dry.
this is quite normal. just imagine              5
icy continental lager sloshing
over your taste buds.

...better?

well, since all 5 senses are now
fully stimulated, your 6th sense                6
should be stirring. the sense that
allows you to know the future.

for example, you know exactly
which lager you're going to ask for
later. ...

uncanny, isn't it?

*Extra Sensory Perfection*

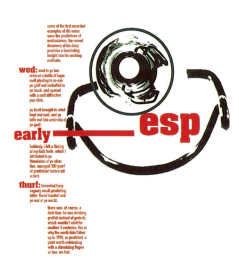

*Extra Sensory Perfection*

some of the first recorded
examples of 6th sense
were the predictions of
nostradamus. the recent
discovery of his diary
provides a fascinating
insight into his working
methods;

**wed:** went to ye bar.
ordered a bottle of lager.
moft pleafing to ye eye.
ye glaff waf embolfed to
ye touch, and opened
with a moft diftinctive
pop clink.

ye fmell brought to mind
hopf and malt, and ye
tafte waf like ambrofia of
ye godf.

**early** ———— **esp**

fuddenly, i felt a ftirring
of my fixth fenfe. which i
attributed to ye
ftimulation of ye other
five. managed 300 yearf
of prediction before laft
orderf.

**thurf:** fomewhat hazy.
vaguely recall predicting
hitler. flared trouferf and
ye end of ye world.

there was, of course, a
fatal flaw. he was drinking
grolfch inftead of grolsch,
which wouldn't exist for
another 3 centuries. this is
why the world didn't blow
up in 1990, as predicted. a
point worth celebrating
with a stimulating flagon
or two. we feel.

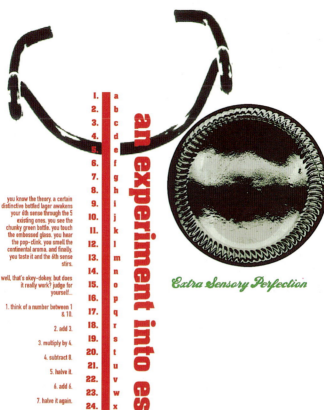

**an experiment into esp**

| | |
|---|---|
| 1. | a |
| 2. | b |
| 3. | c |
| 4. | d |
| 5. | e |
| 6. | f |
| 7. | g |
| 8. | h |
| 9. | i |
| 10. | j |
| 11. | k |
| 12. | l |
| 13. | m |
| 14. | n |
| 15. | o |
| 16. | p |
| 17. | q |
| 18. | r |
| 19. | s |
| 20. | t |
| 21. | u |
| 22. | v |
| 23. | w |
| 24. | x |
| 25. | y |
| 26. | z |

*Extra Sensory Perfection*

you know the theory. a certain distinctive bottled lager awakens your 6th sense through the 5 existing ones. you see the chunky green bottle. you touch the embossed glass. you hear the pop-clink. you smell the continental aroma. and finally, you taste it and the 6th sense stirs.

well, that's okey-dokey. but does it really work? judge for yourself...

1. think of a number between 1 & 10.

2. add 3.

3. multiply by 4.

4. subtract 8.

5. halve it.

6. add 6.

7. halve it again.

8. add 3.

9. subtract the number you first thought of.

10. match the remaining number to its corresponding letter on the mystic chart.

now concentrate on a premium lager beginning with that letter.

absolutely correct. your 6th sense is alive and well. it's probably thirsty, too. so why not pop open a chilled bottle of 7-18-15-12-19-3-0?

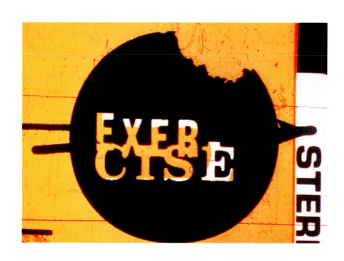

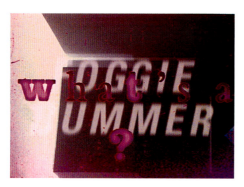

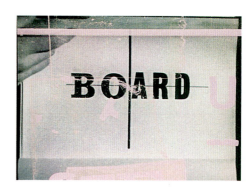

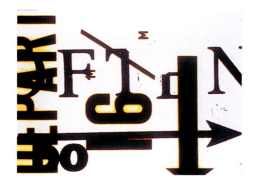

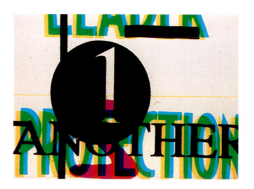

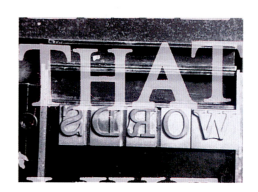

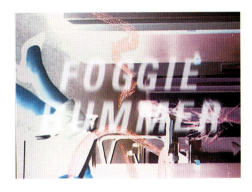

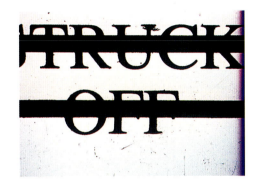

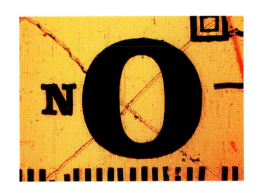

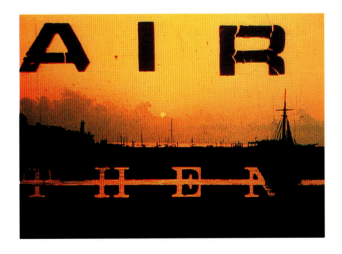

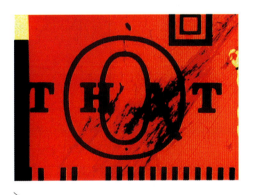

**Foggie Bummer**

Commercial for a spoken-word radio station

DESIGNER     Jonathan Barnbrook
WRITERS     Lindsey Redding, Adrian Jefferey
AGENCY     Faulds
PRINCIPAL TYPEFACES     Clarendon, Times, Franklin Gothic, Eurostile
CLIENT     BBC Radio Scotland

*Great Britain, 1995*

**True Romance**

Commercial for a spoken-word radio station
DESIGNER / Jonathan Barnbrook
WRITERS / Lindsey Redding, Adrian Jeffereys
AGENCY / Faulds
PRINCIPAL TYPEFACES / Manson, Bastard, Nixonscript
CLIENT / BBC Radio Scotland

*Great Britain, 1995*

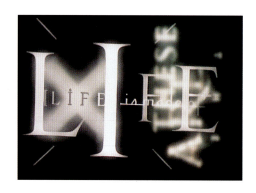

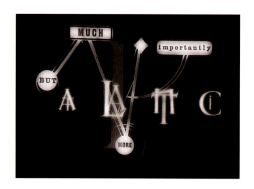

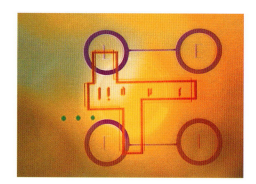

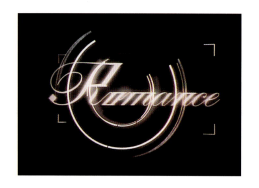

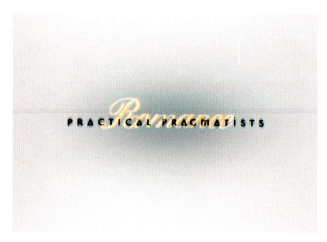

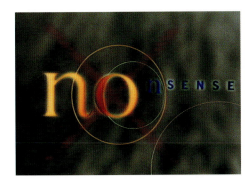
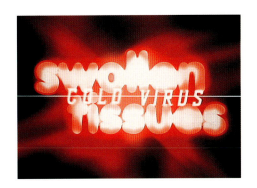
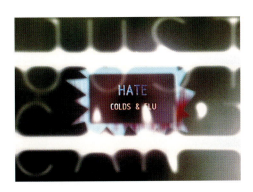
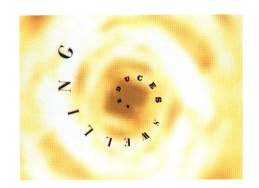
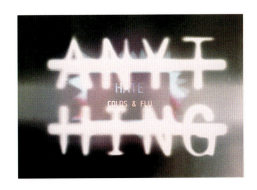
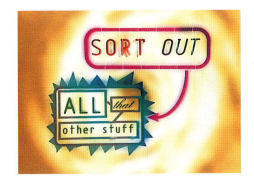

**Vicks Action**

Commercial for a cold remedy
DESIGNER / Jonathan Barnbrook
WRITERS / Stuart Newman, Julian Borra
AGENCY / Leo Burnett
PRINCIPAL TYPEFACES / Letter Gothic, VAG Rounded, Isonorm
CLIENT / Procter & Gamble

*Great Britain, 1995*

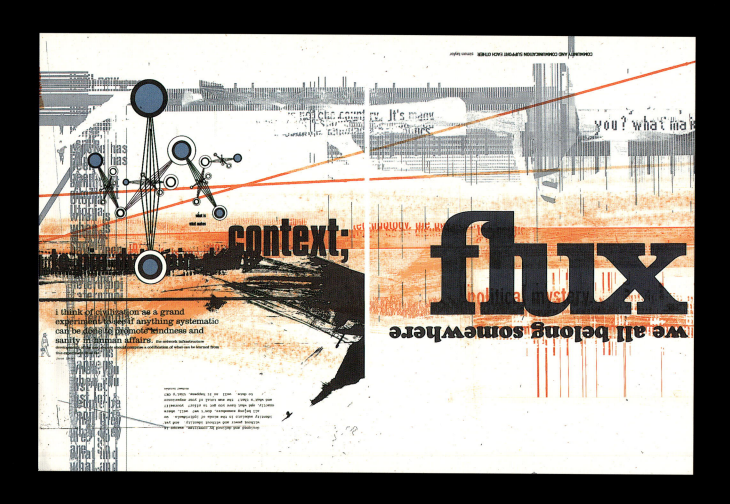

The subject of MTV's first European music awards was "global communication" and the designers' aim was to portray this in typography and image. Working collaboratively, they visualised the collage of quotations and specially written texts as an emotive, flowing stream of consciousness, rather than as a series of separate and possibly disjointed spreads. To enhance the intended humanistic feel, most of the artwork was originated by hand and a variety of papers was used.

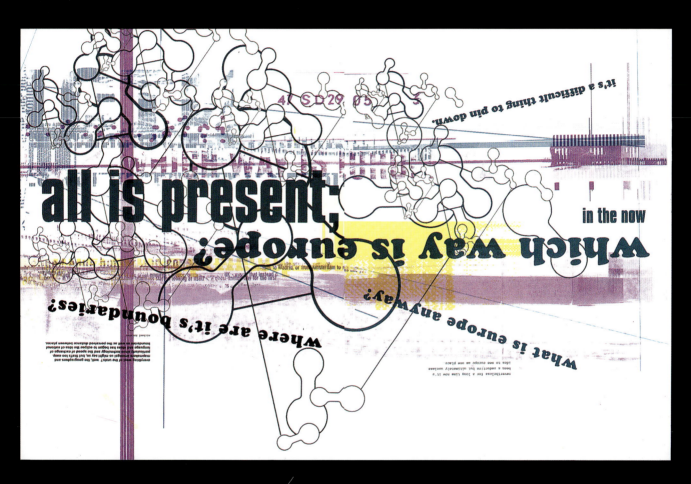

Global Communication: Channel Your Experience

Spreads from a brochure for the MTV Music Awards
*DESIGN DIRECTORS* / John Warwicker, Simon Taylor
*DESIGNERS* / John Warwicker, Simon Taylor, Chris Ashworth, David Smith
*WRITER* / Michael Horsham
*DESIGN COMPANIES* / Tomato, Invisible
*PRINCIPAL TYPEFACES* / Cooper Black, Compacta, Clarendon, Courier, DIN
*CLIENT* / MTV Europe

*Great Britain, 1994*

The complexity I'm interested

I'm not so much interested

layers of meaning . . . I think

society because the conten

complex. Simple black and wh

Graphic design that tries to m

anybody any real benefit. Soci

to deal with the subtlety, con

contemporary life . . . it is po

both complexity and intelli

I'M REALLY I
THIS CONCE
SURFACES". 
MYSTICAL E
INDUSTRIA
OR ALLOYS, C

Most of the time the message isn't worth saying. So when you do get a chance

to say something yourself, you might as well say something you believe in . . .

There's a reason for the way I do things and if you look I hope you'll get the

meaning, though the communication process isn't so direct that you are

necessarily going to get it the first time you look at it.— Jonathan Barnbrook

**d in is complexity of meaning.**
**in the layers of form as the**
**k this approach fits modern**
**nporary world is subtle and**
**nite dualisms no longer work.**
**ake things simple is not doing**
**iety needs to understand how**
**nplexity and contradiction in**
**ssible and necessary to have**
**igibility in graphic design.** *Katherine McCoy*

*NTERESTED IN*
*'T OF "LIVING*
*. . IN MERGING*
*:EMENTS WITH*
*L ELEMENTS*
*ULTURAL ALLOYS.*

P. SCOTT MAKELA

CULTURE:

institutional

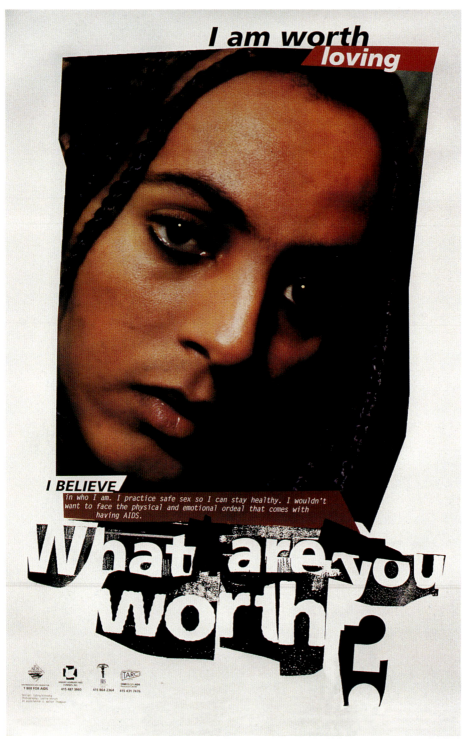

The designers conceived a campaign to reach populations under-served or ignored by San Francisco's AIDS prevention literature. Each poster combines an honest portrait of a local individual, based on the designers' interviews, with the person's own answer to the question. The typography purposely avoids the customary slickness of most citywide advertising in an attempt to capture a hands-on, spontaneous visual language that will appeal to the target group.

**What Are You Worth?**

AIDS prevention poster
DESIGNERS / Martin Venezky, Raul Cabra
DESIGN COMPANY / Diseño
PHOTOGRAPHER / Leslie Hirsch
CLIENT / San Francisco AIDS Foundation

/ USA, 1995

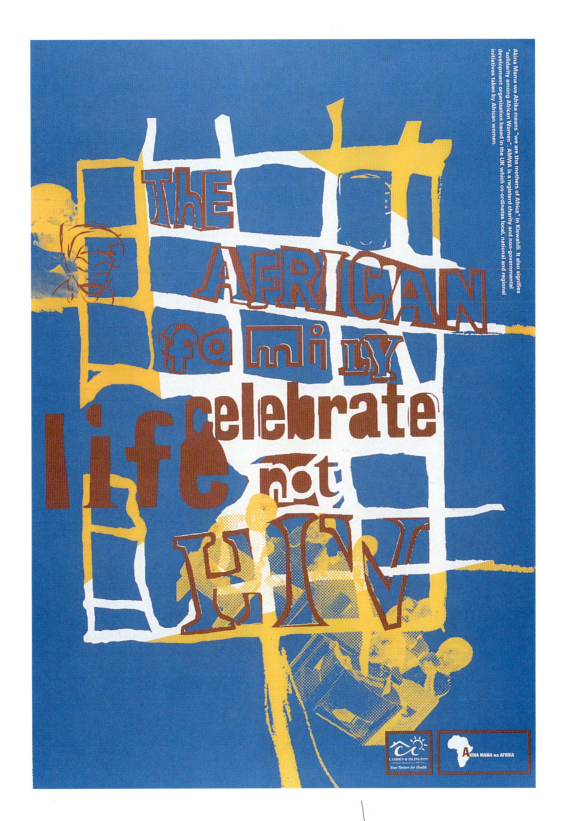

Akina Mama wa Afrika means "we are the mothers of Africa" in Kiswahili. It also signifies "solidarity among African Women". AMWA is a registered charity and non-governmental development organisation based in the UK which co-ordinates local, national and regional initiatives taken by African women.

Poster for World AIDS Day
DESIGNER · Joseph Thomas
DESIGN COMPANY · Push
ILLUSTRATORS · Joseph Thomas, Patrice Gueroult
PRINCIPAL TYPEFACES · Univers, Bureau Grotesque
CLIENT · Akina Mama Wa Africa

*Great Britain, 1994*

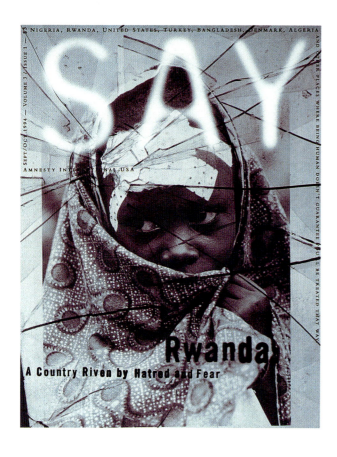

**Say vol. 3 no. 1**

Magazine cover and spread aimed at a student/youth readership

DESIGNERS | Hal Wolverton, Pam Racs
DESIGN COMPANY | Johnson & Wolverton
PHOTOGRAPHER | Stephen Dupont
ILLUSTRATOR | Pam Racs
CLIENT | Amnesty International

USA, 1994

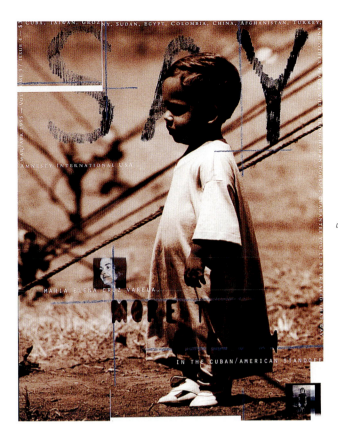

Say vol. 3 no. 4

Magazine cover and spread aimed at a student/youth readership
DESIGNERS / Hal Wolverton, Kat Saito, Robin Muir
DESIGN COMPANY / Johnson & Wolverton
CLIENT / Amnesty International

USA, 1995

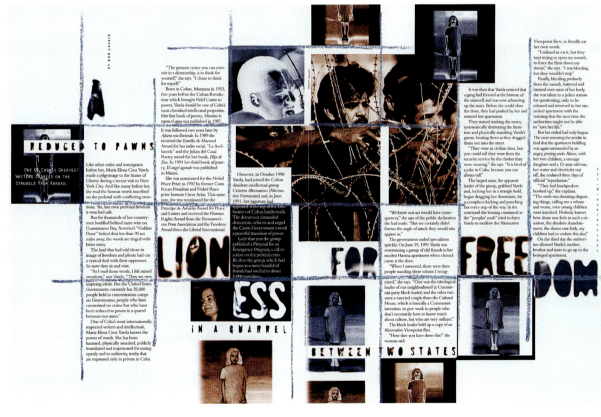

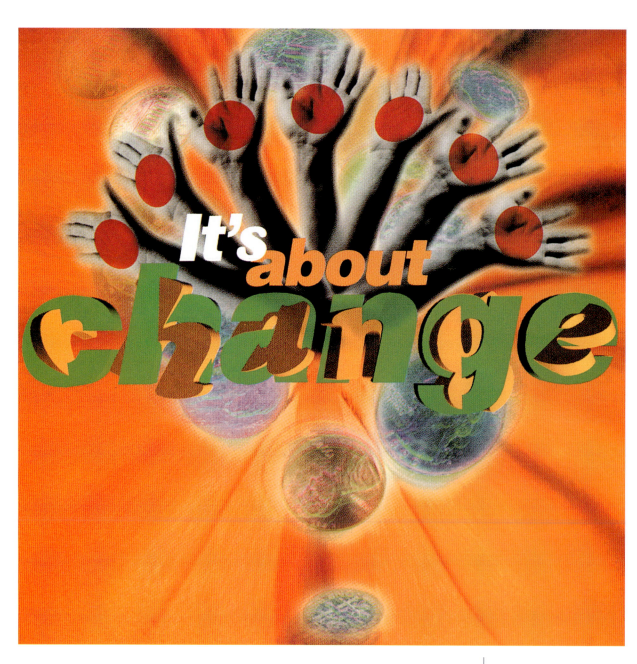

It's About Change

AIDS fundraising poster
DESIGNERS | Richard Bates, Rob Eberhart
DESIGN COMPANY | Bates Hori
PHOTOGRAPHERS | Richard Bates, Allen Hori
PRINCIPAL TYPEFACES | Goudy, Helvetica
CLIENT | Lifebeat

USA, 1994

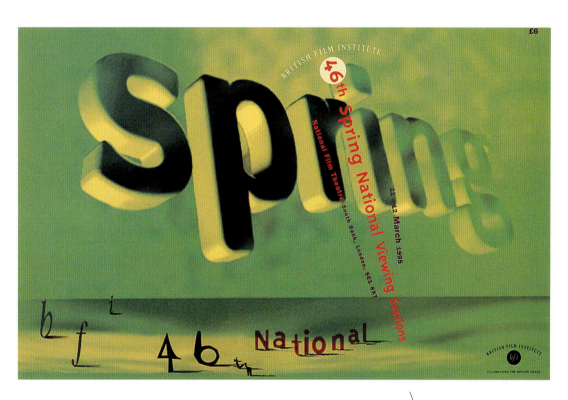

**46th Spring National Viewing Sessions**

Catalogue cover
DESIGNER | Joseph Thomas
DESIGN COMPANY | Push
PRINCIPAL TYPEFACE | Triplex
CLIENT | British Film Institute

*Great Britain, 1995*

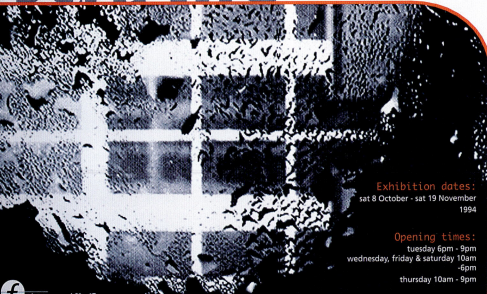

Ruth **MYLIUS**

PHOTOPSY

 **f.stop** Gallery & Darkrooms, Green Park Station, Bath, ba1 1jb.

MYLIUS

**Exhibition dates:**
sat 8 October - sat 19 November
1994

**Opening times:**
tuesday 6pm - 9pm
wednesday, friday & saturday 10am
-6pm
thursday 10am - 9pm

**Exhibition preview:**
saturday 8 October 6 - 8pm

f.Stop Gallery & Darkrooms, Green Park Station, Bath, ba1 1jb.

INVESTMENT
SOUTH WEST ARTS

Green Park
STATION
BATH LIMITED

Design: Julian Harriman-Dickinson.

Photopsy

Poster for photographic exhibition
*DESIGNER* Julian Harriman-Dickinson
*PHOTOGRAPHER* Ruth Mylius
*PRINCIPAL TYPEFACES* Custom-made for the project, Monaco
*CLIENT* f.Stop Gallery

ILLUSTRATOR Andreas Gefe
PRINCIPAL TYPEFACES Custom-made for the proje
CLIENT Rote Fabrik

Switzerland, 1994

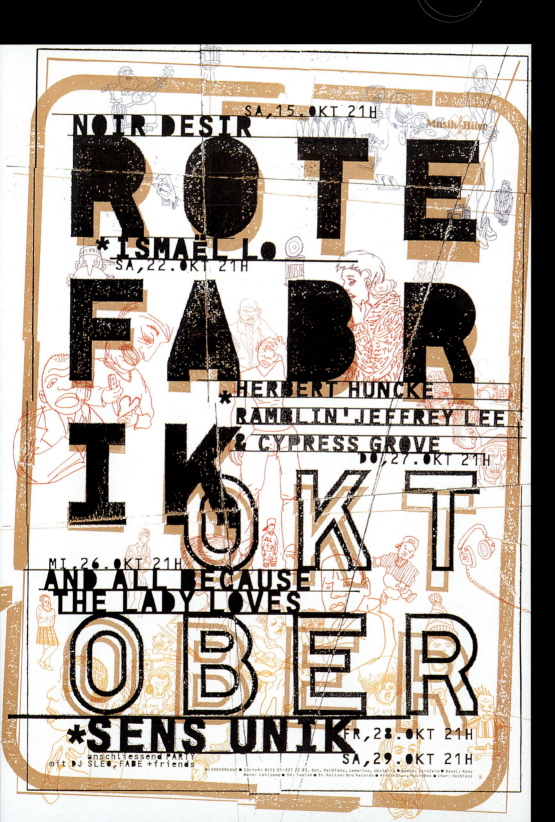

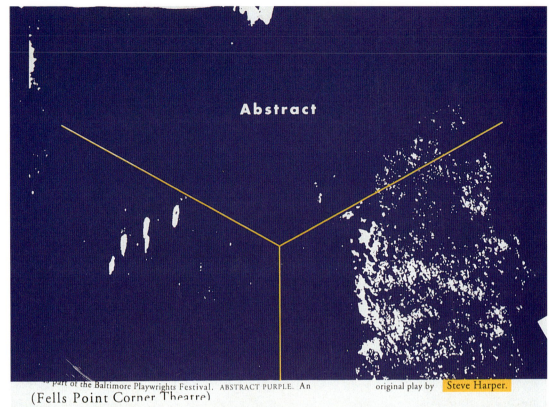

**Abstract**

...part of the Baltimore Playwrights Festival.  ABSTRACT PURPLE.  An   original play by Steve Harper.

(Fells Point Corner Theatre)

JULY 15  3¹   2 76.   CALL   78  3  7   Directed by Miriam Bazensky.

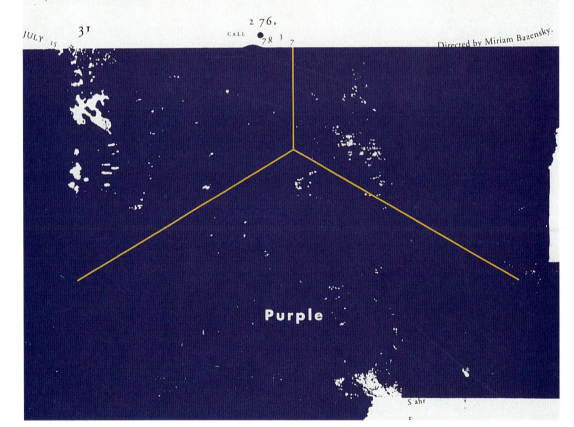

**Purple**

**Abstract Purple**

Theatre poster
DESIGNER Paul Sahre
PRINCIPAL TYPEFACES Garamond, Futura
CLIENT Fells Point Corner Theatre

USA, 1994

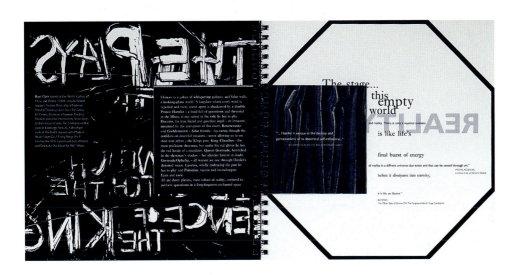

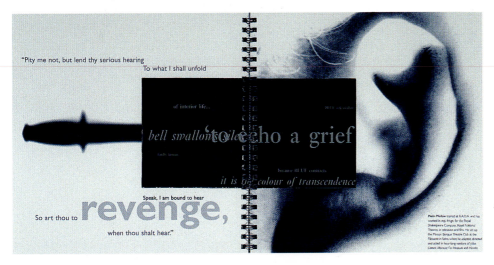

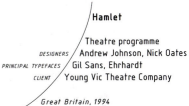

### Hamlet

Theatre programme

DESIGNERS / Andrew Johnson, Nick Oates

PRINCIPAL TYPEFACES / Gil Sans, Ehrhardt

CLIENT / Young Vic Theatre Company

*Great Britain, 1994*

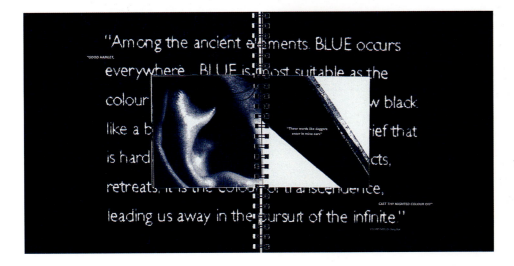

The pages of the wire-bound programme are cut to form a book within a book, allowing viewers to rearrange the pages in any number of permutations and engaging them in a physical, visual, textual and typographic exploration of the complexities of Shakespeare's tragedy.

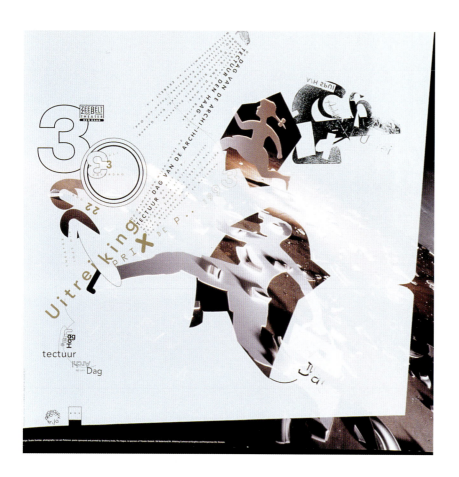

To keep colour printing costs down, Zeebelt Theater posters are conceived by Studio Dumbar as extended series. A photograph is printed in quantity and the monthly calendar or information for a specific event – such as The Hague's "Day of Architecture" – is silkscreened on top. Studio interns undertake many experimental typographic interpretations of the same base image.

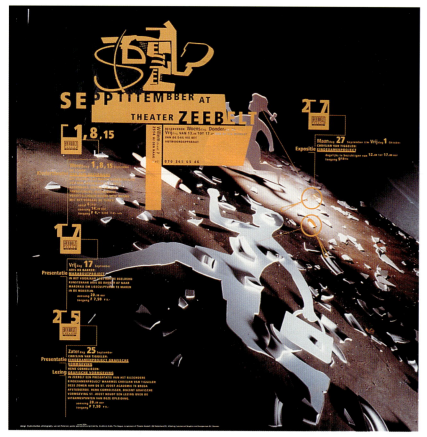

|  |  |
|---|---|
|  | Theatre posters |
| DESIGNER | Martin Venezky |
| DESIGN COMPANY | Studio Dumbar |
| PHOTOGRAPHER | Lex van Pieterson |
| PRINCIPAL TYPEFACE | Frutiger |
| CLIENT | Zeebelt Theater |

*The Netherlands, 1993*

Radix Matrix: The Architecture of Daniel Libeskind

Exhibition poster
DESIGNER Cornel Windlin
PRINCIPAL TYPEFACES Custom-made for the project
CLIENT Museum für Gestaltung, Zurich

Switzerland, 1994

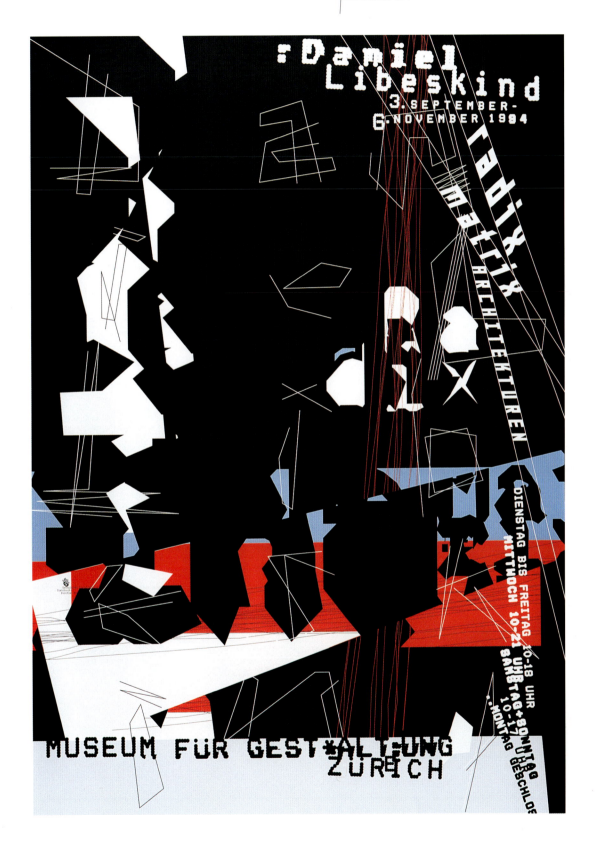

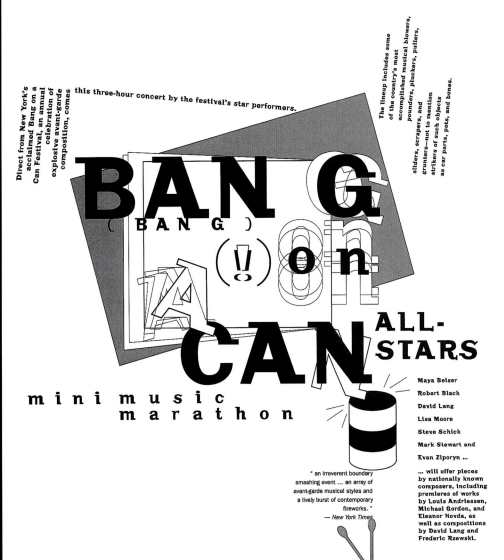

**Walker Art Center**
**and the Minnesota Composers Forum**
present

this three-hour concert by the festival's star performers.

Direct from New York's acclaimed Bang on a Can Festival, an annual celebration of explosive avant-garde composition, comes

The lineup includes some of the country's most accomplished musical blowers, pounders, pluckers, pullers, sliders, scrapers, and grunters—not to mention strikers of such objects as car parts, pots, and bones.

# BANG
( B A N G )
(!) on
# CAN ALL-STARS

m i n i  m u s i c
m a r a t h o n

Maya Beiser
Robert Black
David Lang
Lisa Moore
Steve Schick
Mark Stewart and
Evan Ziporyn ...

" an irreverent boundary smashing event ... an array of avant-garde musical styles and a lively burst of contemporary fireworks. "
— *New York Times*

... will offer pieces by nationally known composers, including premieres of works by Louis Andriessen, Michael Gordon, and Eleanor Hovda, as well as compositions by David Lang and Frederic Rzewski.

**8 pm**

**$ 10 ($8)**
**Saturday, November 21, 1992**
**Walker Auditorium**
For tickets, call the Walker box office at
**375-7622.**

($) = price for Walker and MCF members, seniors, AFDC cardholders, groups of 10 or more

Bang on the Can

Poster for a "noise" music event
DESIGNER          Susan LaPorte
DESIGN COMPANY    Walker Art Center Design Department
ILLUSTRATOR       Susan LaPorte
PRINCIPAL TYPEFACE   Big Girl Bold

A Lie of the Mind

Theatre poster
DESIGNERS | Paul Sahre, David Plunkert
PRINCIPAL TYPEFACE | Futura
CLIENT | Fells Point Corner Theatre

USA, 1993

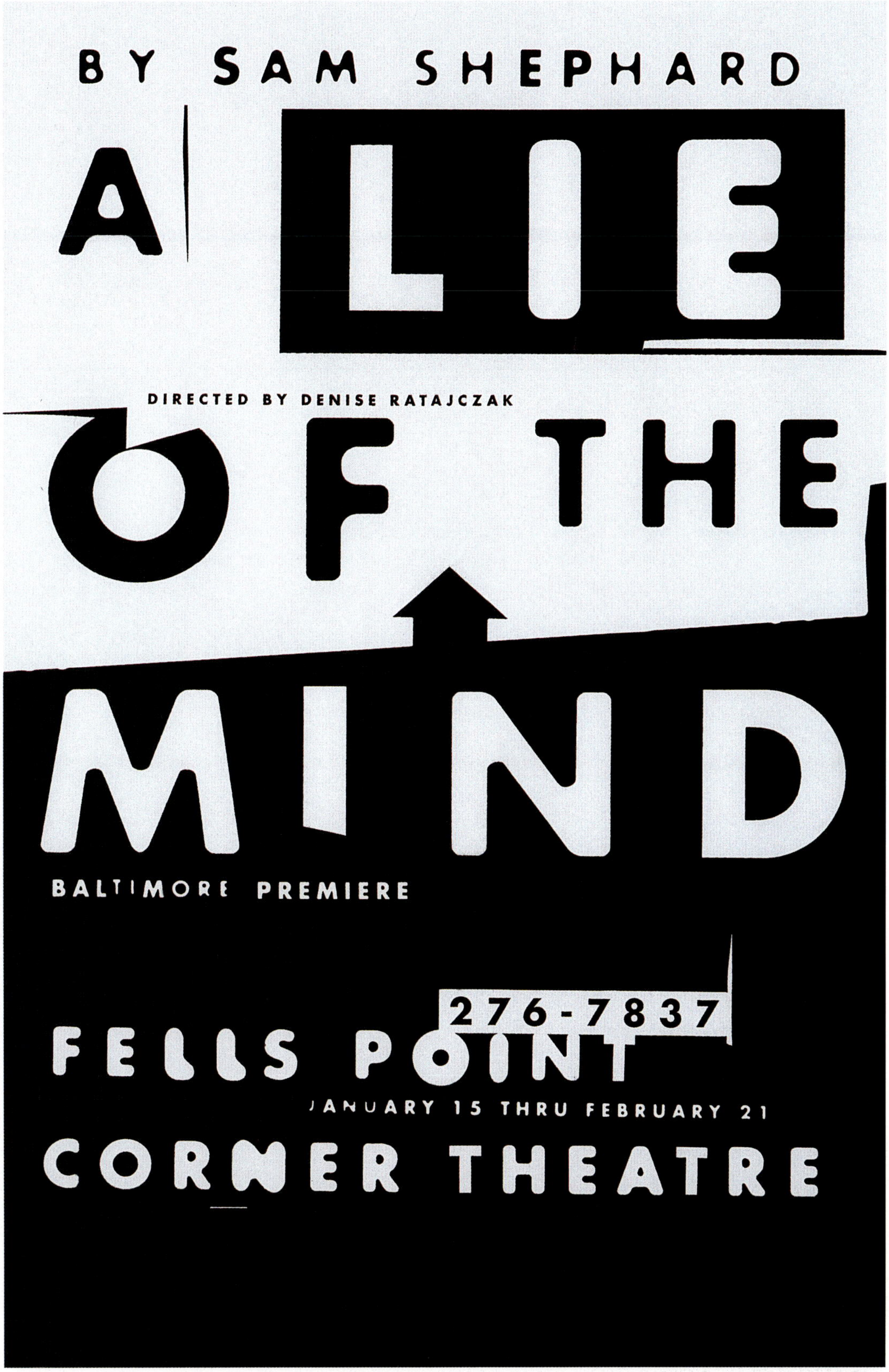

BY SAM SHEPHARD

A LIE

DIRECTED BY DENISE RATAJCZAK

OF THE

MIND

BALTIMORE PREMIERE

276-7837

FELLS POINT

JANUARY 15 THRU FEBRUARY 21

CORNER THEATRE

Spaced Out

Cover and spread from a leaflet for a series of talks on architecture

DESIGNER Jonathan Barnbrook
PRINCIPAL TYPEFACES Delux, Perpetua
CLIENT Institute of Contemporary Arts

Great Britain, 1995

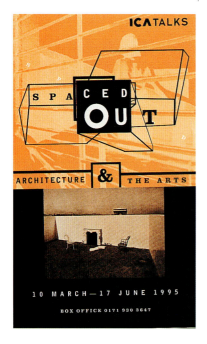

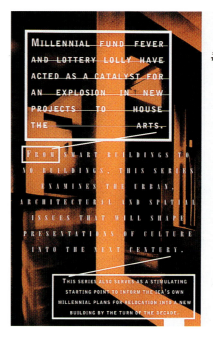

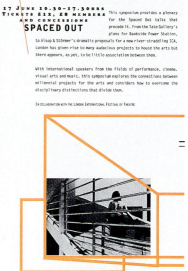

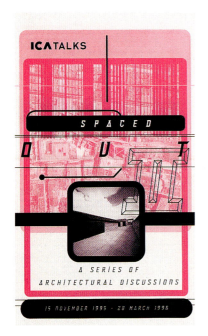

Spaced Out 2

Cover and spread from a leaflet for a series of talks on architecture
DESIGNER Jonathan Barnbrook
PRINCIPAL TYPEFACES Bell Gothic, Clarendon, Bodoni, Cooper Black
CLIENT Institute of Contemporary Arts

Great Britain, 1995

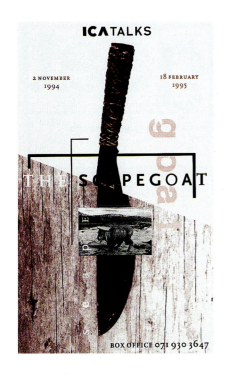

The Scapegoat

Cover and spread from a leaflet for a series of talks on social scapegoats

DESIGNER / Jonathan Barnbrook
PHOTOGRAPHER / Tomoko Yoneda
PRINCIPAL TYPEFACES / Scala, False Idol
CLIENT / Institute of Contemporary Arts

*Great Britain, 1994*

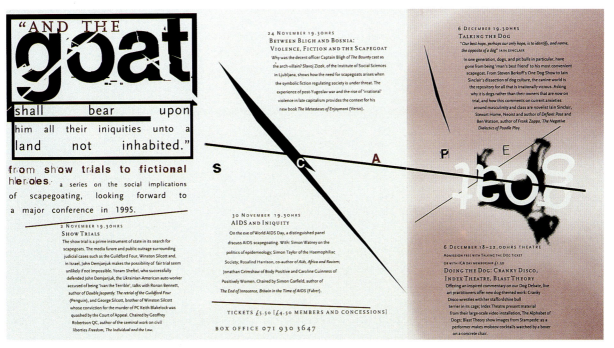

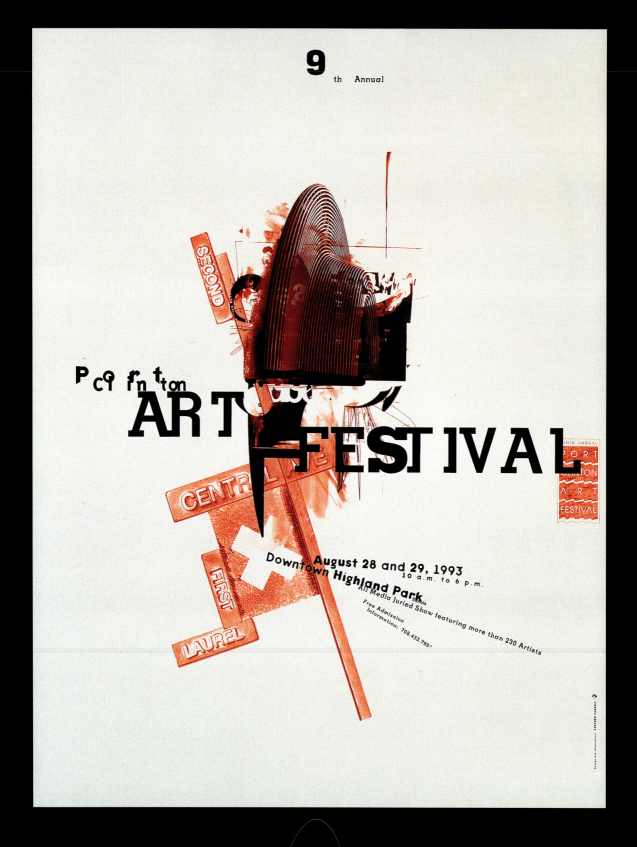

Port Clinton Art Festival

Poster
DESIGNER | Stephen Farrell
DESIGN COMPANY | Stephen Farrell Design
PRINCIPAL TYPEFACES | Carmella, Keedy Sans, Triplex
CLIENT | Highland Park Arts League

*USA, 1993*

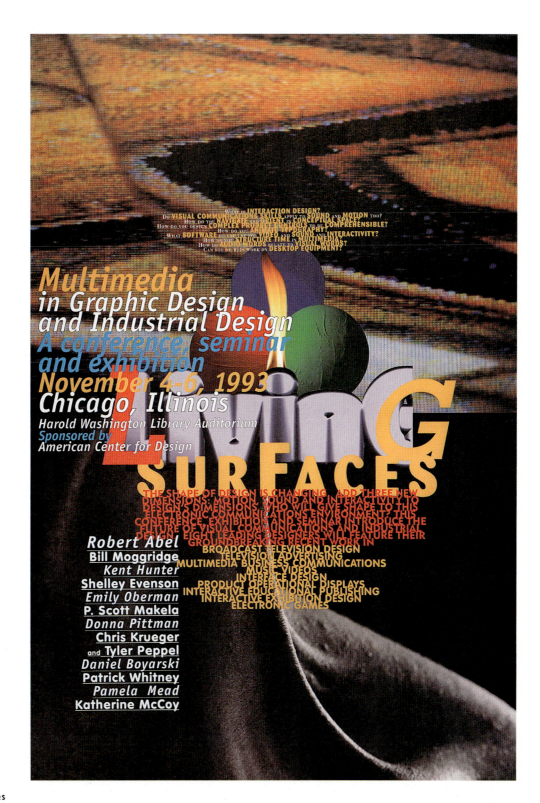

Living Surfaces

Conference poster
DESIGNER          P. Scott Makela
DESIGN COMPANY    Words and Pictures for Business and Culture
PHOTOGRAPHERS     Rik Sferra, P. Scott Makela
PRINCIPAL TYPEFACES  Officina, VAG Rounded, Barmeno
CLIENT            American Center for Design

USA, 1993

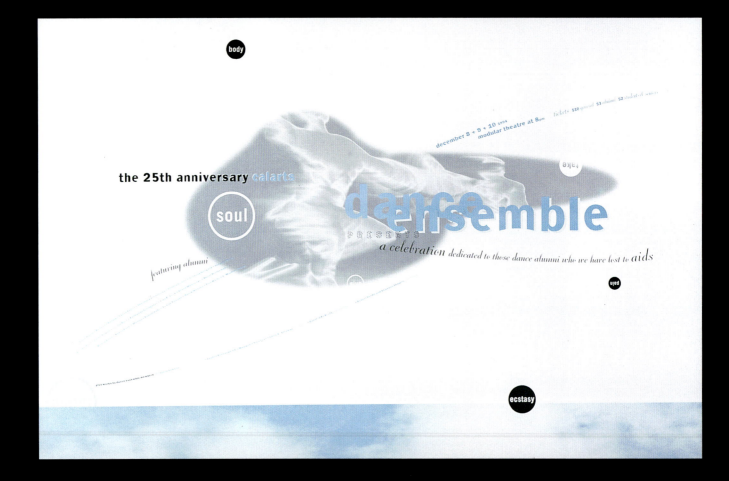

**Dance Ensemble**

Poster to announce a concert dedicated to dance alumni who died from AIDS

*DESIGNER* Jennifer Moody
*DESIGN COMPANY* Office of Public Affairs, California Institute of the Arts
*PHOTOGRAPHER* Steven Gunther
*PRINCIPAL TYPEFACES* Dorchester Script, Scala, Skelter, What the Hell
*CLIENT* School of Dance, California Institute of the Arts

*USA, 1994*

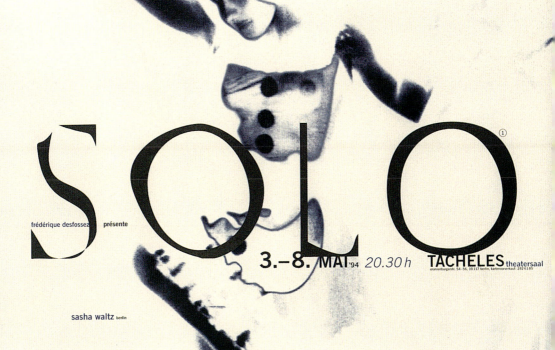

# SOLO ①

frédérique desfossez présente

3.–8. MAI '94 20.30 h **TACHELES** theatersaal
oranienburgerstr. 54–56, 10117 berlin, kartenvorverkauf: 282 61 85

sasha waltz berlin

adria ferrali florenz

kitt johnson kopenhagen

+ newcoming artists...

Film festival poster
DESIGNERS Heike Grebin, Andreas Trogisch
DESIGN COMPANY Grappa Design
PHOTOGRAPHER/ILLUSTRATOR Andreas Trogisch
PRINCIPAL TYPEFACE Eurostile
CLIENT Internationale Kurzfilmtage Oberhausen

Germany, 1995

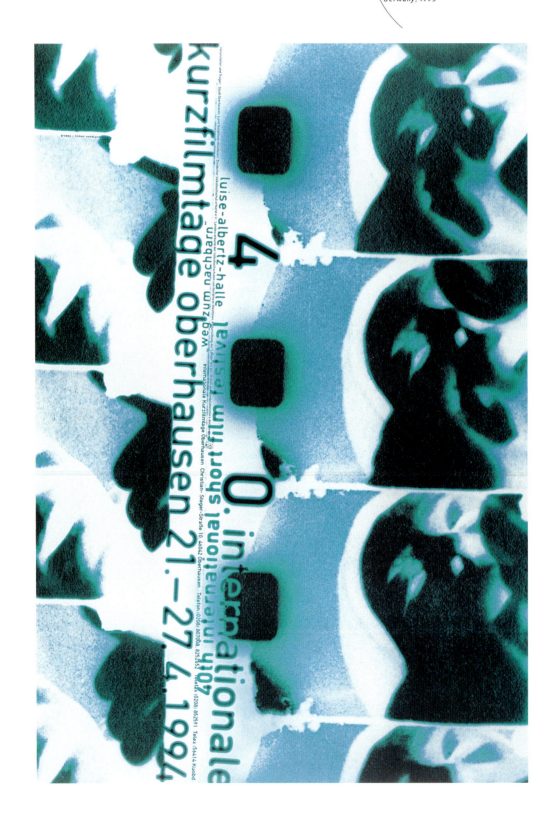

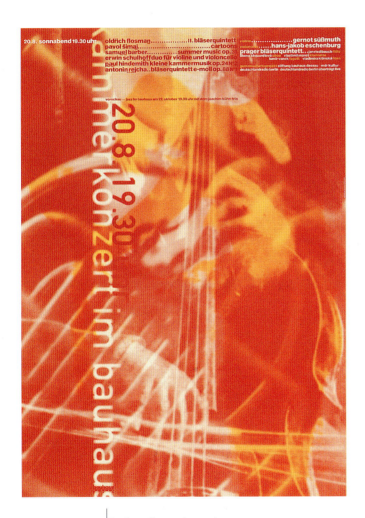

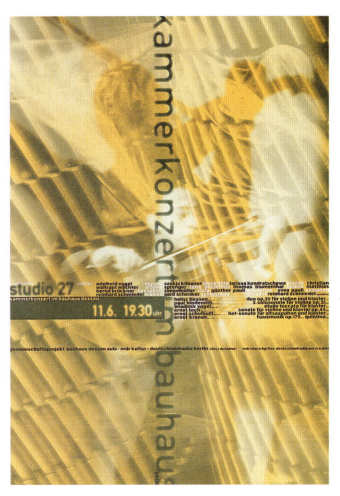

**Bauhaus Kammerkonzert**

Concert posters

DESIGNERS | Daniela Haufe, Detlef Fiedler
DESIGN COMPANY | Cyan
PRINCIPAL TYPEFACE | Akzidenz Grotesk
CLIENT | Bauhaus, Dessau

*Germany, 1994*

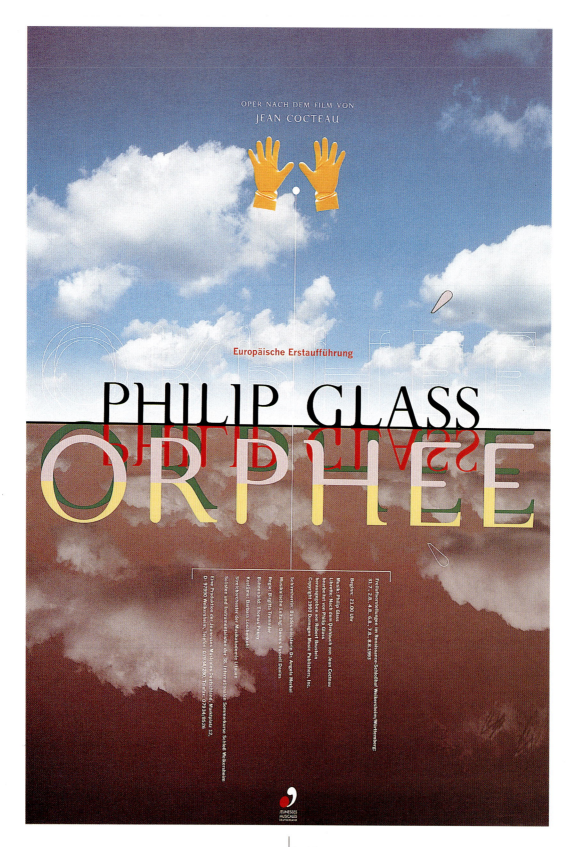

Orphée

Opera poster

DESIGNERS David Ellis, Andy Altmann
DESIGN COMPANY Why Not Associates
PHOTOGRAPHER Image Library
PRINCIPAL TYPEFACE Doddy
CLIENT Lippert Wilkens Partner

*Great Britain, 1993*

**Turangalîla**

Concert poster
DESIGNER | Andrew Johnson
PRINCIPAL TYPEFACE | Univers
CLIENT | Royal Philharmonic Orchestra

*Great Britain, 1993*

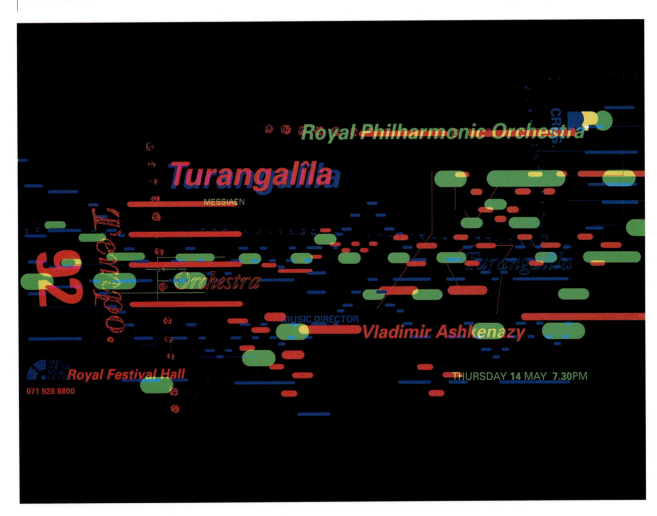

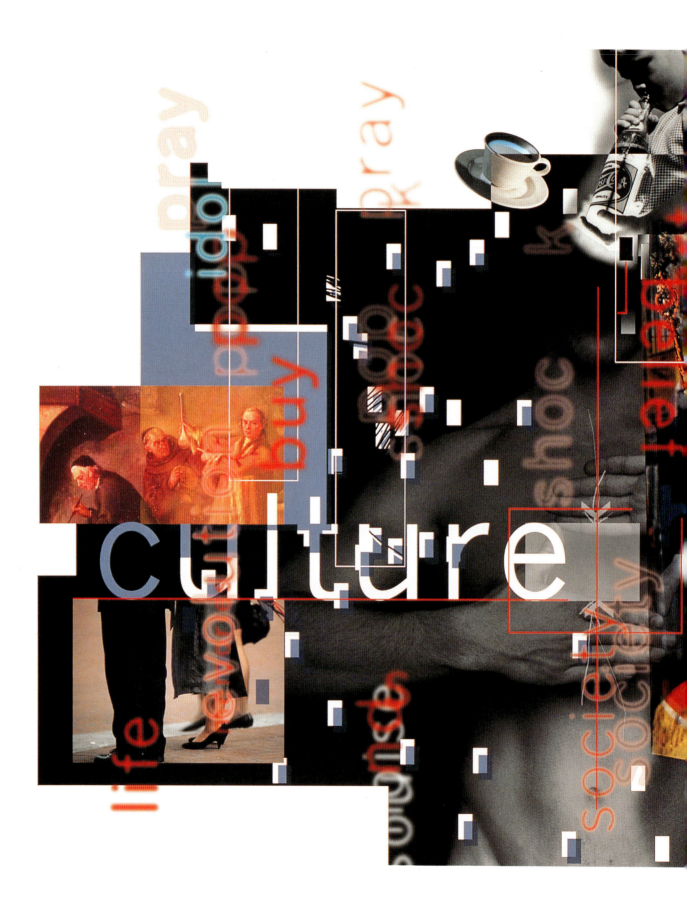

culture

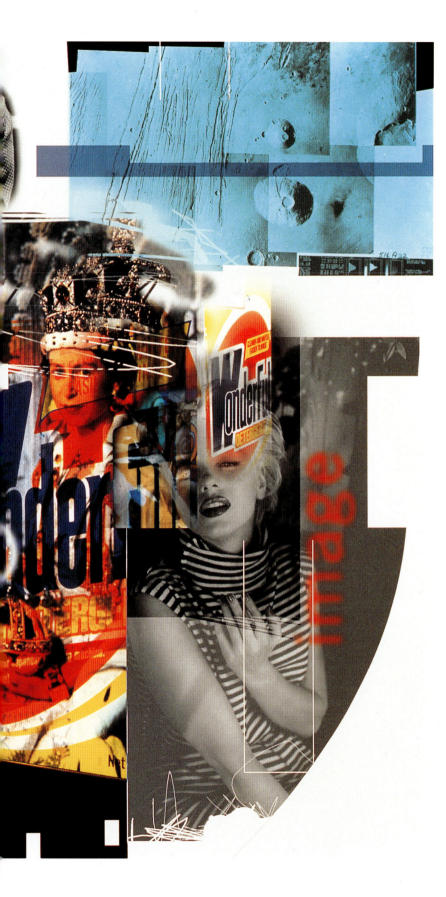

Slide installation for Kobe Fashion Museum

DESIGNERS Andy Altmann, David Ellis, Patrick Morrissey
DESIGN COMPANY Why Not Associates
PHOTOGRAPHERS Rocco Redondo, Richard Woolf, PhotoDisc
PRINCIPAL TYPEFACE Monotype Grotesque
CLIENT Dai Nippon

*Great Britain, 1995*

Since form cannot be separated from content and since form itself carries **meaning,** then the idea is, in fact, structured and inform- ed by its presentation.

Just as the invisible typeface is an impossi- bility, neither can form be invisible.

Louise Sandhaus

THEN

NOW

I love the "POST-MODERN PLURALISM": idea of a post-historical forever: mix and match, past and present, high and low, regular and irregular, "inept" and professional, raw and cooked and everything in between, inside and outsider … and so on and on and on and on.

Edward Fella

We use styles like maniacs but we never use them lock, stock and barrel. We would usually manipulate them to create some kind of tension. No style is either good or bad, it's just another style — whether you use it wholesale or not.

Lorraine Wild

WHY IS "CUTTING EDGE" USUALLY

SYNONYMOUS WITH ILLEGIBILITY?

WHAT WOULD HAPPEN IF THE TWO TERMS

"hip" and "hard to read"

WERE UNCOUPLED?

Can a text be both readerly and experimental?

**J. Abbott Miller**

CULTURE:

educational/publishing

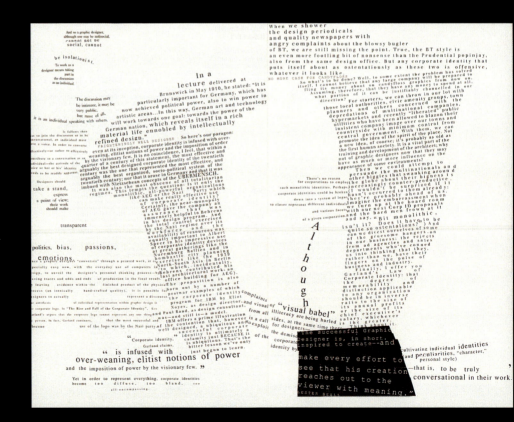

Emigre no. 21

Magazine spreads showing projects by
California Institute of the Arts students

GUEST EDITOR  Jeffery Keedy
DESIGNERS  Margo Johnson, Gail Swanlund
CLIENT  Emigre Graphics

Already a significant force as the 1990s
began, Rudy VanderLans's *Emigre* has
achieved a thoughtfulness, consistency
and rigour in its exploration of
experimental typography that is without
equal in magazine publishing. Completely
redesigned from issue to issue, sometimes
by guest editors, the magazine uses the
type designs of its partner company,
Emigre Fonts, to demonstrate that new
approaches to page structure and textual
flow can be applied in a way that both
encourages and enhances the experience
of reading.

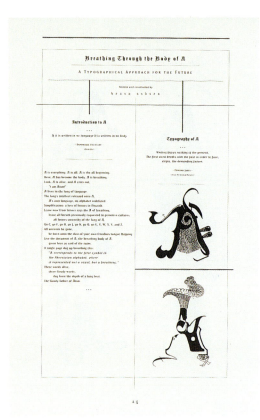

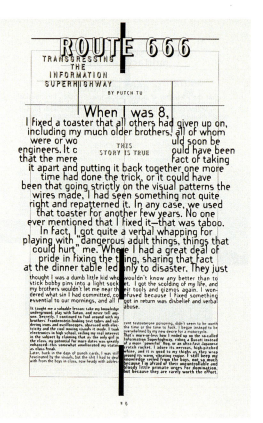

**Emigre no. 32**

Magazine pages

EDITOR/DESIGNER | Rudy VanderLans
DESIGNER AT LARGE | Gail Swanlund
ILLUSTRATOR | Brian Schorn
PRINCIPAL TYPEFACES | Matrix, Template Gothic
CLIENT | Emigre Graphics

USA, 1994

**Emigre no. 28, "Broadcast"**

Magazine page

GUEST EDITOR/DESIGNER | Gail Swanlund
PRINCIPAL TYPEFACES | OutWest, Citizen
CLIENT | Emigre Graphics

USA, 1993

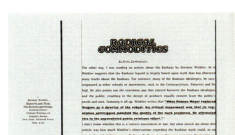
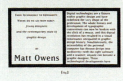
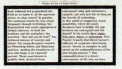

Emigre no. 34, "Rebirth of Design"

Magazine spreads
EDITOR/DESIGNER        Rudy VanderLans
PRINCIPAL TYPEFACES    Arbitrary, Matrix, Keedy Sans, Dogma Outline
CLIENT                 Emigre Graphics

USA, 1995

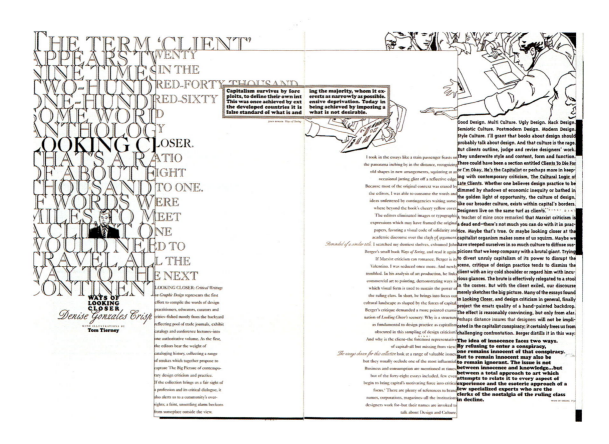

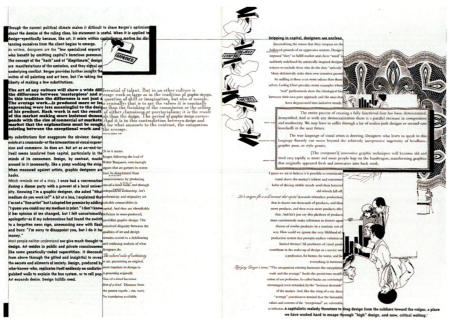

In 1995, *Emigre* made an unexpected change to a smaller page size. While the revised format signalled a new emphasis on writing, the magazine's page structures are still subject to constant reinvention. Issue 34 (previous page) uses the visible grid structures of the later large-format issues to divide the page into horizontal bands so that three articles can proceed in parallel. The two "Mouthpiece" issues mount an examination of the relationship of writing and design with a fluidity unconstrained by the reduced format.

Emigre no. 35, "Mouthpiece" part 1

Magazine spreads for an article about clients

| | |
|---|---|
| GUEST EDITOR | Anne Burdick |
| WRITER/DESIGNER | Denise Gonzales Crisp |
| ILLUSTRATOR | Tom Tierney |
| PRINCIPAL TYPEFACES | Triplex, Bembo, Caslon, Cooper Black, Berthold Script |
| CLIENT | Emigre Graphics |

*USA, 1995*

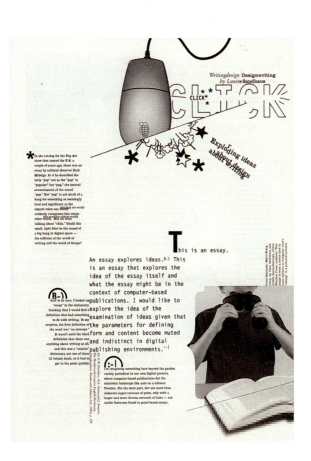

Writingdesign **Designwriting**
by Louise **Sandhaus**

CLICK

Exploding ideas about writing and design

This is an essay.

An essay explores ideas.[B-] This is an essay that explores the idea of the essay itself and what the essay might be in the context of computer-based publications. I would like to explore the idea of the examination of ideas given that the parameters for defining form and content become muted and indistinct in digital publishing environments.[:-]

I'm imagining something here beyond the garden variety periodical in our own digital present, where computer-based publications dot the electronic landscape like ants on a leftover Twinkie. For the most part, few are more than elaborate hyper-versions of print, only with a larger and more diverse network of links — not unlike footnotes found in print-based essays.

**Emigre no. 36, "Mouthpiece" part 2**

Magazine page and spread for an article about writing and design
*GUEST EDITOR* Anne Burdick
*WRITER/DESIGNER* Louise Sandhaus
*PRINCIPAL TYPEFACES* Clarendon, Letter Gothic
*CLIENT* Emigre Graphics

*USA, 1995*

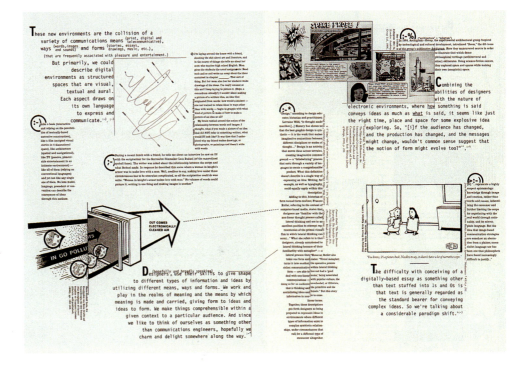

These new environments are the collision of a variety of communications means (print, digital and telecommunicative), ways (words, images and sounds) and forms (stories, essays, drawings, music, etc.), (that are frequently associated with pleasure and entertainment.) But primarily, we could describe digital environments as structured spaces that are visual, textual and aural. Each aspect draws on its own language to express and communicate.

Designers use their skills to give shape to different types of information and ideas by utilizing different means, ways and forms. We work and play in the realms of meaning and the means by which meaning is made and carried, giving form to ideas and ideas to form. We make things comprehensible within a given context to a particular audience. And since we like to think of ourselves as something other than communications engineers, hopefully we charm and delight somewhere along the way.

Combining the abilities of designers with the nature of electronic environments, where _how_ something is said conveys ideas as much as _what_ is said, it seems like just the right time, place and space for some explosive idea exploring. So, "[i]f the audience has changed, and the production has changed, and the messages might change, wouldn't common sense suggest that the notion of form might evolve too?"

The difficulty with conceiving of a digitally-based essay as something other than text stuffed into 1s and 0s is that text is generally regarded as the standard bearer for conveying complex ideas. So we're talking about a considerable paradigm shift.

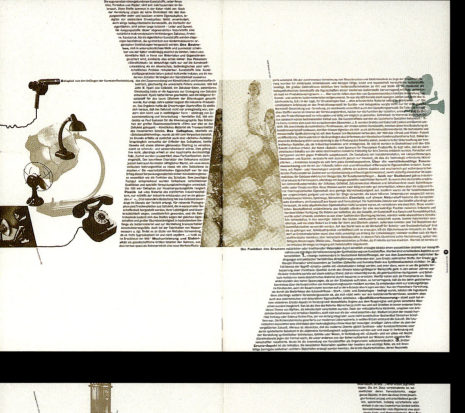

Form + Zweck no. 2/3

Magazine spreads
DESIGNERS Daniela Haufe, Detlef Fiedl
DESIGN COMPANY Cyan
PRINCIPAL TYPEFACE Bureau Grotesque
CLIENT Form + Zweck

Germany, 1991

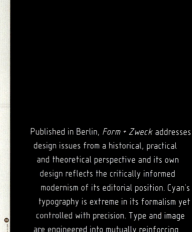

Published in Berlin, *Form + Zweck* addresses
design issues from a historical, practical
and theoretical perspective and its own
design reflects the critically informed
modernism of its editorial position. Cyan's
typography is extreme in its formalism yet
controlled with precision. Type and image
are engineered into mutually reinforcing
structures, while atmospheric photography,
sometimes reminiscent of the 1920s
avant-garde, is used to counterpoint the
textual arabesques. Colour and a high degree
of attention to the material qualities of
paper and binding play an essential role.

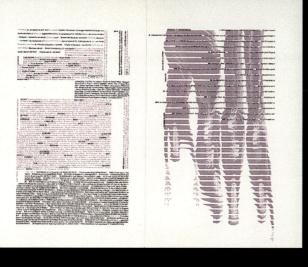

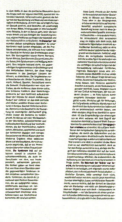

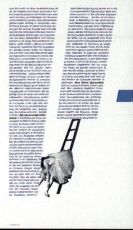

Form + Zweck no. 9/10

Magazine spreads
DESIGNERS          Daniela Haufe, Detlef Fiedler
DESIGN COMPANY     Cyan
PRINCIPAL TYPEFACE Bureau Grotesque
CLIENT             *Form + Zweck*

Germany, 1994

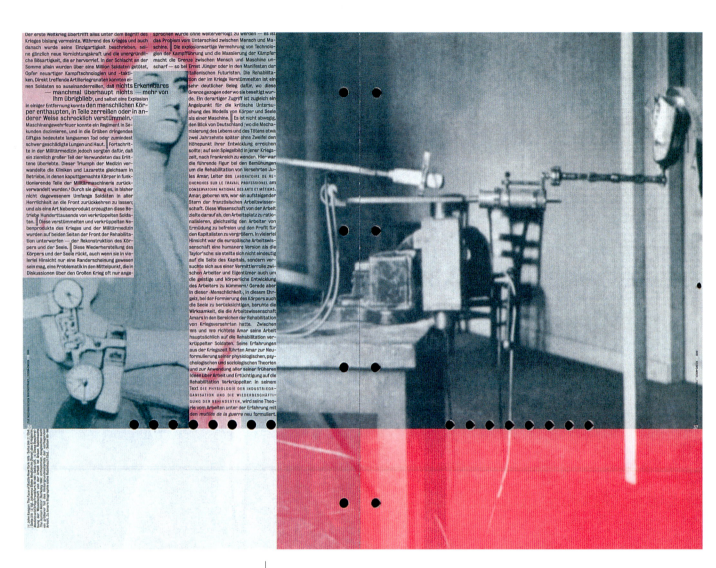

Form + Zweck no. 11/12

Magazine spreads

DESIGNERS Daniela Haufe, Detlef Fiedler
DESIGN COMPANY Cyan
PRINCIPAL TYPEFACE Bureau Grotesque
CLIENT Form + Zweck

Germany, 1995

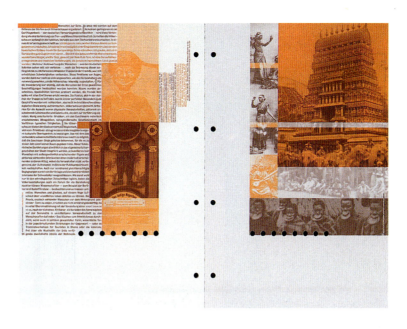

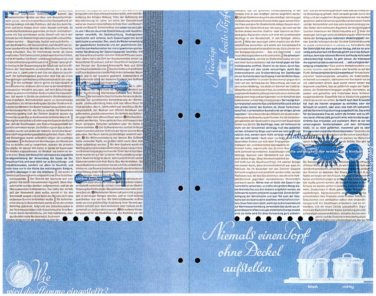

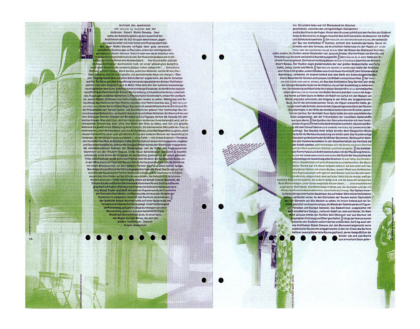

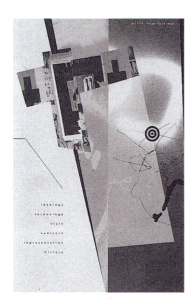

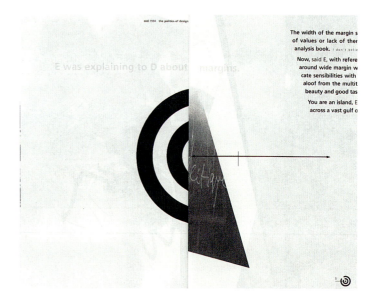

### Zed no. 1, "The Politics of Design"

Journal cover and spreads

EDITOR/DESIGNER Katie Salen
PHOTOGRAPHERS Karen White, Sonya Mead, Katie Salen
PRINCIPAL TYPEFACES Interstate, Frutiger
CLIENT Center for Design Studies,
Communication Arts and Design,
Virginia Commonwealth University

USA, 1994

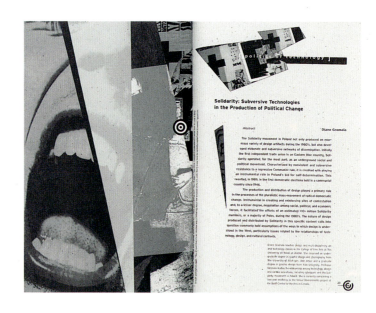

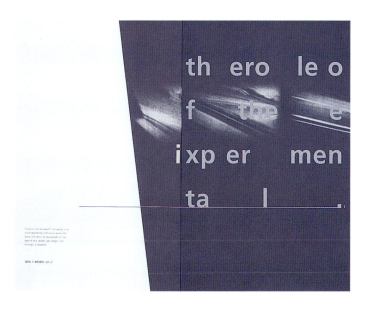

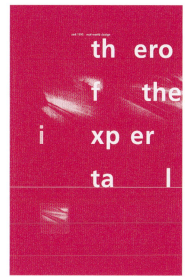

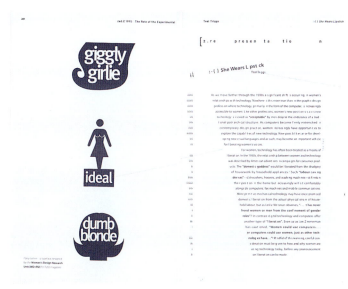

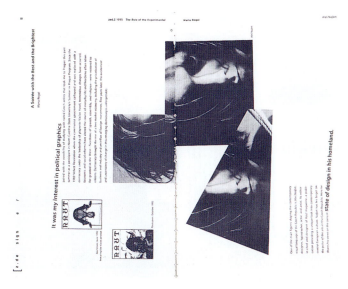

### Zed no. 2, "Real World Design: The Role of the Experimental"

Journal cover and spreads

EDITOR/DESIGNER | Katie Salen
PHOTOGRAPHERS | Nancy Nowacek, Katie Salen
PRINCIPAL TYPEFACES | Interstate, Myriad
CLIENT | Center for Design Studies,
Communication Arts and Design,
Virginia Commonwealth University

USA, 1995

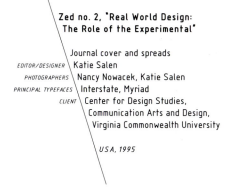

*Zed* is an annual publication that aims to bridge the gap between designer, student and teacher by acting as a vehicle for divergent viewpoints and new voices. While conforming to the conventions of the "design journal" in its booklike proportions and editorial tone, *Zed* manifests a high degree of purposeful experimentation in its design. In the second issue, on the theme of the experimental, the letter "i" is deleted from some articles, requiring readers to "assimilate the unfamiliar" and adapt their method of reading to the modified presentation.

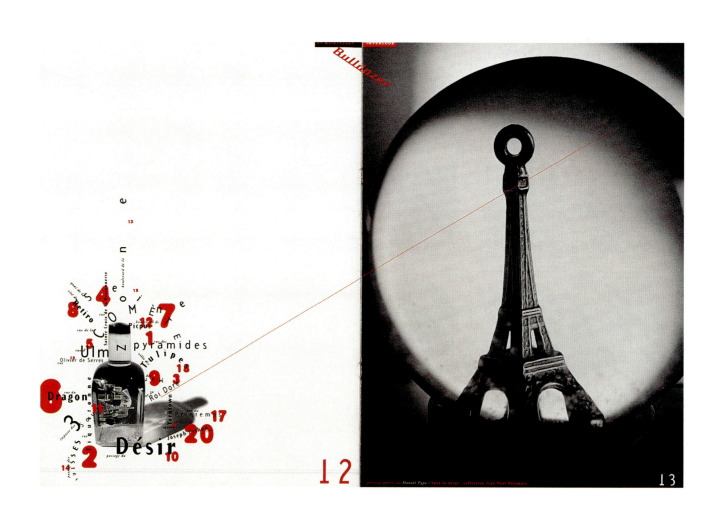

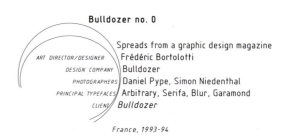

Bulldozer no. 0

|  | Spreads from a graphic design magazine |
| ART DIRECTOR/DESIGNER | Frédéric Bortolotti |
| DESIGN COMPANY | Bulldozer |
| PHOTOGRAPHERS | Daniel Pype, Simon Niedenthal |
| PRINCIPAL TYPEFACES | Arbitrary, Serifa, Blur, Garamond |
| CLIENT | Bulldozer |

France, 1993-94

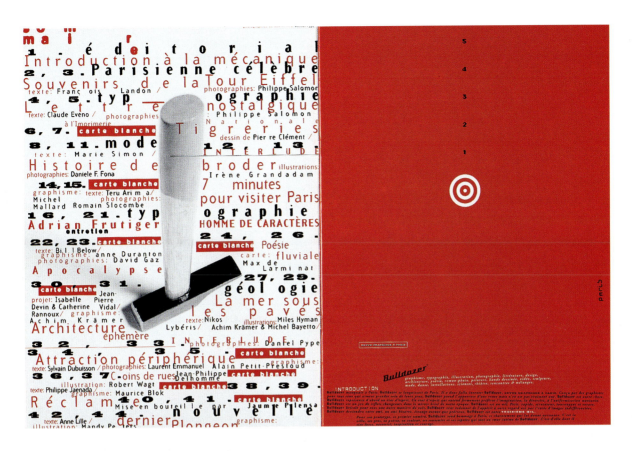

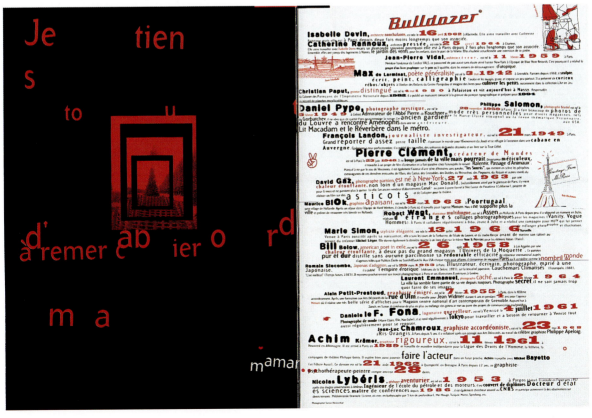

# I like the vernacular NOT!

by Mr. Keedy

The most familiar "use" of vernacular is to produce nostalgia. The problem with the nostalgic vernacular is that it steals from the past to deny the future. The past is robbed of its authenticity and historical context (or specificity) to be rewritten as if it were an episode of Happy Days or a Norman Rockwell painting. Absence makes the heart grow fonder, and there's no fiction like "the good old days." This kind of nostalgic reverie is an escape from the anxiety of an uncertain future, it's not so much historical quotation as it is nostalgic sound bite. Authenticity is NOT a high priority for graphic designers because it's usually the feeling we're after, NOT the fact. This allows us to play fast and loose with history to construct feelings, like that of the art deco thirties or the fifties, that never really correspond to any specific time, place, or people. It's not the past, it's better than the past - and the present and the future. Retreating into nostalgia is turning your back on the present and running in fear of the future. If graphic designers are busy daydreaming about the good old days, then who is going to show us what the future looks like? Who's in charge of inventing tomorrow? Are we all so embarrassed that the modernist visions of Herbert Bayer, Raymond Loewy, and Bucky Fuller didn't exactly come true that we must retreat to some imaginary past life that didn't really exist, either?

The commercial artist was transformed into the graphic designer with the help and encouragement of modernism. Graphic design's identity is so co-dependent on modernism that one does not dare contemplate design outside of the modernist paradigm. Now, in an era of postmodern plurality and technological change, the good old days of the easy and unchallenged answers of modernism are gone for good. That's why graphic design is suffering from an identity crisis. When you are having trouble defining something it is often easier to define what it is NOT, and the vernacular is what we (professional graphic designers) are NOT.

I think much of the current interest in vernacular is a symptom of the lack of direction and groping for self-definition of the design profession. So many times I hear designers waxing poetically about some lovely little matchbook cover, menu design, or hand-lettered sign and how terrific it is—what graphic designer doesn't have a stash of such found goodies to "borrow" from? And there's nothing wrong with that; after all, the capacity to appreciate something will expand your understanding, NOT define it.

Appropriation of the "other" (to use the current art world vernacular) means taking something from a culture "other" than your own. You can appropriate something without reference to its original context (pastiche), or in a way that calls attention to its original context (parody/irony). Other cultures are not just literal; other national cultures but can be high, low, pop, and subculture. When one culture borrows from another there are often problems that arise due to issues of dominance and equality. For example, when the high-culture graphic designer (trained in a design school) borrows clip art illustrations or crude lettering from the low-culture hack (trained in the school of hard knocks) it can be a condescending act of elitism that deliberately draws attention to the difference in status between them as if to say

"Hey, look at what this so-called illustrator did...isn't it corny? I could never do anything that silly, I'm too sophisticated. I really wish I could but I'm just too clever to do anything like that. In fact, I'm too clever to do anything at all, that's why I have to use stuff from these poor hacks."

This appropriation/nostalgia/thing has not only become a bit tiresome lately, but is increasingly mean-spirited as well; but only in the most covert fashion because the plunderers are always the first to proclaim how much they love the one they are plundering. The idea of "borrowing" in graphic design is so pervasive that it's often done unconsciously. What is needed is an awareness of what crossing cultural/historical barriers actually means, as well as an understanding of the importance of context.

The culture that is perceived to be high or dominant is not the only one to be empowered. In this negotiation of status, the plundered underdog is given the unassailable status of the authentic, capable of true, natural, or honest expression. The so designated dominant culture, on the other hand, is a vacuum imitator/manipulator/plunderer, the TRUTH from the real "other" culture. Thus the price of dominance in the culture war is authenticity. They "used to be great" but now that they're mainstream/commercial they're just crap! In this exchange of tit-for-tat, the high and low cultures are leveled out into one pop culture. Is it the graphic designer's task to please everyone in this pan-pop culture? Or to affirm their client's status as the high, and the audience/consumer's status as the low?

You can't please some of the people some of the time, but you can please all of the people all of the time!

Today, cutting-edge vernacular users are the designers creating rave graphics. (For those of you who live in a cave, a rave is an illegal underground party of a thousand kids on ecstasy [DRUG] dancing in puddles of their own sweat to technor-house music until the cows come home, or the cops drop in [FUN].) The old and low cultures that rave designers borrow from are primarily American corporate and package design of the seventies and eighties (now there's some hacks). Rave designers love logos, lots of color, and outlined type, and hey, who doesn't? The fact that the "professional designer's" work is now being reworked like any other bit of ephemera might be some kind of poetic justice, but it fails to be a very interesting design strategy. That's because their work (like their predecessors) is essentially a one-liner that has little resonance beyond the "shock of the old." What little invention there is in rave graphics is provided mostly by the computer.

I remember the late 80s ... now those were the good old days!

At this point it would seem the vernacular idea in graphic design has pretty much played itself out. The only thing the cutting-edge appropriators can do is continuously reuse what they just did last year. This strategy couldn't really be called vernacular design, after all there are already a lot of designers who do this and call it "timeless design." Have you ever seen a dog chasing his own tail? Now that's timeless.

The past used to be considered a classic example or ideal for the present. In the postindustrial postmodern world the past is just another place to go shopping, except most of the past has been bought up, just leaving yesterday's news. Retrofitting a popular old song is the easiest way to get a hit. It is a very different thing to recycle the past for the purposes of "instant gratification" than to reinvent the past as an ideal for the present. Reinventing the past is a lot of hard work (scholarship), and who wants to wait for the future (it may never come). When the general cultural mood is here-today-gone-tomorrow, all history is reduced to one undifferentiated vernacular (no linear hierarchies, please).

Is there a "correct" way to use the idea of vernacular in graphic design, or is the whole idea of the vernacular overly simplistic and not very useful?

Isn't getting "inspiration" from your Print, How, I.D. and Emigre magazines using the vernacular?

Why is it that graphic design history includes cave painting, cuneiform alphabets, and woodblock engravings but doesn't include sign painting or clip art?

When is the vernacular just history?

What is the point of asking all these questions if you aren't going to answer them?

Currently, graphic design practice and history is neither specific nor general in its scope; rather, it is elusively constructed out of fickle self-interest and unchallenged ego. Unchallenged, because for the most part the rest of the world doesn't give a shit about graphic design anyway.

Maybe we should either expand our notion of what constitutes graphic design or become even more specific and rigorous in our self-definition of graphic design practice. Maybe graphic designers should go back to the old business of inventing the future instead of regurgitating a past that's been digested so many times that it has no taste (not to mention style).

Deep down inside I think most designers suspect that "using vernacular" is a chicken shit's easy way out. It's a retreat from style, or at least from expressing your own style forged from your own experience and time. Graphic designers should be responsive to and responsible for the development of their own style. Instead of just "using" the vernacular we are creating it, and it tells us not only who we were and are, but who we hope to be

* I realize most graphic designers today find these two words problematic, since we allegedly are problem-solvers instead of taskmakers and trendsetters, but anyone with half a brain can see what the larger culture values most in graphic design.
Background lettering by Stephen K. McMahon from 100 Meals in Lettering 1947.

Lift and Separate: Graphic Design and the Quote Unquote Vernacular

Essay spreads from an exhibition catalo[g]

EDITOR  Barbara Glauber
WRITER/DESIGNER  Jeffery Keedy
PRINCIPAL TYPEFACE  Manu Sans

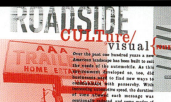

# ROADSIDE

## CULTure/ visual forms & how they were established

by George LaRou

Over the past one hundred years a new American landscape has been built to suit the needs of the automobile. As this environment developed so, too, did businesses need to find new ways to communicate with passersby. With increasing automotive speed, the duration of time allowed each message was continually reduced, and some modes of perception were completely eliminated. At over 50 mph very few could appreciate the goods on display, hear the jukebox, or smell the coffee, let alone see a tiny four-by-eight-foot on-premise sign. Something more substantial was called for to meet the communication needs of free enterprise in the evolving car culture. Some began scientific studies of perception at high velocity to solve the problem. Others, following a less rigorous course, reasoned that if it was big and

In time

shiny and lit up at night those speeding by would be able to make sense of it. In time a vernacular language was developed to communicate to the automotive public, with individual sign artists creating the norms of this visual language based on evolving technology, aesthetics, legislation, and commercial need.

The residue of this birth and growth of a language is the landscape in which we move today, a national roadside culture

made up of a series of zones, each containing on-premise commercial signage shaped as much by specific socioeconomic factors as by signmakers themselves. These general visual zones can be considered singularly or in various combinations to create a basis for understanding complex signage environments.

The first and oldest commercial signage zone is the "old downtown." These are the areas built before the decentralizing influence of the automobile created "strip" cities. In old downtowns the scale and visual impact of architecture greatly outweigh that of signage, much of which is aimed at pedestrian as well as automotive traffic. This is true even in the subset of cities and towns where shopping districts have been unaffected by suburban and shopping mall flight. In these still-viable centers the commercial signage tends to be a true mix of old and new aesthetics and technology.

The majority of downtowns, however, display mainly the residue of abandoned signage as retailers have followed the automobiles further into suburbia, leaving buildings vacant or converted to offices and the odd artists' loft. The retail businesses

---

In its new isolation, the strip became the Madagascar of signage evolution. Despite the economic decline, some of the businesses remained, while other old giants died off or moved to warmer economic zones. Gaps in the economic food chain were filled by businesses more suited to local traffic. After long vacancies, gas stations turned into pizza joints by the thousands. Vacuum cleaner repair shops, liquor stores, and other economic bottom feeders filled in the remaining empty shells. Strange new hybrid forms of signage began to emerge. As signage regulation became more common in the 1970s, many of these areas were considered too poor or too far gone to clean up. The signage dinosaurs

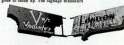

remained intact as originally constructed, some now supporting bizarre new retrofits

or standing as fossilized superstructures. At the same time, hand-painted signs by lettering artists and muralists of wildly varying skill and craft began to compete with new plastic fascias, vinyl letters, mobile signs, and backlit lettered awnings, vying for the attention of motorists in this Grand Canyon of visual historic sediment.

Closely related to these isolated strips, but more highly evolved, are the new or never isolated strips leading to or from the highways and shopping malls. The signage on these strips tends to be much more homogeneous due to their development after sign regulation and their continued economic vitality. Franchise operations, large national or regional retailers in shopping centers, and car dealerships form the core of businesses along this strip. The attendant signage consists almost entirely of lower cost,

## MODULAR

internally illuminated, vacuum-formed colored plastic signage. Modular sign systems and architectural facades are constantly updated to keep the corporate identity current with the zeitgeist of shifting visual mass appeal.

This constant change tends to erase any historic reference more than twenty years old.

---

**Lift and Separate: Graphic Design and the Quote Unquote Vernacular**

Essay spreads from an exhibition catalogue

EDITOR Barbara Glauber

WRITER/DESIGNER George LaRou

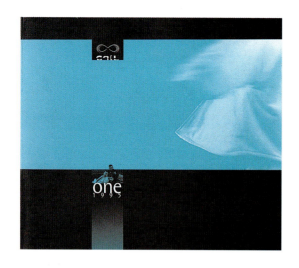

Coil no. 1

Cover and spreads from a
journal of the moving image
DESIGNER | Damian Jaques
DESIGN COMPANY | Proboscis
PRINCIPAL TYPEFACES | Wunderlich, Quadraat,
Disturbance, Coventry, OCRB
CLIENT | Coil

Great Britain, 1995

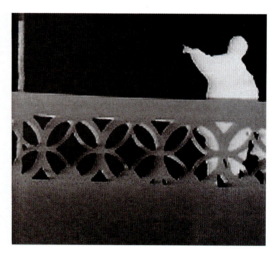

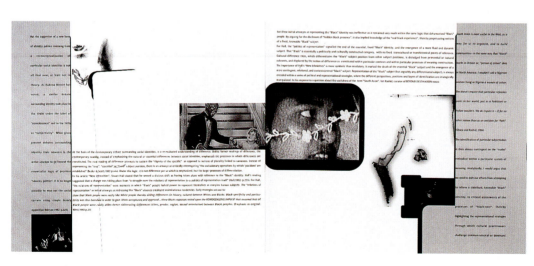

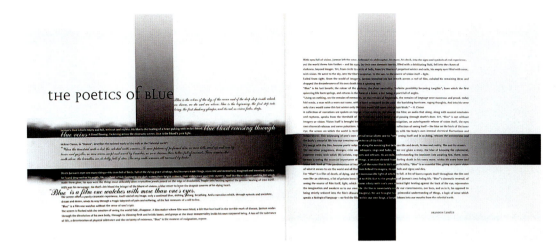

# the poetics of blue

# psi net
rogers

# the perpetual minute
Wayne Sleeth

*Coil* is an independent publication that addresses the cultural, theoretical and practical aspects of the moving image (film, video and digital/ electronic imaging). The contrasting natures and thematic concerns of the different media are reflected in a design which asks for a high degree of involvement from the reader. Early feedback suggests practitioners feel the time is right for a journal presenting this subject matter in a highly activated visual style.

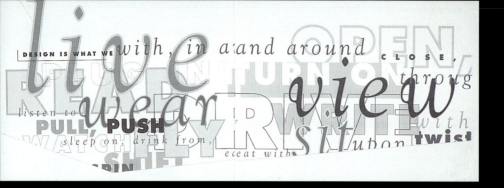

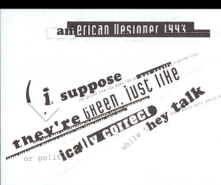

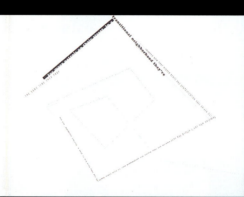

In this celebratory catalogue the ambiguous nature of the creative process is given the same emphasis as the clarity of the designers' philosophies and finished work. The book is structured and paced to reflect the range of rhythms the viewer would experience in exploring the exhibition. Subtle differences between elements and dramatic juxtapositions suggest the eclectic nature of American design.

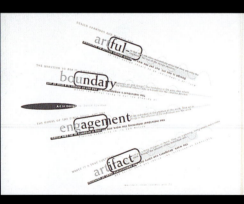

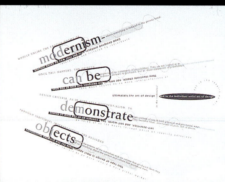

Art of Design 2

Spreads from an exhibition catalogue
DESIGNER Susan Lally
DESIGN COMPANY Lally Design
PRINCIPAL TYPEFACES Futura, Goudy, Franklin Gothic, Garamond
CLIENT Harry Wirth and the American Design Network

Children's illustration exhibition poster/catalogue
DESIGNER \ Carlo Tartaglia
ILLUSTRATORS \ James Jarvis, Sara Fanelli
PRINCIPAL TYPEFACE \ Univers
CLIENT \ Royal College of Art

*Great Britain, 1994*

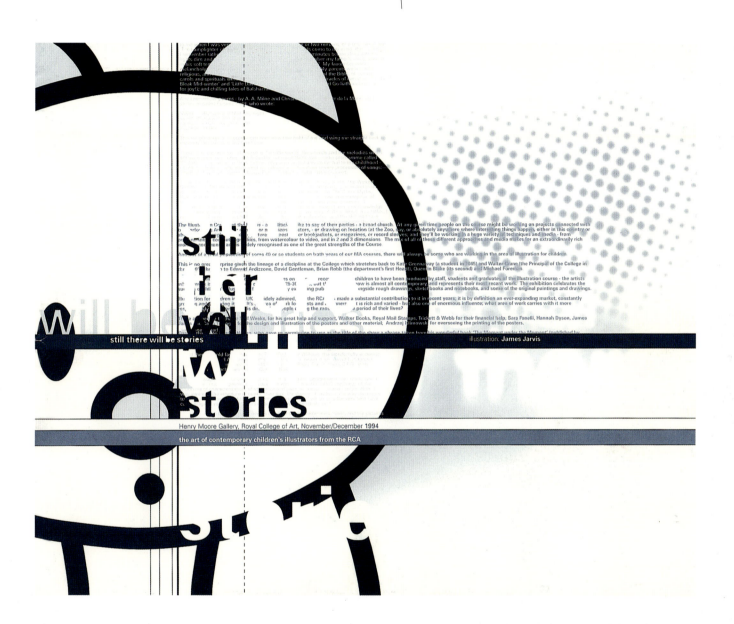

Cut and folded, the poster also
functions as a catalogue. Text is
used as digitally manipulated texture
on the cover, reversing the usual
relationship between word and image
in conventional children's story books.

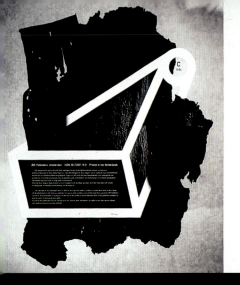
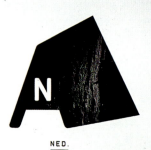

BIS Publishers Amsterdam   ISBN 90-72007-19-8   Printed in the Netherlands

N

NED.

*Architecten*

volume 1

register
index

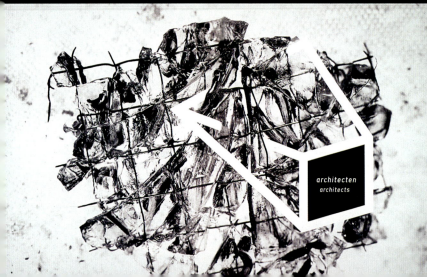

*architecten*

architects

PHOTOGRAPHER | Marc van Praag
PRINCIPAL TYPEFACES | KP DIN, Stone
CLIENT | Uitgeverij BIS

*The Netherlands, 1994*

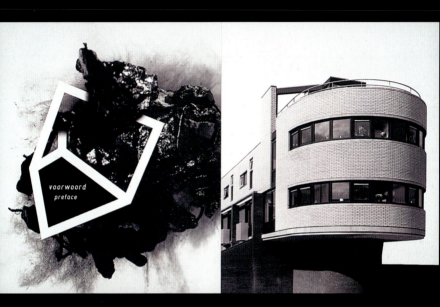

*voorwoord*
*preface*

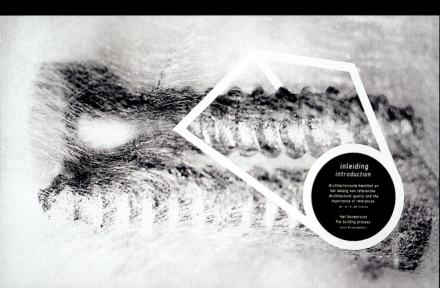

*inleiding*
*introduction*

*Architectonische kwaliteit en
het belang van referenties
Architectural quality and the
importance of references*
dr. ir. h. de Vreeze

*Het bouwproces
The building process*
Olof Koekebakker

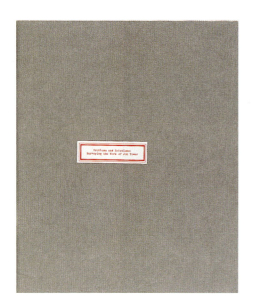

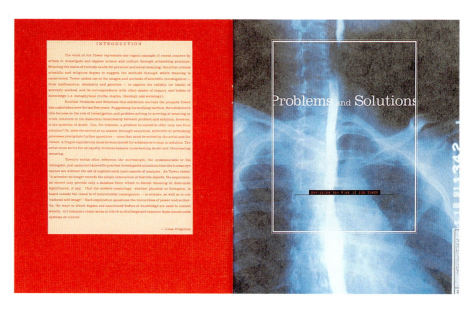

**Problems and Solutions:
Surveying the Work of Jon Tower**

Exhibition catalogue cover and spreads
DESIGNERS | Laura Lacy-Sholly, James Sholly
DESIGN COMPANY | Antenna
PRINCIPAL TYPEFACES | Clarendon, Bell Gothic, STA Portable
CLIENT | Herron Gallery, Indianapolis Center
for Contemporary Art

*USA, 1992*

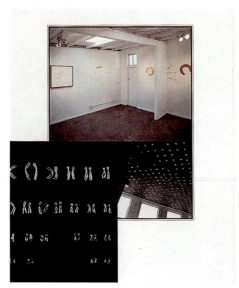

Jon Tower's art deals with the
processes of socialisation that shape
perceptions of religion, education, art
and science. The catalogue represents
the conceptual nature of his work by
distilling elements from the visual
culture of these disciplines into a
document that is part laboratory
report, part text book and part early
volume on art.

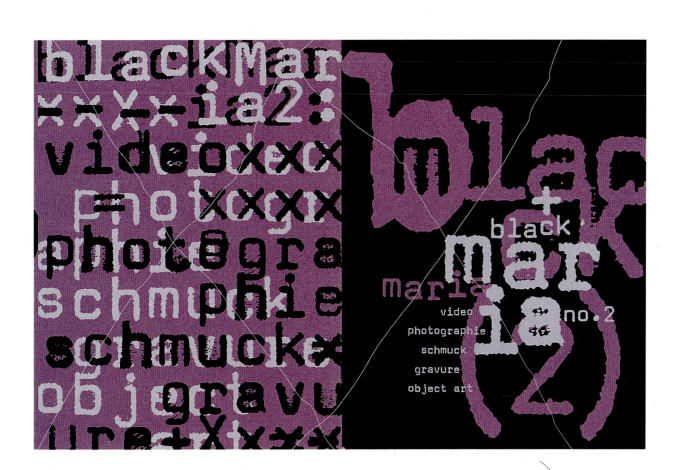

Black Maria no. 2

Magazine cover (front and back)

DESIGNER | Cornel Windlin
PRINCIPAL TYPEFACE | Custom-made for the project
CLIENT | Black Maria

Switzerland, 1994

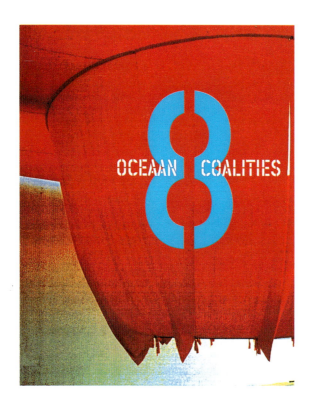

Oceaan Coalities

Catalogue cover and spreads
DESIGNER \ Roelof Mulder
DESIGN COMPANY \ Roelof Mulder Studio
PHOTOGRAPHERS \ Jozee Brouwer, Christa van Kolfschoten
PRINCIPAL TYPEFACE \ Ocean Normal
CLIENT \ Oceaan Galerie

*The Netherlands, 1992*

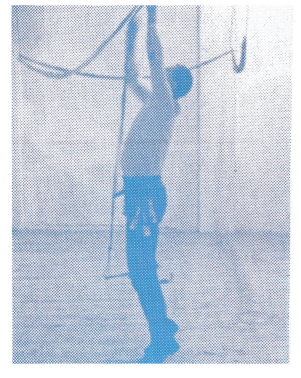

# OCEAAN

COALITIE IS EEN TENTOONSTELLINGSPROJEKT DAT IN 1991 IN OCEAAN PLAATSVOND. TWEE INITIATIEFNEMERS VAN OCEAAN, HESTER OERLEMANS EN NIEK DE JONG BESLOTEN HUN EIGEN KUNSTENAARSCHAP ALS UITGANGSPUNT TE NEMEN VOOR EEN SERIE TENTOONSTELLINGEN. KUNSTENAARS WERDEN UITGENODIGD EEN INHOUDELIJK VERBOND MET ÉÉN VAN HEN AAN TE GAAN OM ZO GEZAMENLIJK TENTOONSTELLINGEN TE REALISEREN. DE TENTOONSTELLINGEN DUURDEN STEEDS DRIE WEKEN EN WERDEN AFGEWISSELD MET ZOGENAAMDE 'ZATERDAGAVONDTENTOONSTELLINGEN' WAARIN JUIST DOOR KUNSTENAARS INGEDIENDE PLANNEN CENTRAAL STONDEN. AAN DE 8 COALITIE-TENTOONSTELLINGEN DIE IN OCEAAN HEBBEN PLAATSGEVONDEN HEBBEN MEER DAN 25 KUNSTENAARS DEELGENOMEN. DAARBIJ ZIJN DE MEEST UITEENLOPENDE DISCIPLINES, ZOALS DESIGN, FOTOGRAFIE, GRAFIEK, SCHILDERKUNST, PERFORMANCE, ARCHITECTUUR, SCULPTUUR, TECHNIEK EN KERAMIEK TE ZIEN GEWEEST. COALITIE HEEFT EEN BIJZONDERE REEKS TENTOONSTELLINGEN OPGELEVERD WAARMEE OCEAAN HAAR HEEL EIGEN VISIE OP HET BEGRIP 'KUNSTENAARSINITIATIEF' HEEFT KUNNEN LATEN ZIEN.

# COALITIES

## BORN TO BE WILD

COALITIE IS EEN COMMUNICATIEPROGRAMMA. TWEE OF MEER KUNSTENAARS GAAN VOOR EEN BEPAALDE TIJD MET ELKAAR IN ZEE EN PROBEREN EEN VERBINDING TUSSEN HUN WERK TOT STAND TE BRENGEN. EEN GESPREK OP ARTISTIEK-INHOUDELIJK NIVEAU MET EEN TENTOONSTELLING ALS RESULTAAT. EEN JAAR LANG HEB IK IEDERE DRIE MAANDEN EEN TENTOONSTELLING GEMAAKT STEEDS IN SAMENWERKING MET ÉÉN OF MEERDERE KUNSTENAARS. ALS KUNSTENAAR NIEK DE JONG ÉN ALS ORGANISATOR. EEN BROEIERIGE DUBBELROL.

MET COALITIE WERD DE RELATIE TUSSEN ORGANISATIE EN KUNSTENAAR TOT EEN MAXIMALE INTENSIVITEIT OPGEVOERD. IK VOND HET NIET MEER ZO INTERESSANT OM VANAF DE ZIJLIJN TOE TE KIJKEN HOE COLLEGAE HET ER IN DE RUIMTE VAN ONS INITIATIEF VANAF BRACHTEN. MIJN IDEALEN REIKTEN VERDER DAN HET SLIJTEN VAN MIJN TIJD ACHTER HET BURO, DE TELEFOON EN DE COMPUTER. IK BEN IN DE WIEG GELEGD VOOR HET KUNSTENAARSCHAP ZELF. DAARBIJ: GALERIES ZIJN ER GENOEG, HET WARE KUNSTENAARSINITIATIEF WORDT STEEDS ZELDZAMER. IK BEDOEL EEN PLEK WAAR GEÏNVESTEERD WORDT IN DE ONTWIKKELING VAN KUNSTENAARS. EEN PLEK DIE NIET ALLEEN MAAR OP ZOEK IS NAAR 'NAMEN', MAAR EEN VERANTWOORDELIJKHEID DRAAGT VOOR EEN ACHTERBAN. EEN PLEK DIE GEEN VOORWAARDEN STELT, MAAR ZE JUIST SCHEPT.

HET BELANGRIJKSTE DOEL VAN COALITIE WAS HET MAKEN VAN PRACHTIGE KUNST, DIT VOOROP. DAARBIJ: DE MANIER WAAROP.
IK VERBAASDE ME ER LAATST OVER WAAROM IK VANAF HET BEGIN VAN OCEAAN OP ÉÉN OF ANDERE MANIER ALTIJD OP ZOEK WAS NAAR DIALOOG, NAAR EEN KLANKBORD. IK VOND HET MAAR NIKS OM IN MIJN ATELIER AAN DINGEN TE WERKEN DIE GEEN DIRECTE FUNKTIE HADDEN, OM ALLEEN MAAR EEN BEETJE IN MIJN EIGEN GEDACHTENWERELDJE TE ZITTEN WROETEN. IK WILDE NAAR BUITEN MET HET SPUL, ZIEN WAT ER GEBEURT ALS JE MENSEN ERMEE KONFRONTEERT. OM JE ALS AANKOMEND KUNSTENAAR DOELEN TE KUNNEN STELLEN MOET JE EERST WETEN WIE JE BENT EN WAAR JE STAAT. OM DAAR ACHTER TE KOMEN MOET JE JE VERHOUDEN MET JE OMGEVING, COLLEGAE EN PUBLIEK, MET DE REALITEIT. EERST IS HET NATUURLIJK MOEILIJK OM DIE DIALOOG OP GANG TE BRENGEN. TOCH BLIJFT HET VOLGENS MIJ VAN LEVENSBELANG OM HET DAARNA OP GANG TE HOUDEN. DE KUNST MOET ZICH STEEDS BLIJVEN VERHOUDEN MET DE REALITEIT. EN IK DENK DAT HET DAAR NOG WEL EENS AAN SCHORT. VEELSTEVEEL MOOIE PLAATJES EN MOOIE PRAATJES.

HET WAS DE BEDOELING VAN COALITIE OM KUNSTENAARS UIT TE DAGEN. HOEVER KUN JE IN EEN SAMENWERKING GAAN ZONDER JEZELF TE BUITEN TE GAAN? KUN JE JEZELF WEL TE BUITEN GAAN? MIJN UITGANGSPUNT WAS NIET TE SNEL BIJ ELKAAR TE WILLEN KOMEN MAAR DE STRIJD JUIST OP TE VOEREN, DAAR HEB JE VEEL MEER AAN. KIJKEN TOT HOEVER JE KUNT GAAN. OP ZOEK NAAR JE GRENS. PROBEREN MEZELF EN DEGENE WAARMEE IK WERKTE TE DWINGEN TOT EEN ZO EXTREEM MOGELIJKE UITSPRAAK TE KOMEN.

DE ENE SAMENWERKING IS NATUURLIJK ANDERS DAN DE ANDERE. DE ENE IS OOK VEEL SPANNENDER ALS DE ANDERE. DIT GELDT VOOR COALITIE MAAR EIGENLIJK VOOR ELKE TENTOONSTELLING IN OCEAAN. STEEDS MOET IK PLAATSBEPALEN. WELKE ROL KAN IK BINNEN DIT GEHEEL SPELEN. SOMS LIJKT HET OF IK MIJN KUNSTENAARSCHAP BUITEN DE DEUR MOET ZETTEN EN SOMS IS MIJN

## 1E COALITIE
### 27 MAART
## ZO WAS HET

VOOR DEZE TENTOONSTELLING HEEFT NIEK DE JONG DEAN BRANNAGAN UIT LONDEN UITGENODIGD NAAR ARNHEM TE KOMEN OM SAMEN AAN EEN TENTOONSTELLING TE WERKEN.
BRANNAGAN WERKTE VEEL MET HET BEGRIP ENGAGEMENT. ENGAGEMENT IS VERLOVING, EEN VERBINTENIS, MAAR OOK BETROKKENHEID BIJ MAATSCHAPPELIJKE ONTWIKKELINGEN. BRANNAGAN WAS ZEER GEÏNTERESSEERD IN DE GESCHIEDENIS VAN ARNHEM TIJDENS DE TWEEDE WERELDOORLOG. GEZAMENLIJK HEBBEN ZIJ EEN AANTAL HISTORISCHE PLEKKEN IN ARNHEM EN OMGEVING BEZOCHT. AL WERKEND ONTSTOND VANUIT DEZE ERVARINGEN EEN PERFORMANCE.
DE PERFORMANCE IS EEN REACTIE OP DE MANIER WAAROP DE GESCHIEDENIS HET VERLEDEN, DIE OP DE BEZOCHTE PLEKKEN NOG HEEL STERK VOELBAAR IS, INTERPRETEERT: ZO WAS HET (NIET).
HET PUBLIEK KOMT BINNEN IN EEN LEGE RUIMTE, NIEK DE JONG EN DEAN BRANNAGAN VOLGEN, BEIDEN IN HET ZWART GEKLEED. NIEK DOOPT EEN KWAST IN EEN EMMER DODEKOPVERF EN BEGINT LEVENSGROTE LETTERS OP DE MUUR TE KALKEN. DEAN ONTROLT INMIDDELS DE BRANDSLANG VAN OCEAAN. HIJ VOLGT DE VORM VAN DE LETTERS MET DE BRANDSPUIT. UITEINDELIJK WORDT DE ZIN 'ZO WAS HET' EVEN LEESBAAR OM HET VOLGENDE MOMENT ONZICHTBAAR TE VERDWIJNEN, DOOR EEN HARDE WATERSTRAAL UITGEWIST.

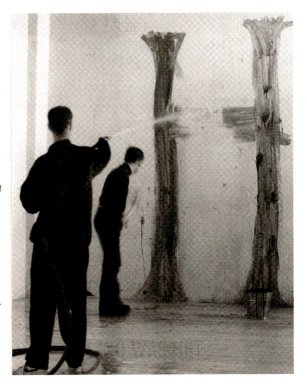

STone UTTERS

Spreads from a book about John Baskerville
WRITER/DESIGNER  Phil Baines
PRINCIPAL TYPEFACES  Monotype Baskerville, Grot

Self-published
Great Britain, 1992

# The ENGLISH form o ress, a n is

f seriffed, varied-weight (stressed) letter, t he norm to which the vernacular form gr avitates unless there is a good reason for it to resist, has a rich full shape, a vertical st nd a fairly sharp gradation from thick to thi n strokes; although it is less abrupt than in the characteristic French form. The differe nce of weight between strokes thick and thi often quite marked; the latter are virtually hairlines. R ich bracketted serifs terminate sharply, if not always a ctually to a point. The tails of the

Apart from the work o f some of t he later W est Countr y tombston e carvers, t he vernacu lar traditio n

Q & R

usually have great ver ve, the tail of the latt er being bowed, not st raight. Proportions te nd to be squarer and more regular than tho se of Roman forms. A, (p.9

The

The ENGLISH letter rance in 1754 when th writing master and ja e began producing his : although there can b signs were based on st eveloped by tombston irty years previously. T ans and **grotesques dense smoke of th tion round about 1** he first definitive form racteristics which now lish could be found in ms of early tombstone dates on houses, and e derived though they w ls.

Whether Bask erville was a cquainted w ith the 'rom ain du roi' it is imposs ible to say, but it is ne arly impossible that h e was not acquainted with Shelley's book: it is inconceivable that a ny professional writin g-master in the time Baskerville was teachi ng writing would not have known of the bo ok. And again, the let

ters

n has been little influe nced by ty pe designs. Indeed, th e influence has often b een very m uch the ot her way ro und. A, p.7 (

T he 'romain du roi' was cut by Gra ndjean for the exclusive use of th e Royal Printing Hou se in France, it was fir st used to print *Medail les sur les Principaux Ev enements du Regne-de-Lo uis le Grand* in 1702. The type certainly is a

break

made its official appea e printer, lettercutter, panner *John Baskervill* innovative letterforms e no doubt that his de yles which had been d e carvers twenty or th he clarendons, egypti **emerged from the e Industrial Revolu 800.** But long before t s appeared, many cha seem particularly Eng the primitive letterfor s, builders' marks and ven in Caslon's types, ere from Dutch mode A, p.10

Much - *I* think too much - h as been mad e of the writ ing masters' influence upon the tombstone c arvers. Probably the fi rst relevant master w as Cocker, whose spec imens were published around 1670; and fro m 1680 to 1741 hardl y a year passed witho ut other masters issui ng specimens. A, p.32

Amongst

Part history and part homage, the book explores John Baskerville's place in the English lettering tradition. The grid structure alludes to gravestones and rubbings but is used differently from page to page to express the subject matter.

ave endeavoured to produce a *Sett of Types* according to what I conceived to be their true proportion. D

The general brilliance

Baskerville's was influenced the design: was

ter. forms elate osely und on tombstones.

actual r cl fo

With generous curves, strongly differentiated thicks and thins, long untapered but bracketed serifs, his types were followed in 1769 by what is known today as *Fry's Baskerville* , (...).
A, p. 11

If he had merely imitated Caslon, even if he had improved on him, there would have been little to say, or to speculate

Finally, after many delays caused by the desire of Baskerville to have the book perfect, the Virgil went to press in 1757, after seven years of careful, patient, persistent work upon it. It was a surprise

peculate about; but he bandoned a] the Caslon tradition, and with Grandjean, Fournier a nd other type-cutters, began a new tradition which, in the eighteenth

rise to the literary world. It was the first fine book printed in England. (...) Every part of the volume was in harmony with every other part. There was no dissproportion. The book has been well said to be a landmark in the history of typography. In looking at it today we wonder how it was done when it was done. It seems as though the Birmingham artist had come before his time.
E, p. 39

enth c e mart s

ntury revolutionised the appearance of the printed page. (...)
The revolution which Grandjean and Baskerville brought about was in the relationship between the thick and thin parts of a letter, in the position of the thickest parts of the letter, and in the treatment of the serifs. All these are minutiae; but type design is a matter of minutiae. Baskerville thickened the thick parts of his roman letter and made the thin parts thinner, giving them a sharper, s

er appearance. (...)
He pulled the thickest part of a curved letter away from the position of being 45° to the horizontal and raised it higher up the curve. (...)
He made more of the serifs of the letters, making them more noticeable by giving them a sharper, spiky quality. (...)
These minute changes of detail would probably have gone unnoticed (...) if it had not been for his

sup erb p r e

*He had a constant succession of hot plates of copper ready, b*

etween which, a s soon as printed (...) the sheets w ere inserted. The

*wet was thus expelled, the ink set, and a glossy surface put on all simultaneously.*
E, p. 65

superior ink, and smooth paper. Baskerville made other innovations in design. The type of the late seventeenth century was, on the whole, rather compressed —whether for reasons of aesthetic appeal or economy it is difficult to say—but Baskerville gave his letters a rounded, open appearance. They take up a lot of room.
B, p. 161

The type was cut for him by John Handy (d. 1792) who, by the time of Baskerville's death, had worked for

S W O r k , s o k ,

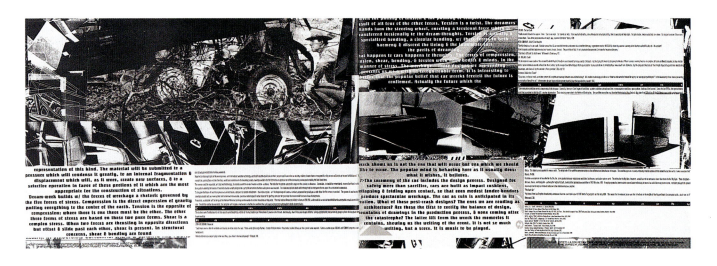

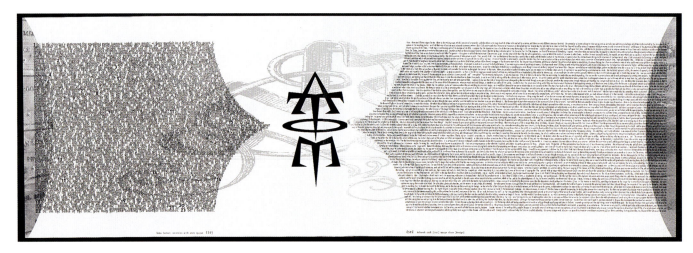

Semiotext(e) Architecture

Book spreads

EDITOR/DESIGNER  Hraztan Zeitlian
DESIGNERS  Reverb Struere, Margo Chase, David Carson, Barry Deck
CLIENT  *Semiotext(e)*

*USA, 1992*

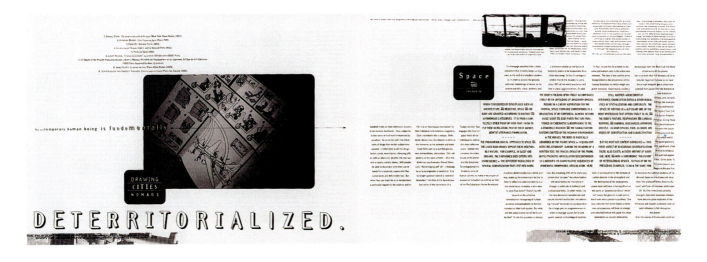

The large-format edition of the theoretical journal *Semiotext(e)* devoted to architecture achieved instant notoriety on its publication. Editor and project designer Hraztan Zeitlian enlisted a cast of American designers known for their experimental approaches to typography to construct a demandingly visual, not to say overloaded, examination of theory's role in architectural design.

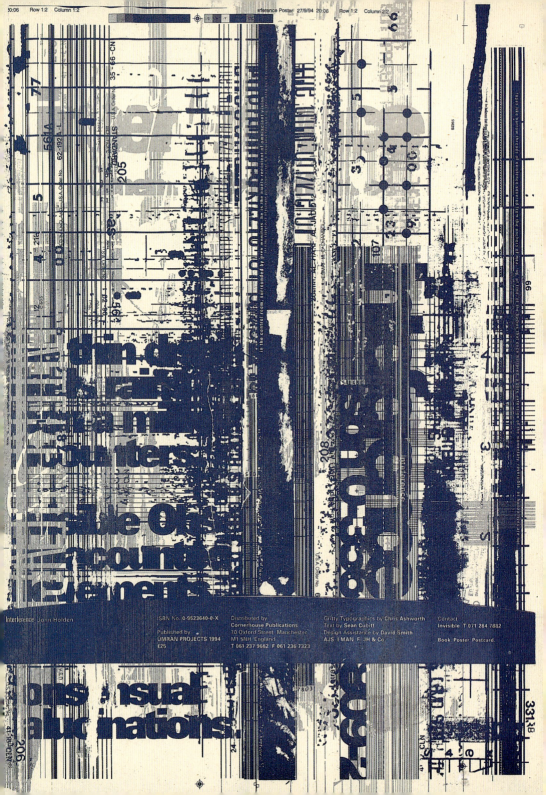

Interference  John Holden

ISBN No. 0-9523640-0-X

Published by
UMRAN PROJECTS 1994
£25

Distributed by
Cornerhouse Publications
70 Oxford Street  Manchester
M1 5NH  England
T 061 237 9662  F 061 236 7323

Gritty Typographics by Chris Ashworth
Text by Sean Cubitt
Design Assistance by David Smith
AJS  I MAN  F  JH & Co.

Contact
Invisible  T 071 284 7882

Book. Poster. Postcard.

## Interference

Book spreads
DESIGNERS | Chris Ashworth, Neil Fletcher, Amanda Sissons, John Holden
PHOTOGRAPHER | John Holden
PRINCIPAL TYPEFACES | Custom-made for the project
CLIENT | Ümran Projects

*Great Britain, 1994*

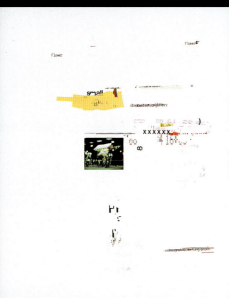
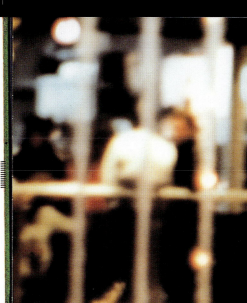
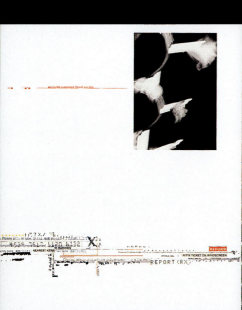
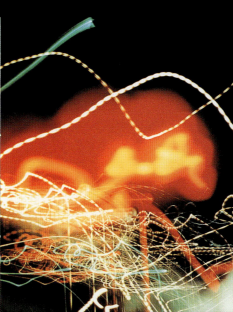

*Interference* is a photographic essay on surveillance in the city. In response to John Holden's lushly sinister images the designers created typographic illustrations of technological

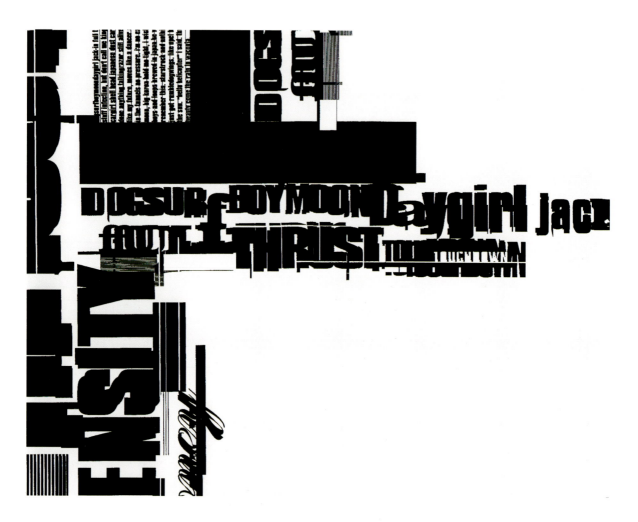

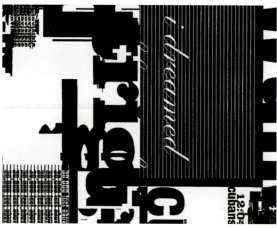

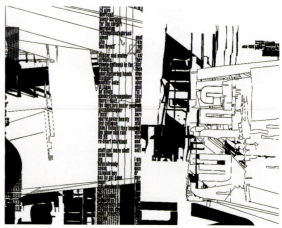

Mmm ... Skyscraper I Love You

Spreads from a typographic journal of New York

WRITERS/DESIGNERS John Warwicker, Karl Hyde
DESIGN COMPANY Tomato
PRINCIPAL TYPEFACES Compacta, Clarendon, Bureau Grotesque, Shelley
CLIENT Booth-Clibborn Editions

*Great Britain, 1994*

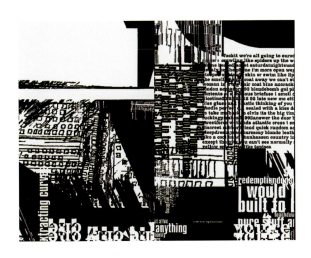
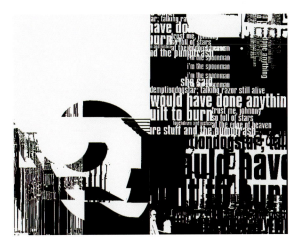
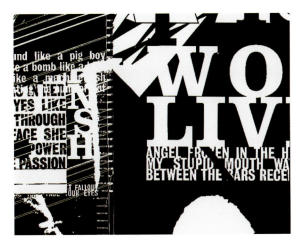
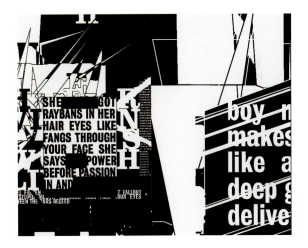

Randomly spliced together, the pages of *Skyscraper* record the sights, sounds, "crosstalk and chaos" of a journey through the streets of New York. Material was first developed during the recording of Underworld's album *dubnobasswithmyheadman* (two of the group, including Karl Hyde, are members of Tomato). Subsequently published, the project is closely related to the artist's book genre, except that it is available in ordinary bookshops.

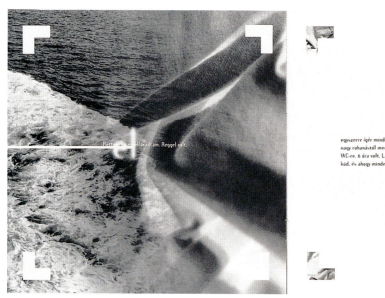

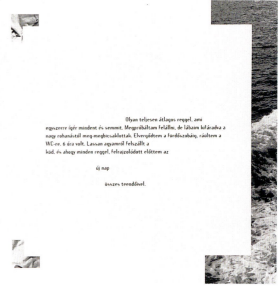

Olyan teljesen átlagos reggel, ami
egyszerre ígér mindent és semmit. Megpróbáltam felállni, de lábaim kifáradva a
nagy rohanástól meg-megbicsaklottak. Elvergődtem a fürdőszobáig, ráültem a
WC-re. 6 óra volt. Lassan agyamról felszállt a
köd, és ahogy minden reggel, felrajzolódott előttem az

új nap

összes teendőivel.

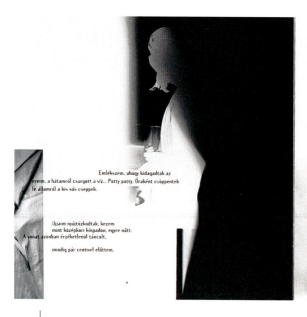

Le-ma-radt, le-ma-radt, le-ma-radt, le-ma-radt

üvöltötte egy

kegyetlen hang belülről. Egy kéz fehér lappal takarta le a tájat

és az eget, a vonat képe egyre egyszerűsödött a szemem előtt. Sziluettjét mintha

fekete ceruzával vagy tussal húzták volna át. Nem volt ott már más, csak a

száguldozó monstrum és egy absztrakt fájó rohanás. Ez azonban kínjaimon nem

enyhített és a Feladat sem tűnt értelmetlenebbnek. A lényegen nem változtathat

semmi, amikor az ember tudja, hogy rohannia kell, mert lemarad.

**Rövidülni Kezdet**

Spreads from a literary booklet

DESIGNER Zsolt Czakó
WRITER Krisztina Somogyi
PRINCIPAL TYPEFACE Template Gothic

*Self-published
Hungary, 1995*

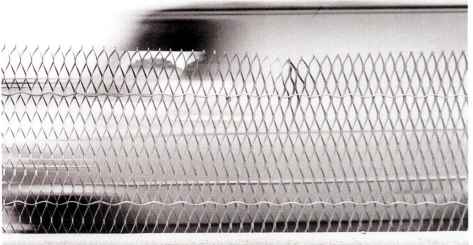

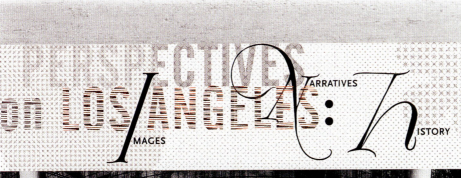

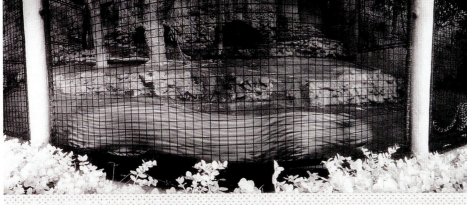

PERSPECTIVES on LOS ANGELES: *Narratives, Images, History*

THE GETTY CENTER FOR THE HISTORY OF
ART AND THE HUMANITIES
1996–1997
SCHOLARS AND SEMINARS PROGRAM

The Getty Center for the History of Art and the Humanities is dedicated to advanced research in the history of art, broadly defined as an integral part of human history and society. The goal of the Center is to cross the traditional boundaries imposed on academic institutions by bringing together international scholars to reexamine the meaning of art and artifacts and to reassess their importance within the full scope of the humanities and social sciences.

The Center's 1996–1997 Scholars and Seminars Program, *Perspectives on Los Angeles: Narratives, Images, History*, will be dedicated to research on Los Angeles and Southern California. Potential areas for exploration within this context include not only traditional forms of artistic and cultural expression, such as painting, sculpture, and architecture, but also journalism, photography, film, literature, the book arts, performance, urban studies, and all forms of popular and mass culture—each viewed in relationship to the ecologies, historical conditions, communities, and institutions that have affected its development. Research is understood in broad and inclusive terms that embrace the pursuits of scholars, artists, and cultural workers.

The Center solicits research proposals on all aspects of the artistic, cultural, social, economic, and political history of Los Angeles. Candidates may apply as Predoctoral or Postdoctoral Fellows, Getty Scholars, or Visiting Scholars. To receive an Application Packet with a detailed description of the Center's 1996–1997 scholar year, please contact your department administrator or:

THE SCHOLARS AND SEMINARS PROGRAM
THE GETTY CENTER FOR THE HISTORY OF ART AND THE HUMANITIES
401 Wilshire Blvd., Ste. 700, Santa Monica, CA 90401-1455, USA
(310) 458-9811, ext. 6000 (telephone)
(310) 395-1515 (facsimile)
Fellowships@getty.edu (e-mail)

**Perspectives on Los Angeles: Narratives, Images, History**

Poster

| | |
|---|---|
| DESIGNER | Lisa Nugent |
| DESIGN COMPANY | ReVerb |
| PHOTOGRAPHER | Dennis Keeley |
| PRINCIPAL TYPEFACES | Alternate Gothic, Scala Sans |
| CLIENT | The Getty Center for the History of Art and the Humanities |

*USA, 1995*

The Getty Center's 1996-97 Scholars and Seminars Program was dedicated to research on Los Angeles and Southern California. ReVerb's brief, for a poster to be displayed primarily at educational institutions, was to represent LA and its diverse cultures. The photographs compare two urban landscapes: a freeway system and a caged animal. The typography reinforces the visual language of the photography by mimicking the barriers and screens as well as the organic.

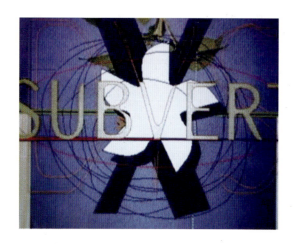

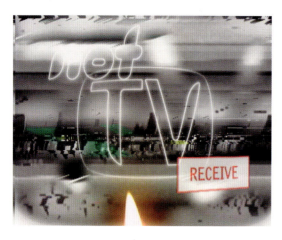

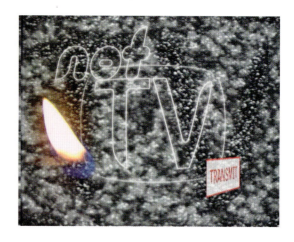

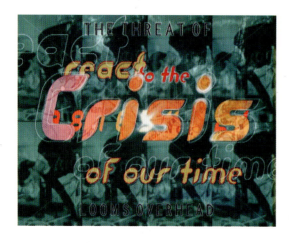

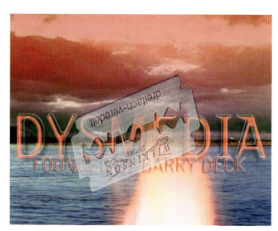

Dysmedia

Self-promotional video
DESIGNER Barry Deck
EDITOR AND EXTRA SHOOTING Uwe Wiesemann
PRINCIPAL TYPEFACES Truth, Cyberotica

USA/Germany, 1995

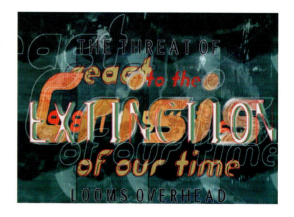

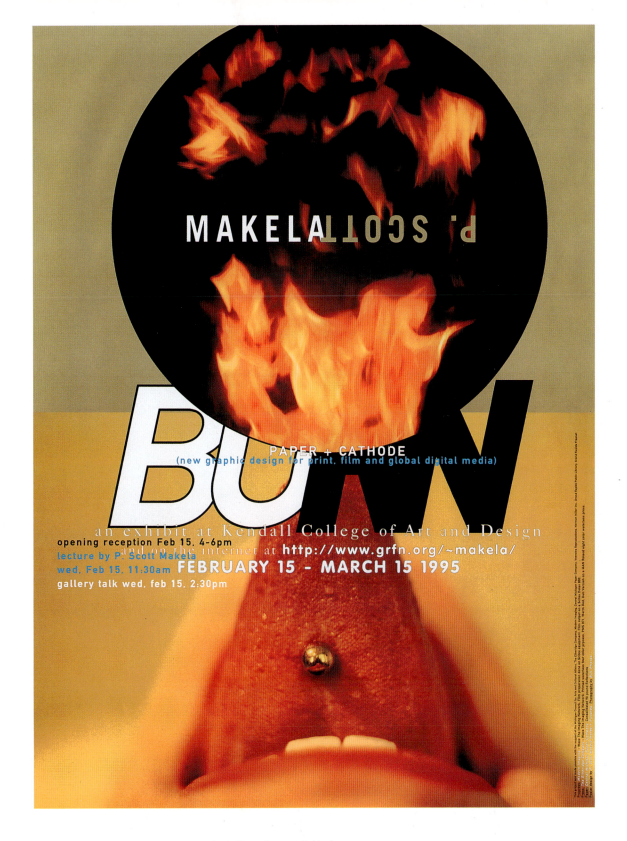

Born/Burn: Paper + Cathode

|  | Exhibition poster |
| DESIGNER | P. Scott Makela |
| DESIGN COMPANY | Words and Pictures for Business and Culture |
| PHOTOGRAPHER | Billy Phelps |
| PRINCIPAL TYPEFACES | Officina, VAG Rounded, Trade Gothic, WAC Mittelschrift |
| CLIENT | Kendall College of Art and Design |

*USA, 1995*

National Portfolio Day 1992

Poster inviting prospective students to show their work
DESIGNER/PHOTOGRAPHER/ILLUSTRATOR | Alexei Tylevich
PRINCIPAL TYPEFACES | Blur, Template Gothic, custom-made for the project
CLIENT | Minneapolis College of Art and Design

USA, 1992

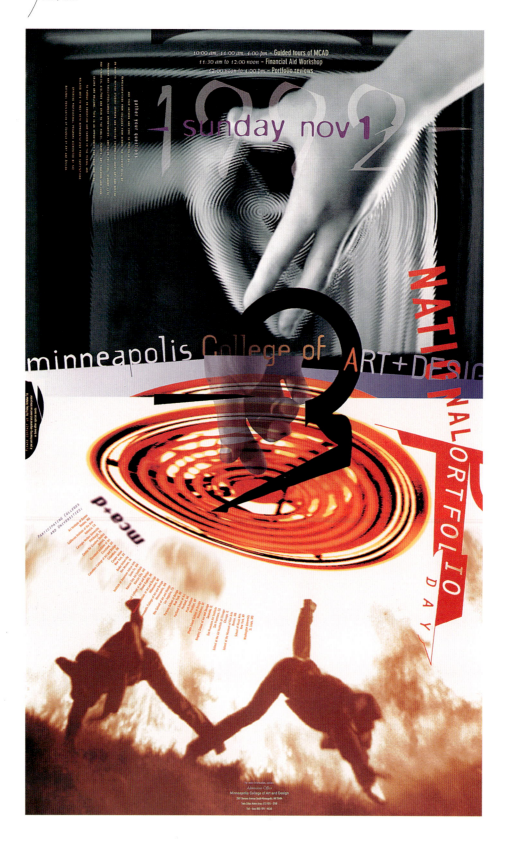

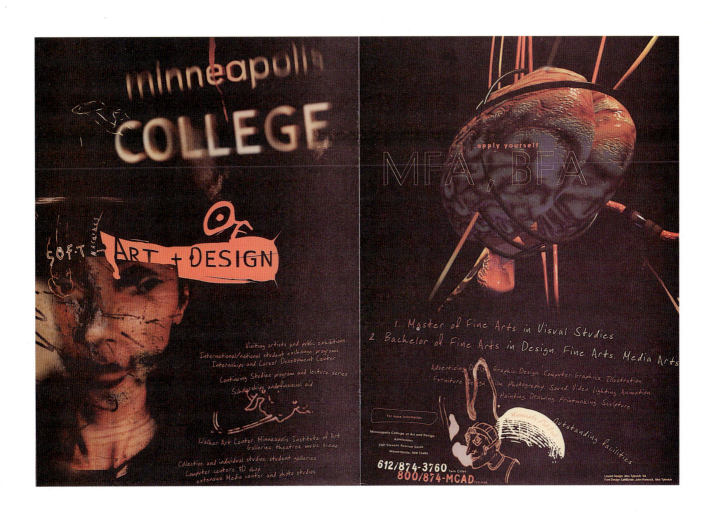

Magazine advertisement aimed at high school advisers and students

DESIGNER/ILLUSTRATOR Alexei Tylevich

PRINCIPAL TYPEFACES Calculus, Hancock, Stamp Gothic

CLIENT Minneapolis College of Art and Design

USA, 1993

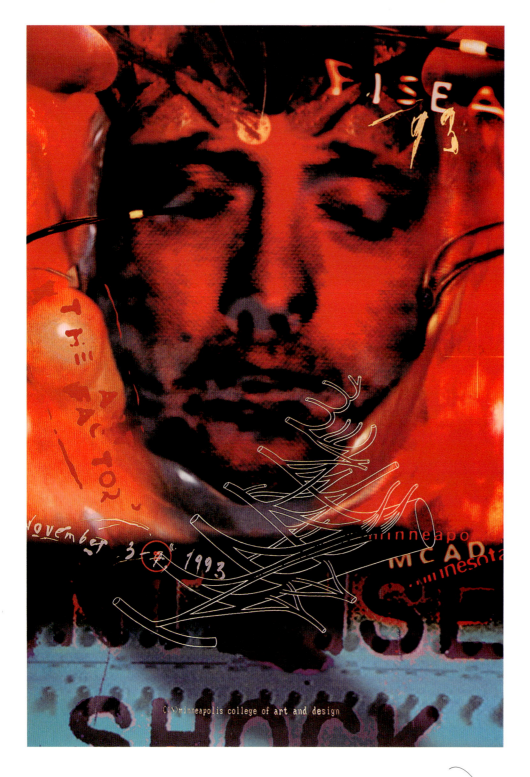

Alexei Tylevich's poster for the Fourth
International Symposium on Electronic
Art expresses the contemporary merging
of art, technology and the body as a
brutal "cyborg icon" – an anonymous,
wired, Christlike figure immersed in fluid
tissue, through which the type itself
seems to course like a new kind of
informational blood.

## FISEA '93

Conference poster
DESIGNER/PHOTOGRAPHER/ILLUSTRATOR Alexei Tylevich
PRINCIPAL TYPEFACE Custom-made for the project
CLIENT Minneapolis College of Art and Design,
International Symposium on Electronic Art

USA, 1993

**Visual Language '94**

| | |
|---|---|
| | Exhibition poster |
| DESIGNER/ILLUSTRATOR | Alexei Tylevich |
| PRINCIPAL TYPEFACE | Custom-made for the project |
| CLIENT | Minneapolis College of Art and Design |

USA, 1994

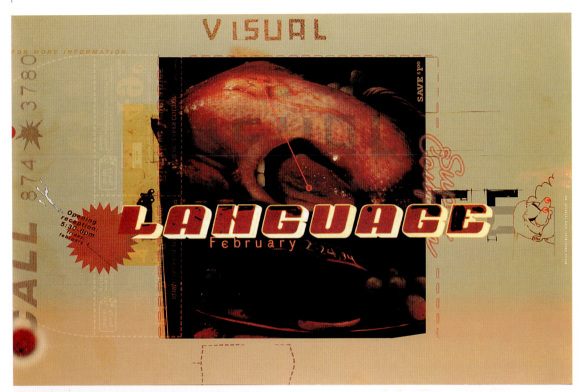

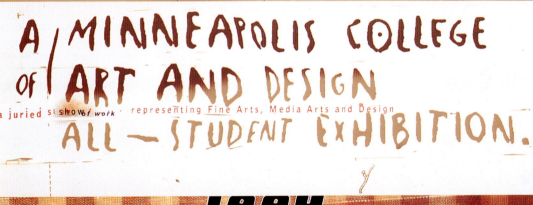

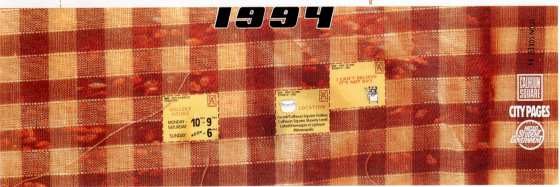

INTERDISCIP-
LINARY
ARTS /
FELLOWSHIP
S

INTERMEDIA
MCKNIGHT

AZANDE, RICARDO BLOCH,
LAURIE BETH CLARK, DAVID DUNLAP,
WENDY MORRIS

and music? Can a found object be sculpture? And the relevant question for critics and viewers often seemed to be "Yes, but is it ART?"

Interdisciplinary Fellowships 1994

Catalogue
DESIGNER | Jan Jancourt
DESIGN COMPANY | Jancourt & Associates
PHOTOGRAPHER | Warwick Green
PRINCIPAL TYPEFACES | Franklin Gothic, Officina
CLIENT | Intermedia Arts

USA, 1994

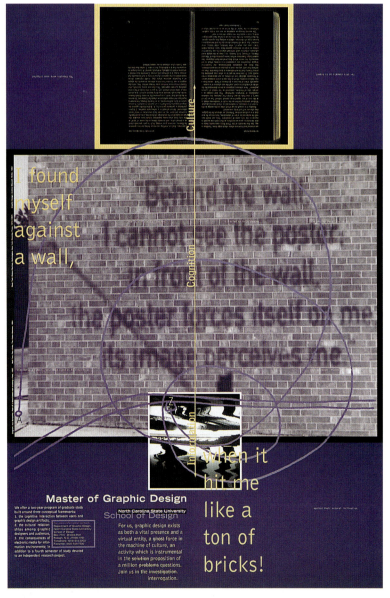

I found
myself
against
a wall,

"Behind the wall,
I cannot see the poster.
In front of the wall,
the poster forces itself on me,
its image perceives me."

when it
hit me
like a
ton of
bricks!

Master of Graphic Design
North Carolina State University
School of Design

We offer a two-year program of graduate study built around three conceptual frameworks:
1. the cognitive interaction between users and graphic design artifacts,
2. the cultural relationships among graphic designers and audiences,
3. the consequences of electronic media for information environments; in addition to a fourth semester of study devoted to an independent research project.

For more information contact:
Department of Graphic Design
North Carolina State University,
School of Design
Box 7701, Brooks Hall
Raleigh, N.C. 27695-7701
Telephone: (919) 515-2203
Facsimile: (919) 515-7330

For us, graphic design exists as both a vital presence and a virtual entity, a ghost force in the machine of culture, an activity which is instrumental in the solution proposition of a million problems questions. Join us in the investigation. interrogation.

Conceptually, the poster/brochure uses a number of "texts" or "voices" to create a dialogue with the reader. Since the graphic design programme's philosophy is divided into three frameworks (cognitive interaction, cultural dynamics, information media environments), three images were chosen to represent these areas. The only proviso was that they should all relate to the statement "I found myself against a wall, when it hit me like a ton of bricks", intended to suggest the student's moments of frustration and discovery.

Master of Graphic Design Recruitment

Poster/brochure
DESIGNER/PHOTOGRAPHER | Andrew Blauvelt
PRINCIPAL TYPEFACES | Bell Gothic, Trade Gothic, Letter Gothic
CLIENT | Department of Graphic Design,
North Carolina State University

USA, 1995

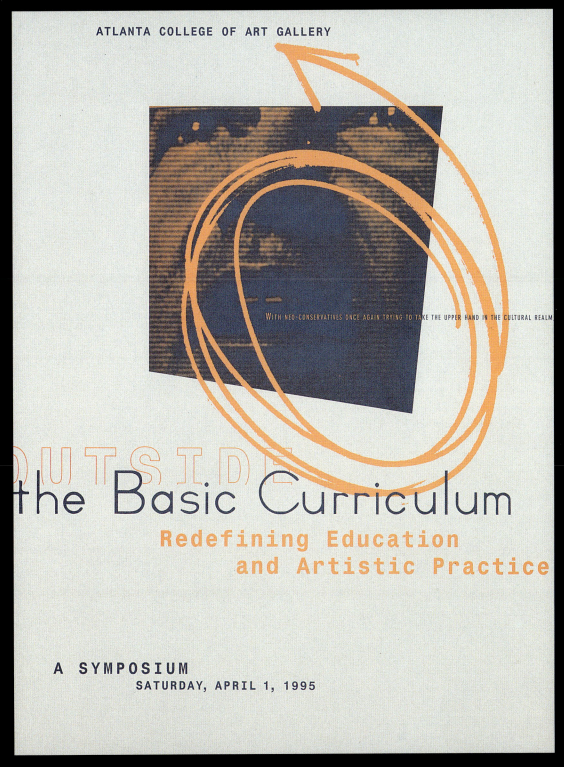

ATLANTA COLLEGE OF ART GALLERY

WITH NEO-CONSERVATIVES ONCE AGAIN TRYING TO TAKE THE UPPER HAND IN THE CULTURAL REALM

OUTSIDE
the Basic Curriculum
Redefining Education
and Artistic Practice

A SYMPOSIUM
SATURDAY, APRIL 1, 1995

Based on a TV image of US Speaker of the House Newt Gingrich, whose controversial history course was broadcast by satellite, the poster announces a symposium on the ways educators and artists can begin to counteract the political advances made by America's right wing, which now defines the agenda on cultural issues. The designers scanned in a copy of the standardised handwriting model for students ("the Basic Curriculum") but let the program's outline recognition software redefine their shapes according to its parameters.

Outside the Basic Curriculum:
Redefining Education and Artistic Practice

Conference poster
DESIGNERS          Andrew Blauvelt, Anne Burdick
PHOTOGRAPHER       Anne Burdick
PRINCIPAL TYPEFACES Monospace 821, DIN Neuzeit Grotesk, Manuscript
CLIENT             Atlanta College of Art Gallery

USA, 1995

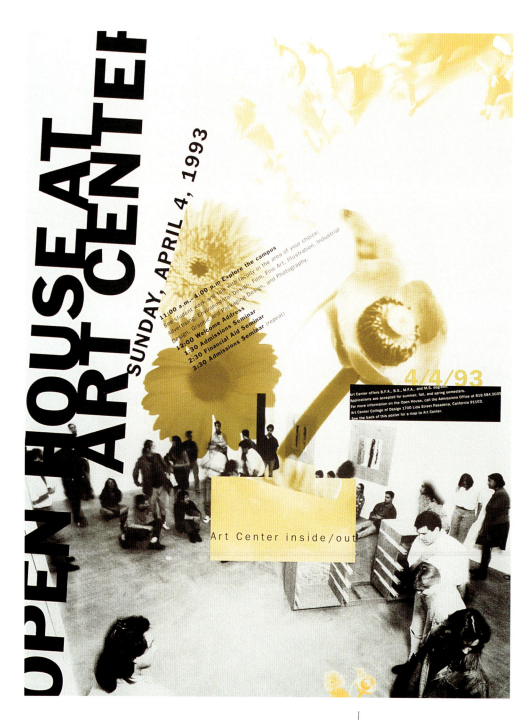

OPEN HOUSE AT ART CENTER

SUNDAY, APRIL 4, 1993

**11:00 a.m.– 4:00 p.m Explore the campus**
See student work and talk with faculty in the area of your choice:
Advertising, Environmental Design, Film, Fine Art, Illustration, Industrial
Design, Graphic and Packaging Design, and Photography.
**12:00 Welcome Address**
**1:30 Admissions Seminar**
**2:30 Financial Aid Seminar**
**3:30 Admissions Seminar** (repeat)

4/4/93

Art Center offers B.F.A., B.S., M.F.A. and M.S. degrees.
Applications are accepted for summer, fall, and spring semesters.
For more information on the Open House, call the Admissions Office at 818.584.5035
Art Center College of Design 1700 Lida Street Pasadena, California 91103.
See the back of this poster for a map to Art Center.

Art Center inside/out

Open House at Art Center

Poster
DESIGN DIRECTOR | Rebeca Méndez
DESIGNERS | Rebeca Méndez, Darin Beaman
DESIGN COMPANY | Art Center College of Design
PHOTOGRAPHER | Steven A. Heller
PRINCIPAL TYPEFACE | Franklin Gothic
CLIENT | Art Center College of Design

USA, 1993

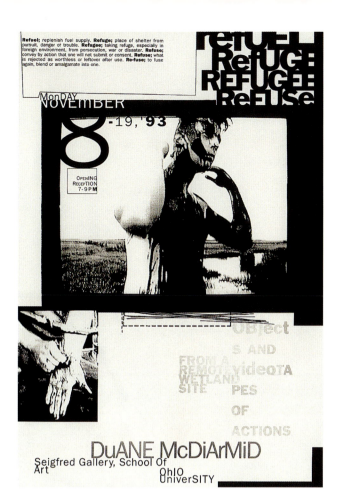

Refuel; replenish fuel supply. **Refuge;** place of shelter from pursuit, danger or trouble. **Refuge;** taking refuge, especially in foreign environment, from persecution, war or disaster. **Refuse;** convey by action that one will not submit or consent. **Refuse;** what is rejected as worthless or leftover after use. **Re-fuse;** to fuse again, blend or amalgamate into one.

**Refuel, Refuge, Refugee, Refuse**

Exhibition poster
DESIGNER | Joan Dobkin
DESIGN COMPANY | Joan Dobkin Design
VIDEO STILLS | Gadi Gofbarg
PRINCIPAL TYPEFACE | Franklin Gothic
CLIENT | Seigfred Gallery, School of Art, Ohio University

*USA, 1993*

**Text/Image**

Promotional poster for a new course offered by the faculties of Design and Photography
DESIGNER | Joan Dobkin
DESIGN COMPANY | Joan Dobkin Design
PHOTOGRAPHER | Patty Mitchell
PRINCIPAL TYPEFACE | Franklin Gothic
CLIENT | School of Art, Ohio University

*USA, 1993*

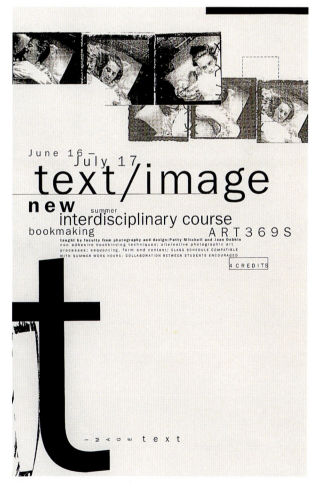

de Program 1992

Poster

DESIGNER/PHOTOGRAPHER Doug Kisor
PRINCIPAL TYPEFACE City
CLIENT Eastern Michigan University Design Department

USA, 1992

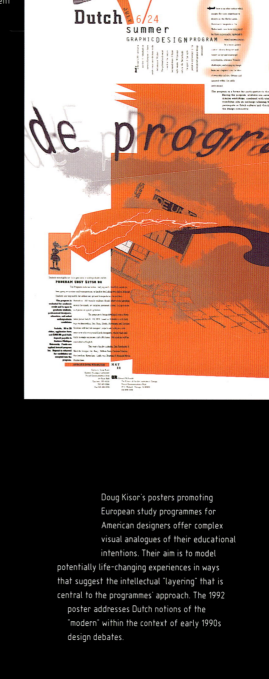

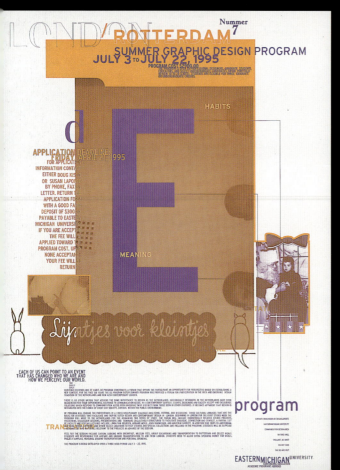

Doug Kisor's posters promoting
European study programmes for
American designers offer complex
visual analogues of their educational
intentions. Their aim is to model
potentially life-changing experiences in ways
that suggest the intellectual "layering" that is
central to the programmes' approach. The 1992
poster addresses Dutch notions of the
"modern" within the context of early 1990s
design debates.

London/Rotterdam Design Program

Poster

DESIGNER/PHOTOGRAPHER Doug Kisor
PRINCIPAL TYPEFACES Interstate, One Iota
CLIENT Eastern Michigan University Design Department

USA, 1995

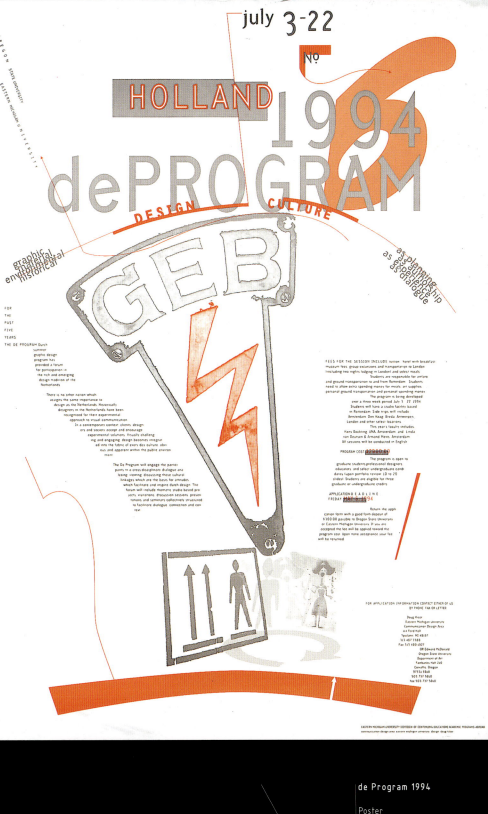

de Program 1994

Poster
Doug Kisor
Industry
Eastern Michigan University Design Depa

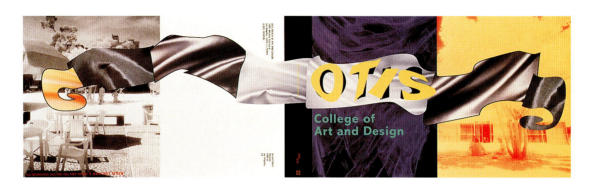

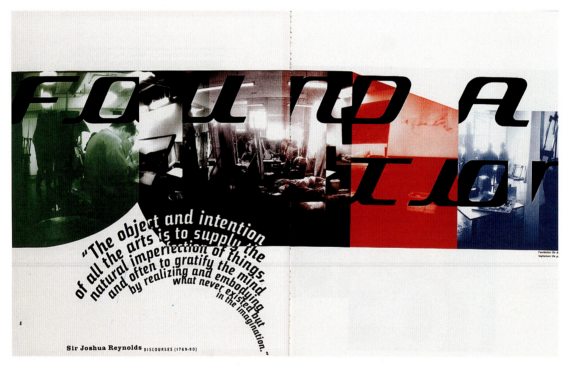

Otis College of Art and Design 93-94/94-95

Fold-out cover and catalogue spreads

DESIGNERS Lisa Nugent, Whitney Lowe, Somi Kim
DESIGN COMPANY ReVerb
PHOTOGRAPHER Dennis Keeley
PRINCIPAL TYPEFACES Clarendon, Steile Futura, Script
CLIENT Otis College of Art and Design

USA, 1993

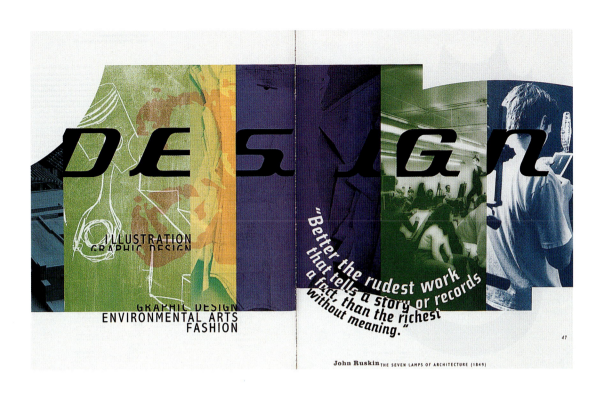

"Better the rudest work that tells a story or records a fact, than the richest without meaning."

47

John Ruskin THE SEVEN LAMPS OF ARCHITECTURE (1849)

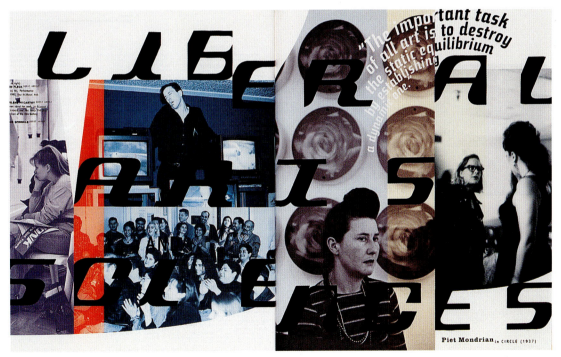

"The important task of all art is to destroy the static equilibrium by establishing a dynamic one."

Piet Mondrian in CIRCLE (1937)

The catalogue's theme, "set things in motion", is expressed through the use of shifting type and flowing, banner-inspired shapes. The density of type and image is intended to reflect the energy of campus activity.

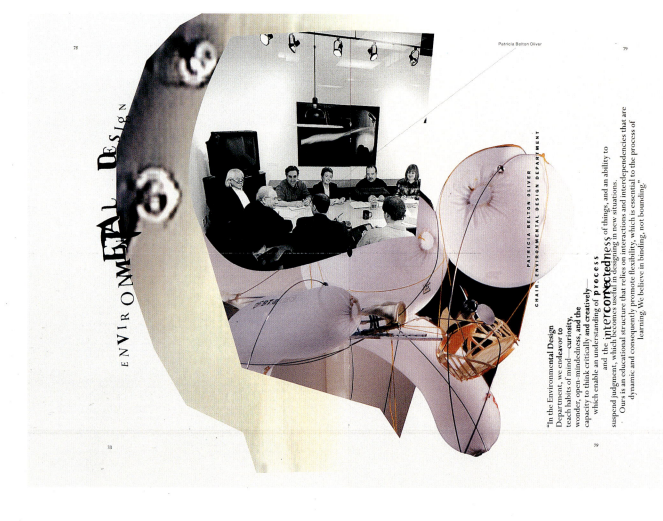

ENVIRONMENTAL DESIGN

"In the Environmental Design
Department, we endeavor to
teach habits of mind —curiosity,
wonder, open-mindedness, and the
capacity to think critically and creatively—
which enable an understanding of process
and the interconnectedness of things, and an ability to
suspend judgment, which becomes useful in designing in new situations.
Ours is an educational structure that relies on interactions and interdependencies that are
dynamic and consequently promote flexibility, which is essential to the process of
learning. We believe in binding, not bounding."

PATRICIA BELTON OLIVER
CHAIR, ENVIRONMENTAL DESIGN DEPARTMENT

**ENVIRONMENTAL DESIGN**

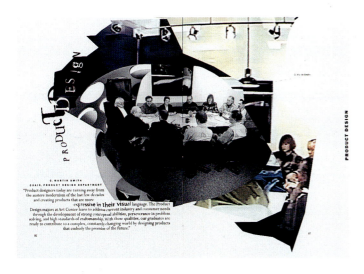

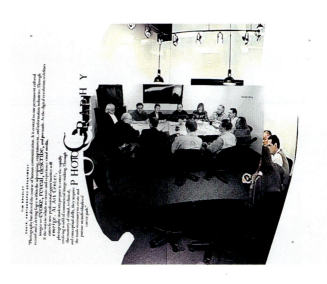

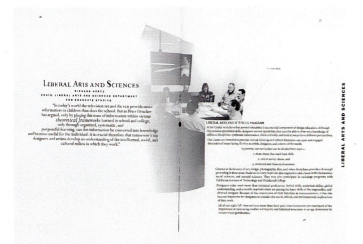

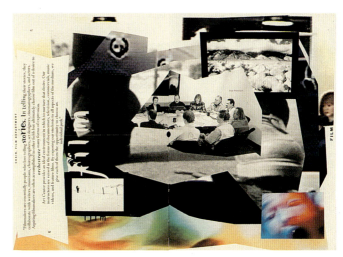

Art Center College of Design Catalog 1995-96

Catalogue spreads
DESIGN DIRECTOR  Rebeca Méndez
DESIGNER  Darin Beaman
ASSOCIATE DESIGNER  Chris Haaga
PHOTOGRAPHER  Steven A. Heller
PRINCIPAL TYPEFACES  Perpetua, Minion, Franklin Gothic, Helvetica, Tema Cantante, Lip
CLIENT  Art Center College of Design

USA, 1994

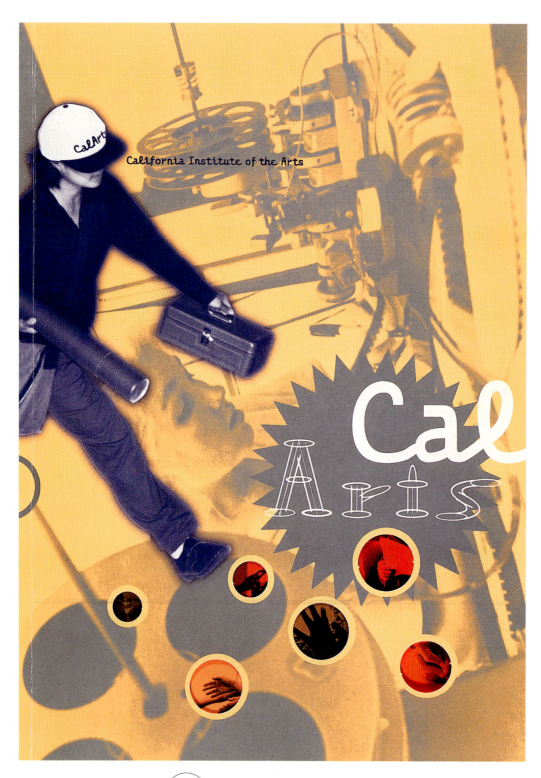

California Institute of the Arts

CalArts

**CalArts**

| | |
|---|---|
| | Cover and spreads from California Institute of the Arts catalogue, 1995-97 |
| DESIGNERS | Somi Kim, Barbara Glauber |
| DESIGN COMPANIES | ReVerb, Heavy Meta |
| PHOTOGRAPHERS | Steven A. Gunther, Paula Riff, Raymond Hahn, Stephen Callis |
| PRINCIPAL TYPEFACES | Arbitrary, Jot, One Iota, OutWest, Platelet, Tribulation, Wormwood |
| CLIENT | California Institute of the Arts |

*USA, 1994*

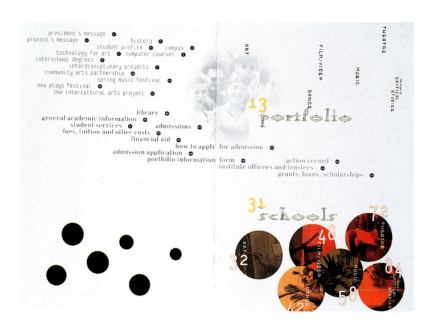

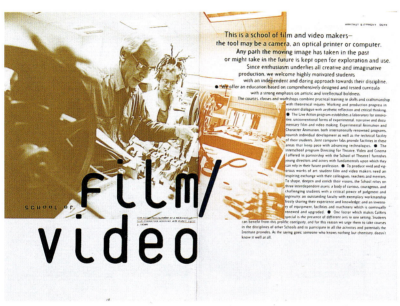

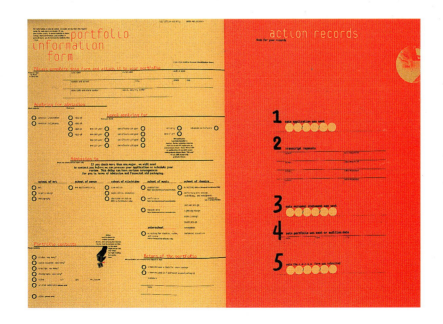

Flyer for a lecture by Edward Fella
DESIGNER | Edward Fella
PRINCIPAL TYPEFACES | By Fella's CalArts students
CLIENT | Art Center College of Design

USA, 1995

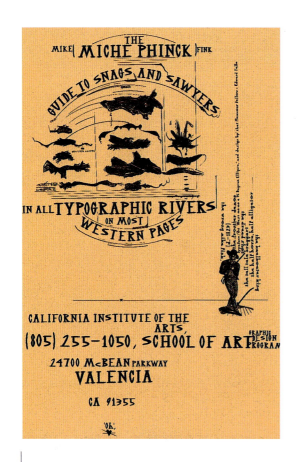

Flyer for a lecture by Mike Fink
DESIGNER | Edward Fella
PRINCIPAL TYPEFACE | OutWest
CLIENT | Graphic Design Program, California Institute of the Arts

USA, 1993

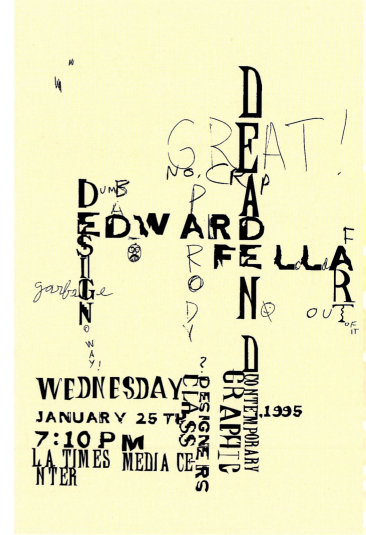

Edward Fella's lecture "announcements"
are made, with some perversity, long
after the event itself is over. As with
his earlier Detroit Focus Gallery series,
their defiantly non-digital, hand-
lettered inventions refer not to the
visiting artists and designers (except in
the case of his own lectures) but to
Fella's pet themes and predilections.
The poster for graphic designer Mike
Fink featuring Fella's typeface OutWest
takes its cue from another historical
"Miche Phinck", who in the early 1800s
earned a wild west reputation as a
brawler, braggart and marksman.

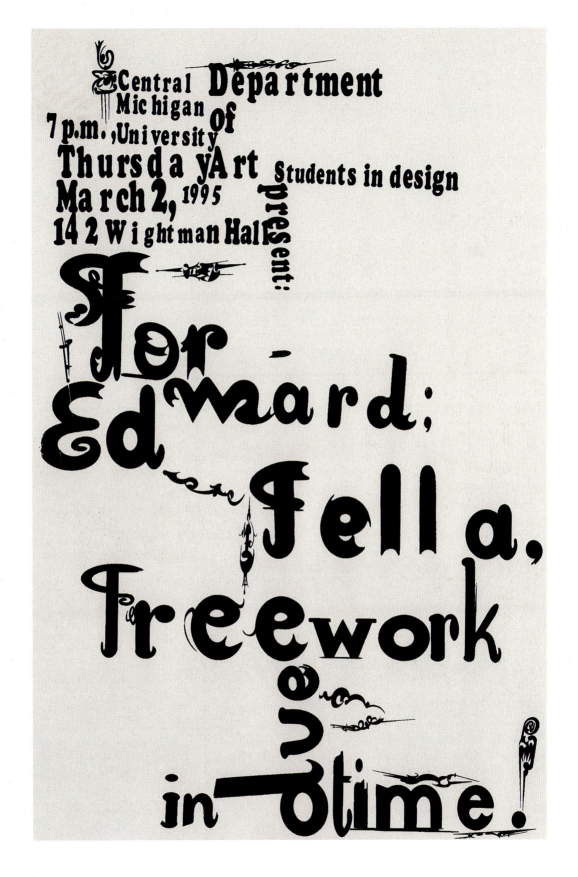

Central Michigan University Department of Art Students in design present:

7 p.m., Thursday March 2, 1995
142 Wightman Hall

for Edward; Fella, Freework on in time!

Flyer for a lecture by Edward Fella
DESIGNER Edward Fella
PRINCIPAL TYPEFACES Custom-made for the project, Cooper Black
CLIENT Central Michigan University Department of Art

USA, 1995

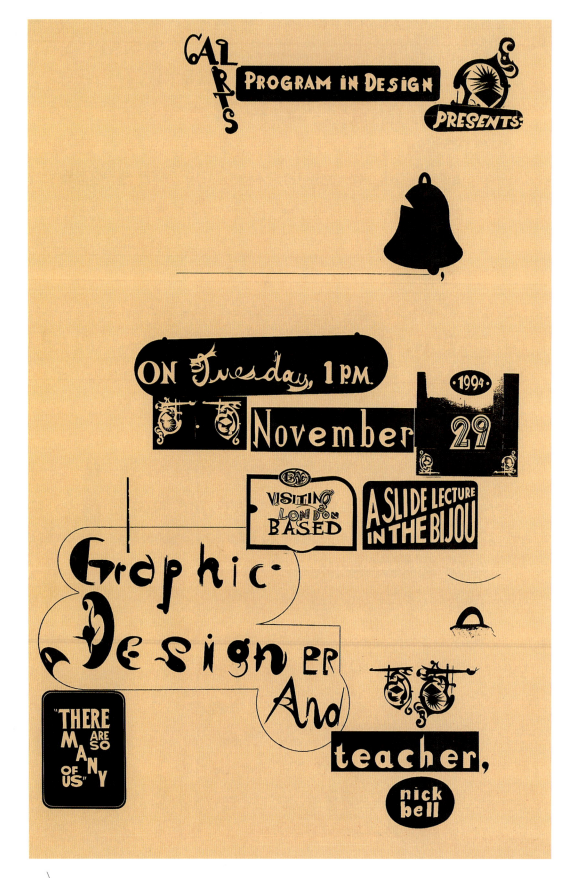

CAL ARTS PROGRAM iN DESIGN PRESENTS:

ON Tuesday, 1 P.M. · 1994 · November 29

VISITING LONDON BASED

A SLIDE LECTURE IN THE BIJOU

Graphic Designer And teacher, nick bell

"THERE ARE SO MANY OF US"

Flyer for a lecture by Nick Bell
*DESIGNER* Edward Fella
*PRINCIPAL TYPEFACES* Custom-made for the project
*CLIENT* Graphic Design Program, California Institute of the Arts

*USA, 1994*

Flyer for a lecture by Rebeca Méndez

DESIGNER | Edward Fella
PRINCIPAL TYPEFACES | Custom-made for the project
CLIENT | Graphic Design Program, California Institute of the Arts

*USA, 1993*

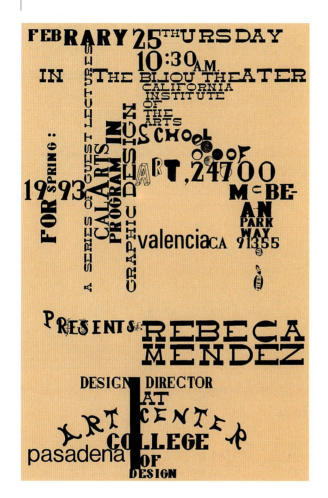

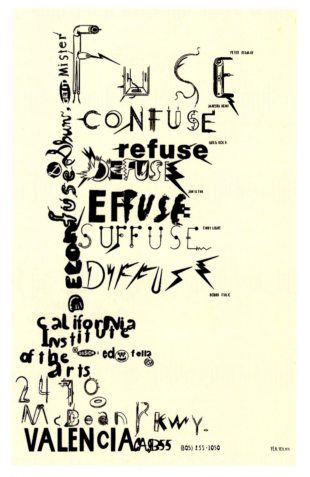

Flyer for a lecture by Neville Brody

DESIGNER | Edward Fella
PRINCIPAL TYPEFACES | Peter Regular, Marsha Demi, Greg Bold,
Jan Ultra, Cindy Light, Bobby Italic
CLIENT | Graphic Design Program, California Institute of the Arts

*USA, 1994*

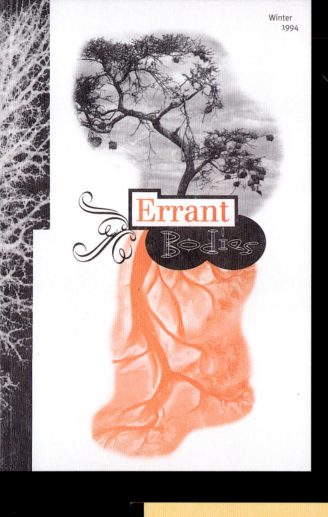

Winter
1994

# Errant
## Bodies

**Errant Bodies**

Cultural journal cover
DESIGNER Louise Sandhaus
PRINCIPAL TYPEFACES OutWest, Walbaum
CLIENT Brandon LaBelle

U S A, 1994

**Errant Bodies**

Cultural journal cover
DESIGNER Louise Sandhaus
PRINCIPAL TYPEFACES Suburban, Monoline Script, Grotesque
CLIENT Brandon LaBelle, Louise Sandhaus

U S A, 1994

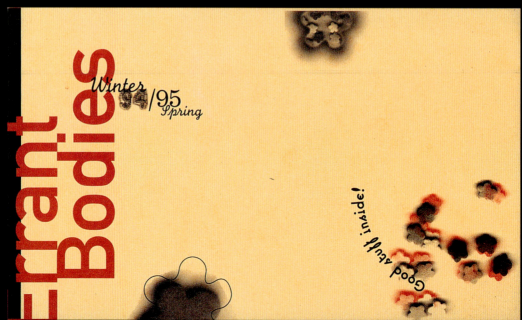

# Errant Bodies

Winter 94/95 Spring

Good stuff inside!

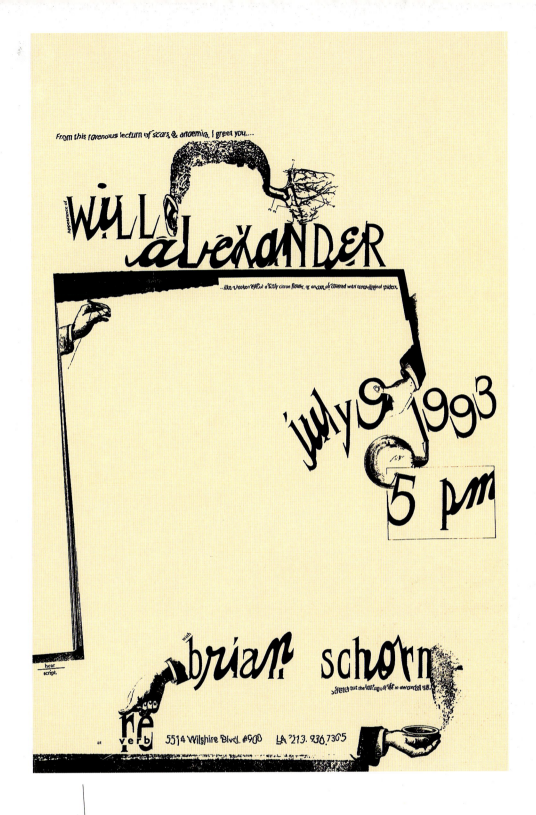

Poster for a literary reading
DESIGNER Brian Schorn
DESIGN COMPANY ReVerb
PRINCIPAL TYPEFACES Letraset Sourcebook, Gill Sans

*Self-published*
*USA, 1993*

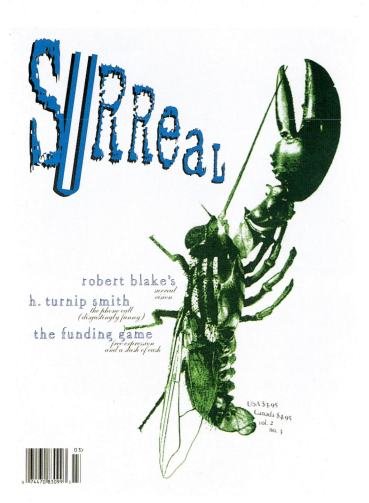

robert blake's
*surreal
vision*

h. turnip smith
*the phone call
(disgustingly funny)*

the funding game
*free expression
and a stash of cash*

USA $3.95
Canada $4.95
vol. 2
no. 3

Surreal vol. 2 no. 3

Arts magazine cover
DESIGNER  Brian Schorn
PRINCIPAL TYPEFACES  Harting, Madrid, Onyx, Blackoak, Kaufmann
CLIENT  *Surreal*

*USA, 1994*

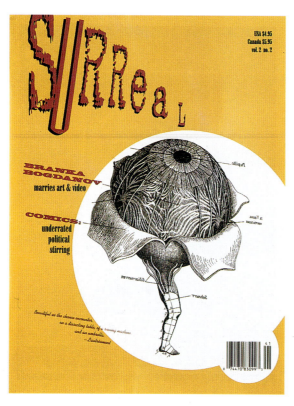

USA $4.95
Canada $5.95
vol. 2 no. 2

BRANKA
BOGDANOV
marries art & video

COMICS:
underrated
political
stirring

*Beautiful as the chance encounter
on a dissecting table, of a sewing machine
and an umbrella.
— Lautréamont*

Surreal vol. 2 no. 2

Arts magazine cover
DESIGNER  Brian Schorn
PRINCIPAL TYPEFACES  Harting, Madrid, Technocrat, Shelley
CLIENT  *Surreal*

*USA, 1994*

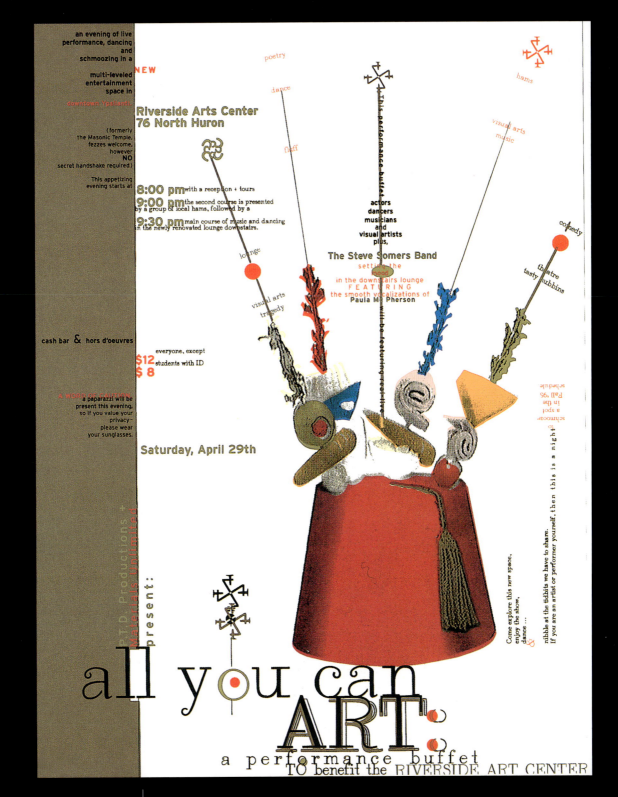

an evening of live performance, dancing and schmoozing in a

multi-leveled entertainment space in

downtown Ypsilanti

**Riverside Arts Center**
**76 North Huron**

(formerly the Masonic Temple, fezzes welcome, however **NO** secret handshake required)

This appetizing evening starts at

**8:00 pm** with a reception + tours

**9:00 pm** the second course is presented by a group of local hams, followed by a

**9:30 pm** main course of music and dancing in the newly renovated lounge downstairs.

cash bar **&** hors d'oeuvres

everyone, except
**$12** students with ID
**$ 8**

A WORD: paparazzi will be present this evening, so if you value your privacy— please wear your sunglasses.

**Saturday, April 29th**

NEW

poetry

dance

fluff

hams

visual arts
music

actors
dancers
musicians
and
visual artists
plus,

**The Steve Somers Band**
setting the mood
in the downstairs lounge
FEATURING
the smooth vocalizations of
Paula McPherson

comedy

theatre
tasty nibbins

visual arts
tragedy

lounge

This performance buffet will be featuring real tidbits

Come explore this new space, enjoy the show, dance . . .

nibble at the tidbits we have to share. If you are an artist or performer yourself, then this is a night to schmooze a spot in the Fall '95 schedule

P.T.D. Productions +
Materials Unlimited
present:

**all you can**
**ART:**
*a performance buffet*
TO benefit the RIVERSIDE ART CENTER

**All You Can Art**

Poster for a performance buffet

DESIGNERS/PHOTOGRAPHERS  Susan LaPorte, George LaRou
DESIGN COMPANY  Exquisite Corps
PRINCIPAL TYPEFACES  Fancy Single, Interstate
CLIENT  P.T.D. Productions

*USA, 1995*

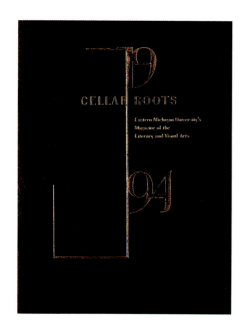

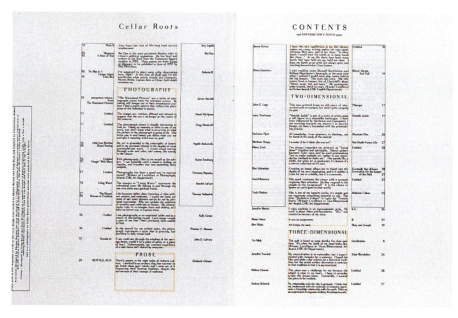

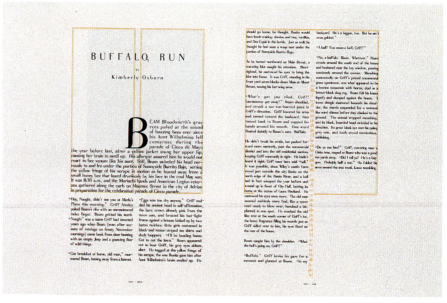

The 1994 *Cellar Roots* was designed as a response to conservative criticism of the design of previous issues. The golden mean, the Arts and Crafts movement and nuances found in letterpress were used as references and the typefaces Flattop and Procession also contain a historical reference to the structure and proportions of Bodoni. The satirical aim was to produce a "beautiful magazine" to showcase the art and literature department's work.

**Cellar Roots**

Cover and spreads from a magazine
of literary and visual arts

FACULTY ADVISER George LaRou
DESIGNERS Craig Steen, Sharon Marson
DESIGN COMPANY Eastern Michigan University Design Department
PRINCIPAL TYPEFACES Flattop, Procession
CLIENT Eastern Michigan University Student Media

*USA, 1994*

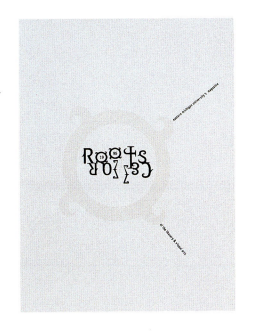

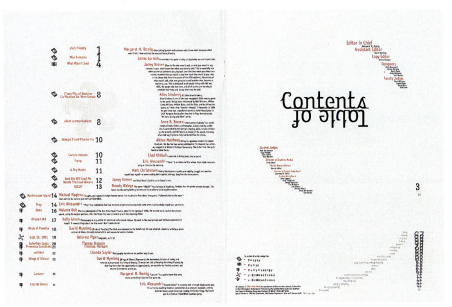

# Contents of Table

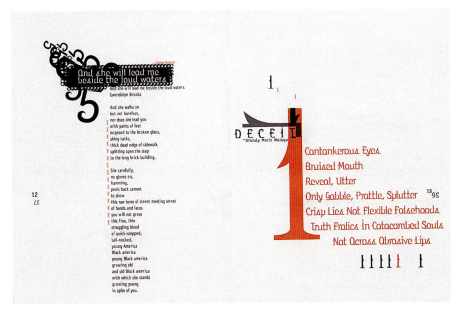

## Cellar Roots

Cover and spreads from a magazine
of literary and visual arts

FACULTY ADVISER George LaRou
DESIGNERS Anne Bourselth, Kindra Murphy, Kevin Sams, Andy Slopsema, Lori Young
DESIGN COMPANY Eastern Michigan University Design Department
PRINCIPAL TYPEFACES Celly, Starlight
CLIENT Eastern Michigan University Student Media

USA, 1995

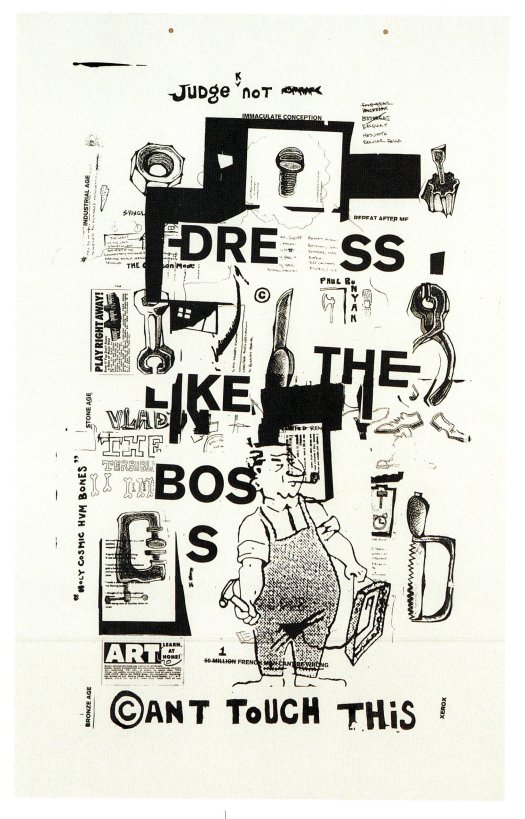

Dress Like the Boss

|  | Poster |
| DESIGNER | Elliott Peter Earls |
| DESIGN COMPANY | The Apollo Program |
| PRINCIPAL TYPEFACE | Helvetica |

*Self-published*
*USA, 1993*

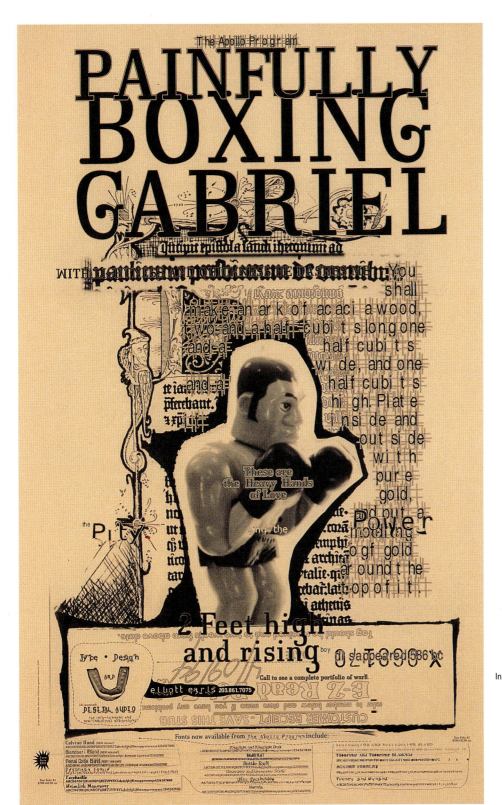

Painfully Boxing Gabriel

Poster
DESIGNER / Elliott Peter Earls
DESIGN COMPANY / The Apollo Program
PHOTOGRAPHER / The Apollo Program
PRINCIPAL TYPEFACES / Calvino Hand, Bland Serif Bland

*Self-published*
*USA, 1995*

In his self-published posters, often designed to promote his own typefaces, Elliott Peter Earls poses fundamental questions about experimental design. "How do we restore radicality to the creative process when pluralism renders all work valid and no work taboo?" he asks. "How can we deal with the pervasive 'legitimation of the subversive'?" Earls's personal answer is the literary concept of defamiliarisation. With his bizarre typography he makes the familiar strange and the strange familiar and in the process questions the viewer's assumptions about "form" itself.

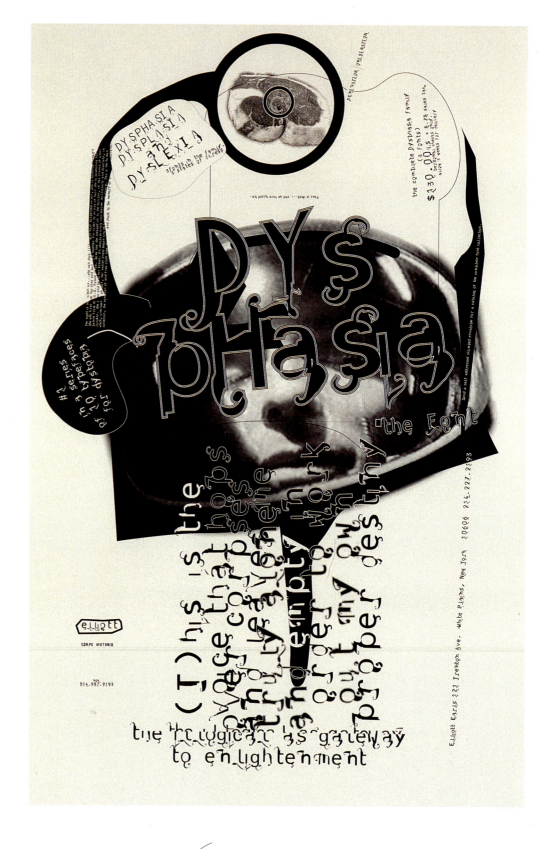

Dysphasia, Dysplasia, Dyslexia

Poster advertising three typefaces

DESIGNER Elliott Peter Earls
DESIGN COMPANY The Apollo Program
PHOTOGRAPHER The Apollo Program
PRINCIPAL TYPEFACES Dysphasia, Dysplasia, Dyslexia

Self-published
USA, 1995

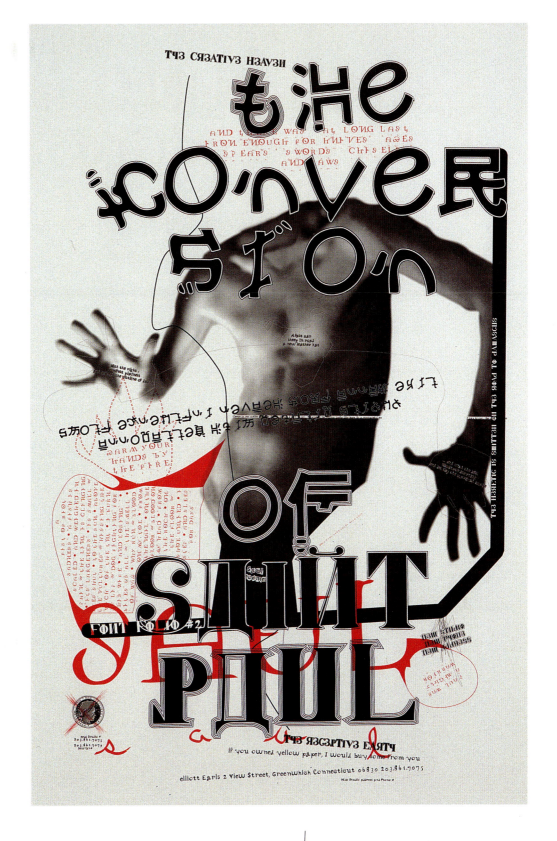

The Conversion of Saint Paul

| | |
|---|---|
| | Poster |
| DESIGNER | Elliott Peter Earls |
| DESIGN COMPANY | The Apollo Program |
| PHOTOGRAPHER | The Apollo Program |
| PRINCIPAL TYPEFACES | Mothra Paralax, Toohey, Wynand |

*Self-published*
*USA, 1995*

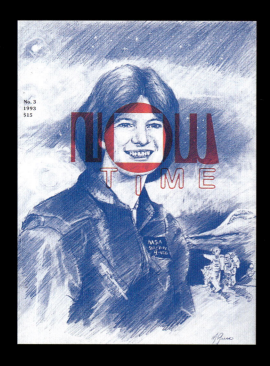

**Now Time no. 3**

Cover and contents spread from a magazine of social and cultural criticism

DESIGNERS  Somi Kim, Whitney Lowe, Susan Parr, Lorraine Wild, Caryn Aono, Andrea Fella
DESIGN COMPANY  ReVerb
ILLUSTRATOR  Michael Greco
PRINCIPAL TYPEFACES  Antique Olive, Souvenir
CLIENT  A.R.T. Press

USA, 1993

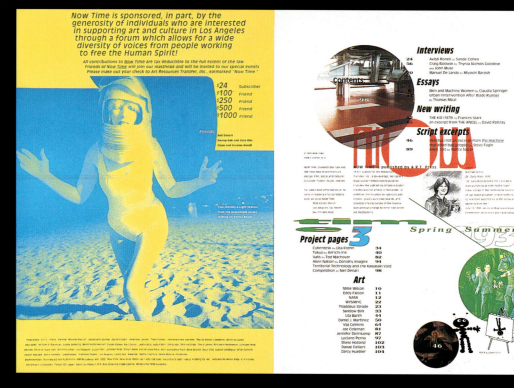

## The Crystal Goblet.The Big Spit

Pages from a visual essay published in the promotion
*Rethinking Design II: The Future of Print*

| | |
|---|---|
| DESIGNER | Allen Hori |
| EDITORS | Michael Bierut, Emily Hayes |
| DESIGN COMPANY | Bates Hori |
| PHOTOGRAPHERS | Christopher Weil, Allen Hori |
| PRINCIPAL TYPEFACES | Akzidenz Grotesk, Melior, Garamond |
| CLIENT | Mohawk Paper Mills |

*USA, 1995*

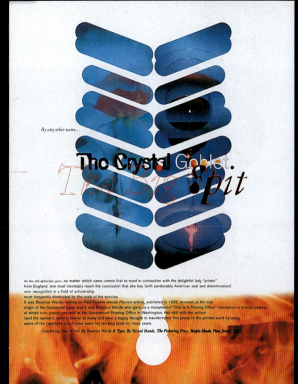

By any other name...

The Crystal Goblet.
The Big Spit

As the old aphorism goes, no matter which name comes first to mind in connection with the delightful lady "printer" from England, one must inevitably reach the conclusion that she has (with pardonably American zeal and determination) won recognition in a field of scholarship most frequently dominated by the male of the species.

It was Beatrice Warde, writing as Paul Fleuron whose *Fleuron* article, published in 1926, showed us the true origin of the Garamond types and it was Beatrice Warde who gave us a monumental "This Is A Printing Office" inscription—a bronze casting of which now graces one wall in the Government Printing Office in Washington. Her skill with the written (and the spoken) word is known to many and what a happy thought to transform her fine prose to the printed word by using some of the typefaces which have been her working tools for many years.

*Concerning These Words: By Beatrice Warde & Types By Varied Hands, The Pickering Press, Maple Shade, New Jersey, 1955*

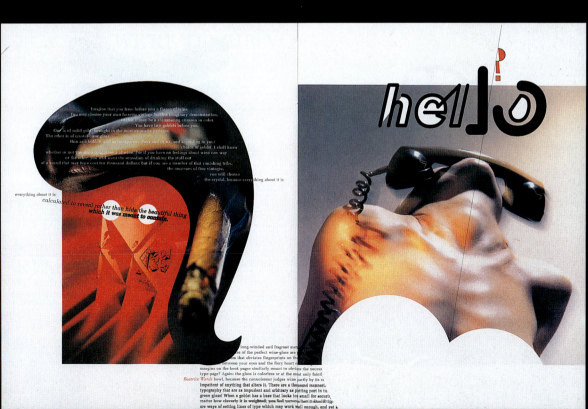

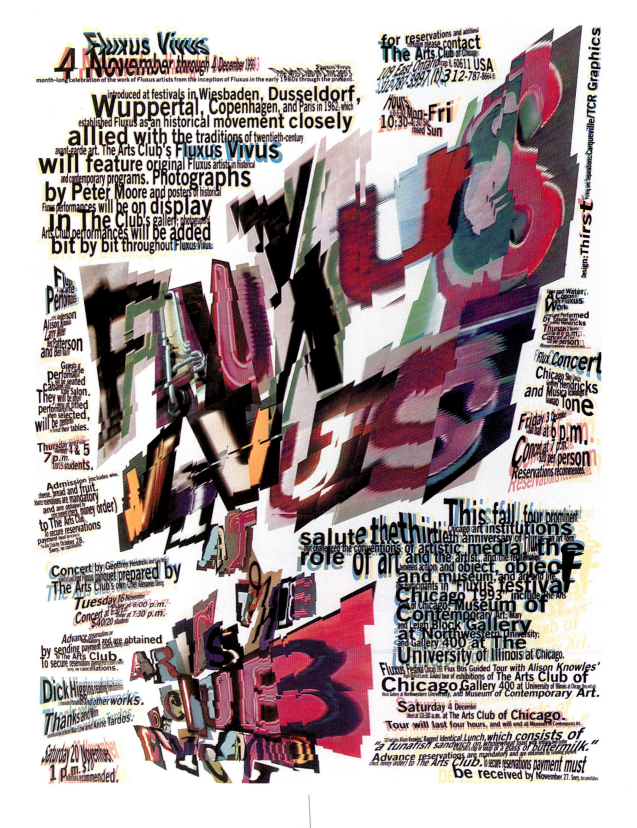

Fluxus Vivus

Poster for a month-long Fluxus festival

DESIGNERS/DIGITAL IMAGING  Rick Valicenti, Mark Rattlin
DESIGN COMPANY  Thirst
PRINCIPAL TYPEFACES  News Gothic, random video grabs
CLIENT  Arts Club of Chicago

USA, 1993

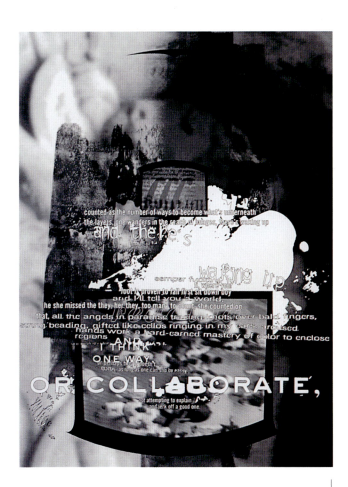

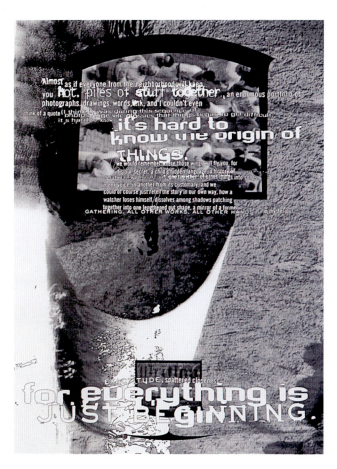

**A House Swarming!**

Pages from a poem/foreword for a journal of literature and art

*DESIGNER/PHOTOGRAPHER* Stephen Farrell

*WRITER* D. R. Heiniger

*PRINCIPAL TYPEFACES* Beach Savage, Werkman Round, Evangelic, typewriter

*CLIENT* *Private Arts*

*USA, 1994*

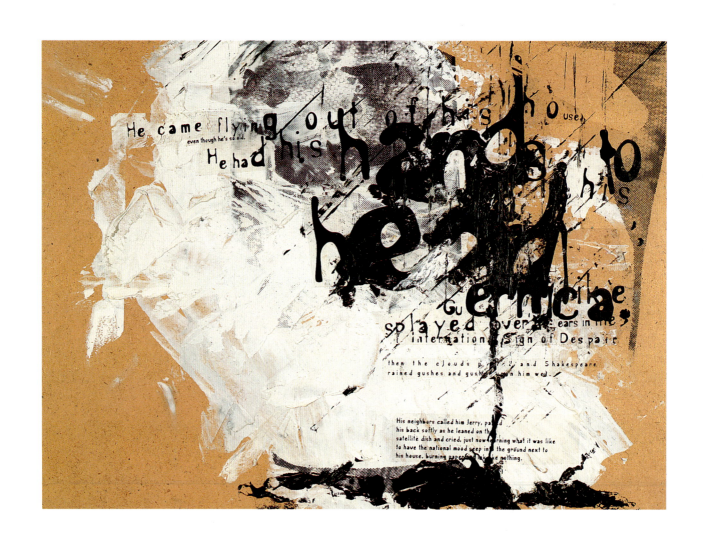

**Fire at J. D. Salinger's House**

Unpublished poetry promotion/font specimen poster

DESIGNER  Stephen Farrell
WRITER  Daniel X. O'Neil
PRINCIPAL TYPEFACE  Tetsuo Organic

USA, 1993

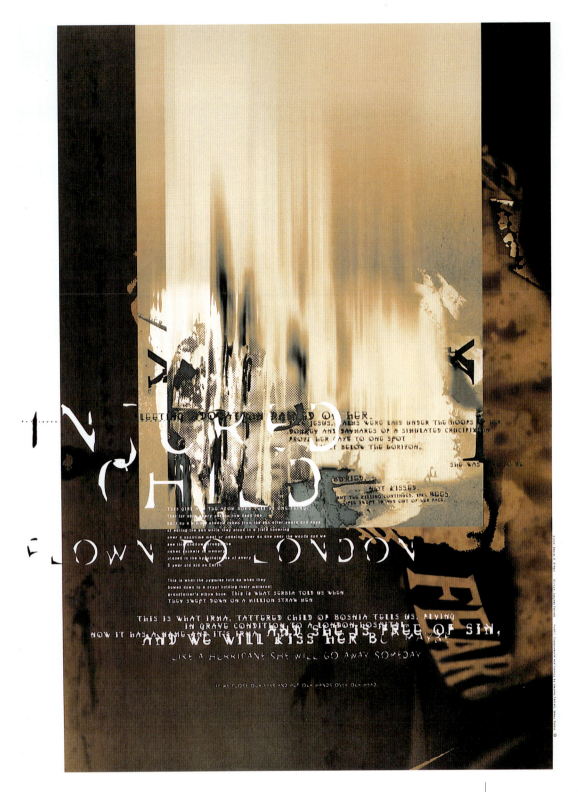

Stephen Farrell's pieces with the poet
Daniel X. O'Neil are rare but highly
suggestive examples of close creative
collaboration between designer and
writer. In *Injured Child*, text and
typeface illustrate each other. Both
are commentaries on brokenness: the
poem on the broken social and political
structures of Europe, the typefaces –
Farrell's own designs – on the fractured
nature of communication in English.

**Injured Child Flown to London**

Limited edition print
*DESIGNER/ILLUSTRATOR* Stephen Farrell
*WRITER* Daniel X. O'Neil
*PRINCIPAL TYPEFACES* Entropy, Commonworld, Stamp Gothic

*Self-published*
*USA, 1994*

ALTHOUGH THE COMPUTER AIDS IN
CERTAIN DESIGN TASKS, MUCH AS THE
TECHNOLOGY OF LASERS AIDS THE
SURGEON, ULTIMATELY THE HAND AND
EYE ARE THE PRIMARY TOOLS.

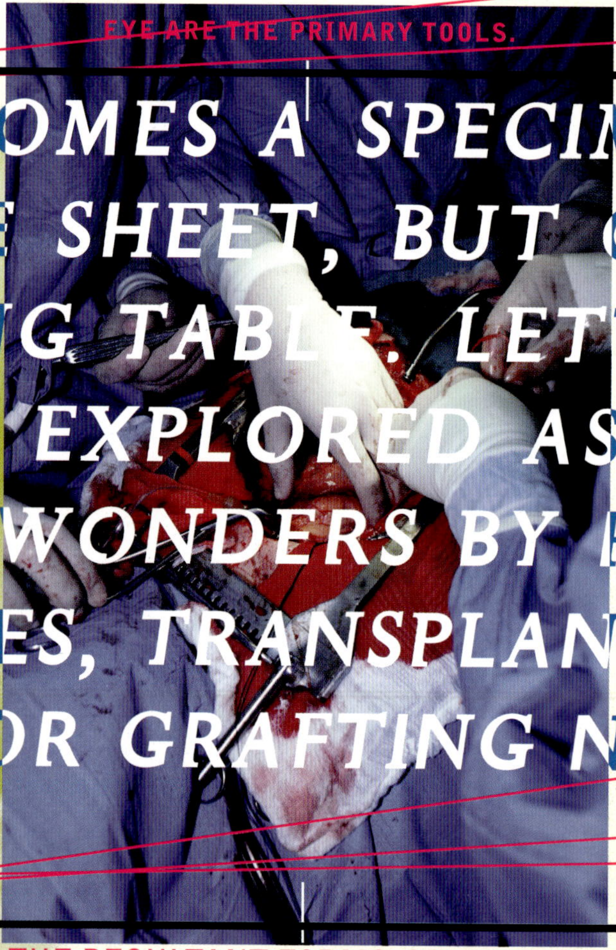

TYPE BECOMES A SPECIMEN, NOT
ON THE SHEET, BUT ON THE
OPERATING TABLE. LETTERS CAN
NOW BE EXPLORED AS LIVING,
ORGANIC WONDERS BY REMOVING
OLD TISSUES, TRANSPLANTING NEW
ORGANS, OR GRAFTING NEW LIMBS

THE RESULTANT FORMS, SOMETIMES
CURIOUS ANOMALIES, SOMETIMES
FLORAL BEAUTIES, INEVITABLY
CHALLENGE THE CONCEPTION OF
TYPOGRAPHY TODAY.

BRIAN SCHORN

# TYPOGRAPHY

IN THE INTERACTIVE WORLD IS FLUID,
AND BOTH THE

## TEXT AND THE DESIGN

CAN BE OPEN TO

RE-INTERPRETATION & RE-CONFIGURATION

BY THE

## READER/USER.

THE OPTIONS MAY EXIST AS VARIABLES CREATED BY THE

## AUTHOR/DESIGNER,

OR DESIGN MAY BE ALLOWED TO ROAM FREE, OPEN TO

## CROSS-FERTILIZATION.

MICHAEL WORTHINGTON

THE DOMINANT AND REPRESSIVE ROLE OF THE TEXT OVER
THE IMAGE IS BREAKING DOWN. AS THE DESIRE TO FIX
IMAGE CONNOTATION IS REPLACED BY A MORE INCLUSIVE
AND OPEN UNDERSTANDING, THE BOUNDARIES BETWEEN
WORDS, SOUNDS AND IMAGES DISSOLVE INTO THE
ELECTRONIC FLOW.

JEFFERY KEEDY

student

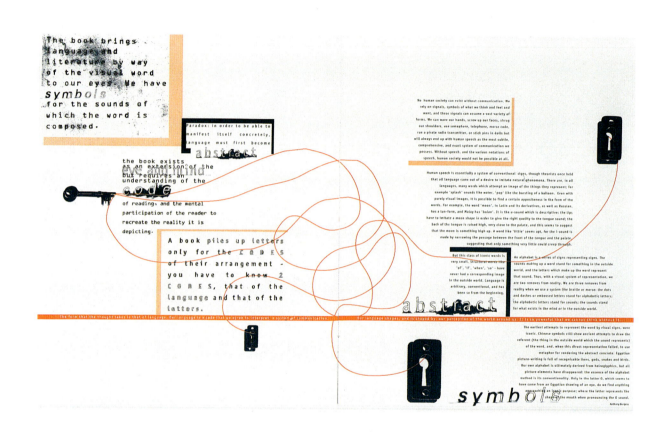

The book brings language and literature by way of the visual word to our eyes. We have *symbols* for the sounds of which the word is composed.

Paradox: in order to be able to manifest itself concretely, language must first become abstract

the book exists as an extension of the eye and mind but requires an understanding of the code of reading, and the mental participation of the reader to recreate the reality it is depicting.

A book piles up letters only for the CODES of their arrangement — you have to know 2 CODES, that of the language and that of the letters.

No human society can exist without communication. We rely on signals, symbols of what we think and feel and want, and these signals can assume a vast variety of forms. We can wave our hands, screw up our faces, shrug our shoulders, use semaphore, telephone, morse code, run a pirate radio transmitter, or stick pins in dolls but will always end up with human speech as the most subtle, comprehensive, and exact system of communication we possess. Without speech, and the various notations of speech, human society would not be possible at all.

Human speech is essentially a system of conventional signs, though theorists once held that all language came out of a desire to imitate natural phenomena. There are, in all languages, many words which attempt an image of the things they represent; for example 'splash' sounds like water, 'pop' like the bursting of a balloon. Even with purely visual images, it is possible to find a certain appositeness in the form of the words. For example, the word 'moon', in Latin and its derivatives, as well as Russian, has a *lun*-form, and Malay has 'bulan'. It is the u-sound which is descriptive; the lips have to imitate a moon shape in order to give the right quality to the tongue sound; the back of the tongue is raised high, very close to the palate, and this seems to suggest that the moon is something high up. A word like 'little' seems apt, for the i-sound is made by narrowing the passage between the front of the tongue and the palate, suggesting that only something very little could creep through.

But this class of iconic words is very small. Structural words like 'of', 'if', 'when', 'so' – have never had a corresponding image in the outside world. Language is arbitrary, conventional, and has been so from the beginning.

An alphabet is a series of signs representing signs. The sounds making up a word stand for something in the outside world, and the letters which make up the word represent that sound. Thus, with a visual system of representation, we are two removes from reality. We are three removes from reality when we use a system like braille or morse: the dots and dashes or embossed letters stand for alphabetic letters; the alphabetic letters stand for sounds; the sounds stand for what exists in the mind or in the outside world.

abstract

The earliest attempts to represent the word by visual signs, were iconic. Chinese symbols still show ancient attempts to draw the referent (the thing in the outside world which the sound represents) of the word, and, when this direct representation failed, to use metaphor for rendering the abstract concrete. Egyptian picture-writing is full of recognisable lions, gods, snakes and birds. Our own alphabet is ultimately derived from heiroglyphics, but all picture elements have disappeared: the essence of the alphabet method is its conventionality. Only in the letter O, which seems to have come from an Egyptian drawing of an eye, do we find anything approaching an iconic purpose; where the letter represents the shape of the mouth when pronouncing the O sound.

Anthony Burgess

symbols

The form that the thought takes is that of language. Our language is a code that we agree to interpret: a system of communication. Our language shapes, and is shaped by, our perception of the world around us. It is so powerful that we cannot think without it.

**The Magazine of the Book**

Magazine spreads presenting research from the project "When is a book not a book?"

DESIGNERS  Vivienne Cherry, Seònaid MacKay

PRINCIPAL TYPEFACES  Custom-made for the project

*Royal College of Art*
*Great Britain, 1995*

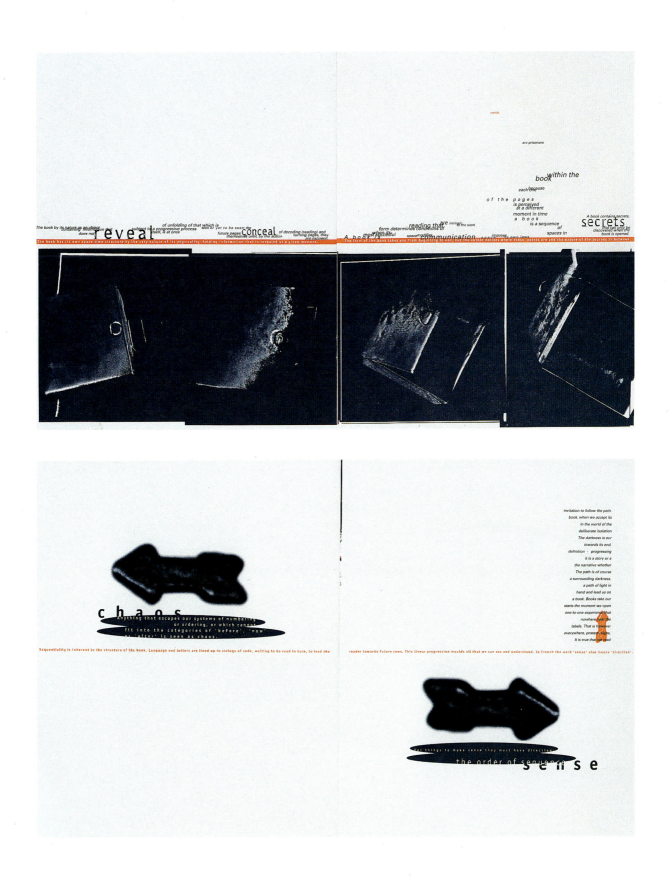

words

are prisoners

book within the

each other

because

of the pages
is perceived
at a different
moment in time
a book
is a sequence
of
spaces in

A book contains secrets,
that can only be
discovered when the
book is opened.

secrets

reveal

conceal

The book by its nature as an object that
does not

of unfolding of that which is
subject to a progressive process
itself, is at once

yet to be seen.
seen or

of decoding (reading and
future pages
themselves until, by the action
turning pages, they
are exposed

reading that

intrinsic to the work
form determines conditions of

A book
most successful

space

communication
imposes
own laws

The book has its own space-time structure by the very nature of its physicality, holding information that is revealed at a given moment. The form of the book takes you from beginning to end, but the author decides where these points are and the nature of the journey in between.

chaos

Anything that escapes our systems of numbering
or ordering, or which cannot
fit into the categories of 'before', 'now'
or 'after' is seen as chaos.

Sequentiality is inherent to the structure of the book. Language and letters are lined up in strings of code, waiting to be read in turn, to lead the reader towards future rows. This linear progression moulds all that we can see and understand. In French the word 'sense' also means 'direction'.

invitation to follow the path.
book, when we accept its
in the world of the
deliberate isolation
The darkness is our
towards its end.
definition - progressing
it is a story or a
the narrative whether
The path is of course
a surrounding darkness.
a path of light in
hand and lead us on
a book. Books take our
starts the moment we open
one-to-one experience that
nowhere near the
labels. That is however
everywhere, posters, signs.
It is true that we read

for things to make sense they must have direction

the order of sequence

sense

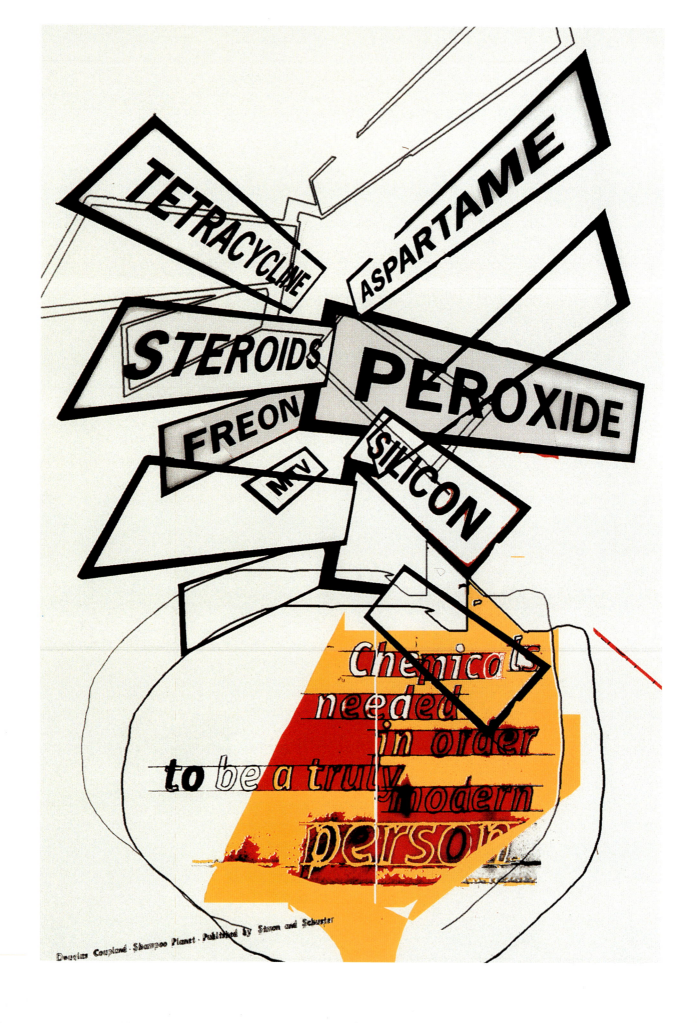

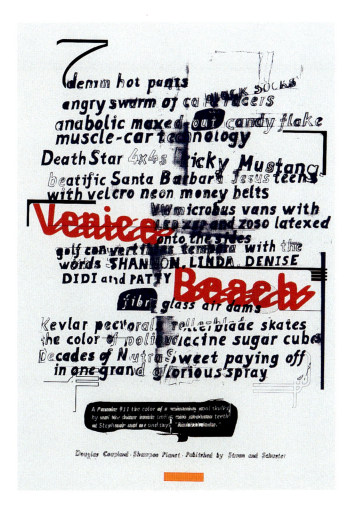

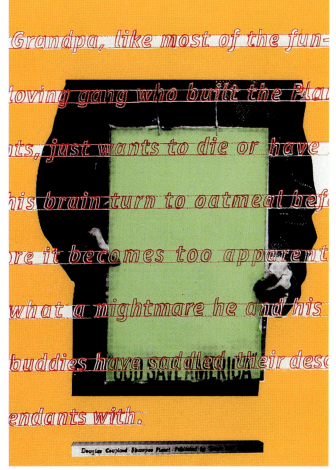

Chemicals
Venice Beach
Grandpa

Poster project based on Douglas Coupland's novel *Shampoo Planet*
DESIGNER | Martin Carty
PRINCIPAL TYPEFACES | Custom-made for the project

*Royal College of Art*
*Great Britain, 1995*

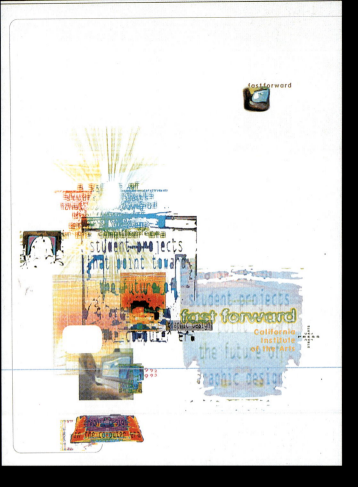

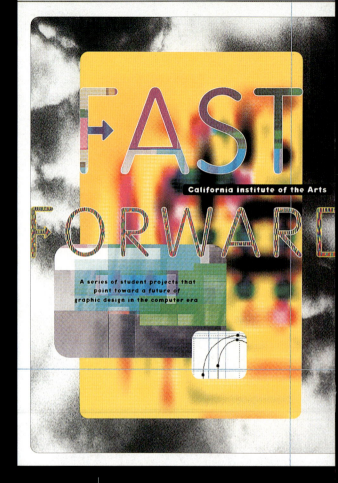

## Fast Forward

Book documenting a series of lectures and
projects about graphic design in the computer era

ART DIRECTOR Jeffery Keedy
DESIGNERS James Stoecker (front), Margo Johnson (back)
PRINCIPAL TYPEFACES Keedy Sans, VAG Rounded

*California Institute of the Arts*
*USA, 1993*

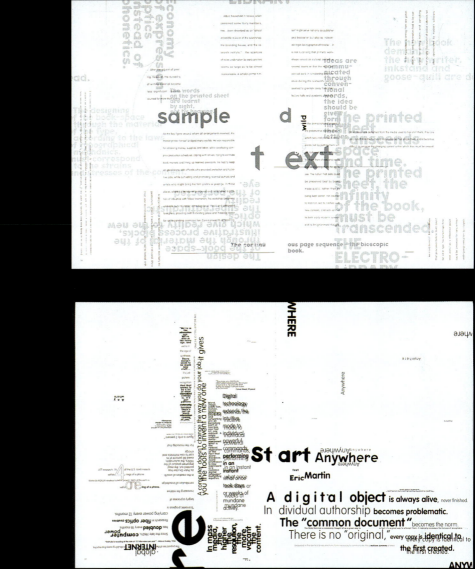

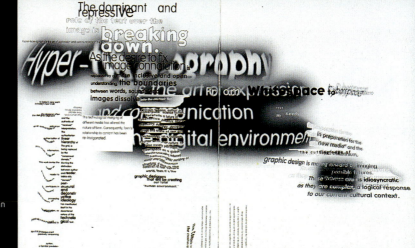

**Fast Forward**

Essay spreads
Jeffery Keedy
Lorraine Wild, Eric Martin, Jeffery Keedy
Shawn Mckinney, Shelley Stepp, Scott Saltsman
Keedy Sans, VAG Rounded

*California Institute of the Arts*
*USA, 1993*

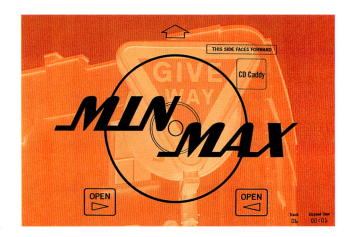

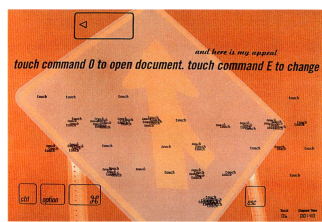

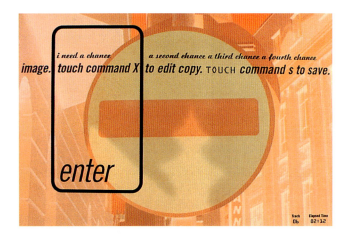

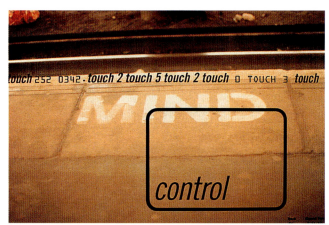

In this short self-published book,
the vernacular type of the computer
keyboard is juxtaposed with banal imagery
to question the nature of binary touch and
our relationship with digital technology. Is
escape from this seductive environment
possible? asks the designer.
Who controls whom?

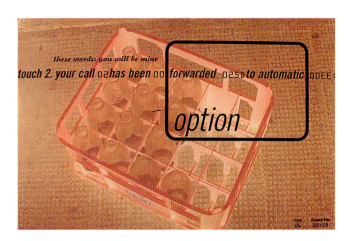

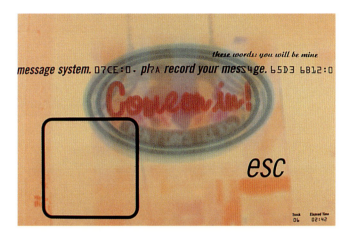

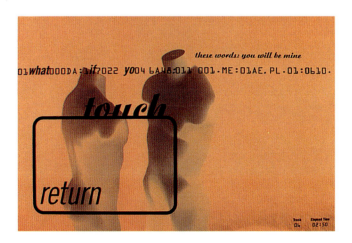

**MIN/MAX**

Book pages
WRITER/DESIGNER    Liisa Salonen
PRINCIPAL TYPEFACES    OCRA, Ariston, Trade Gothic,
Peignot

*Cranbrook Academy of Art*
*USA, 1995*

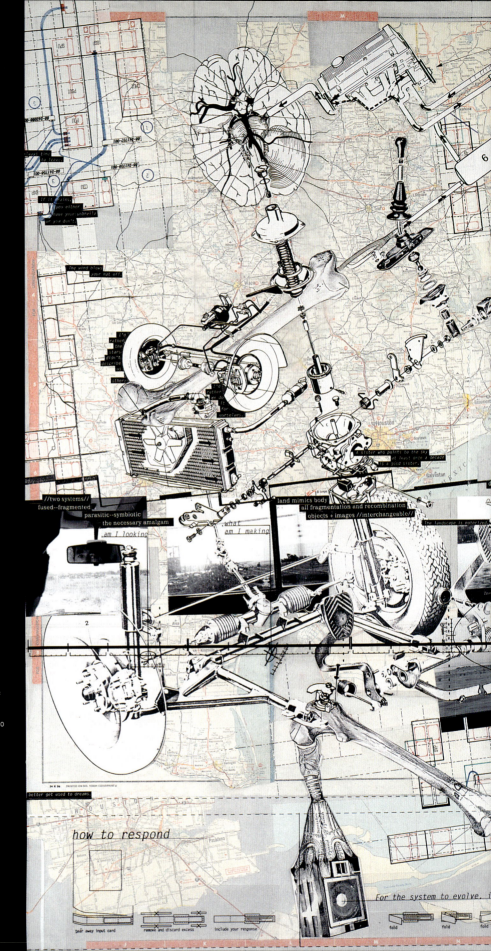

**Systems**

Poster/mailer
DESIGNER/PHOTOGRAPHER Jeremy Francis Mende
PRINCIPAL TYPEFACE Univers

*Cranbrook Academy of Art*
*USA, 1994*

The self-published poster discusses
cultural and individual fragmentation
and the contemporary schizophrenia of
identity and memory. The piece invites
viewer response via a mail-back card so
that both emotional and analytical
information can be re-entered into the
creative process, thereby evolving it.

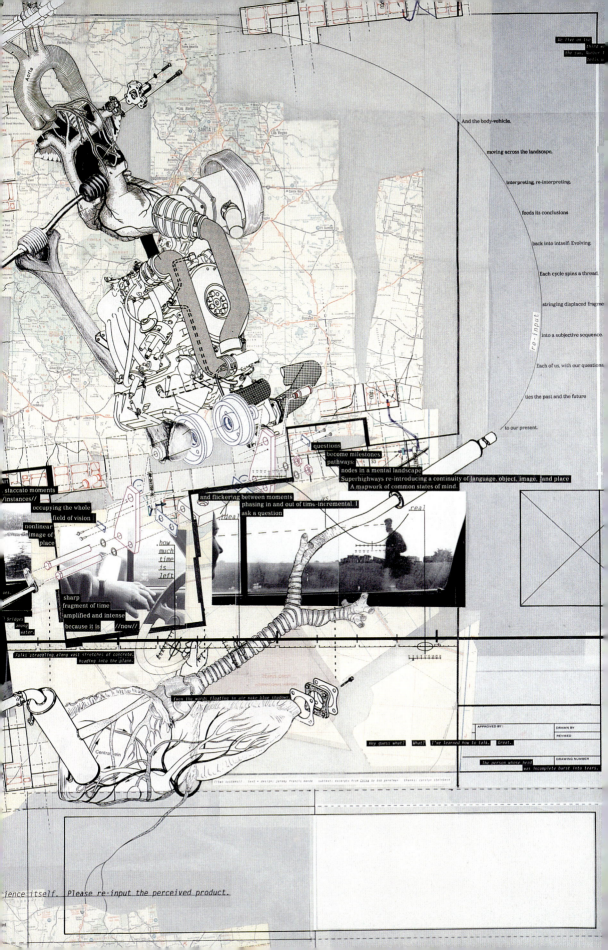

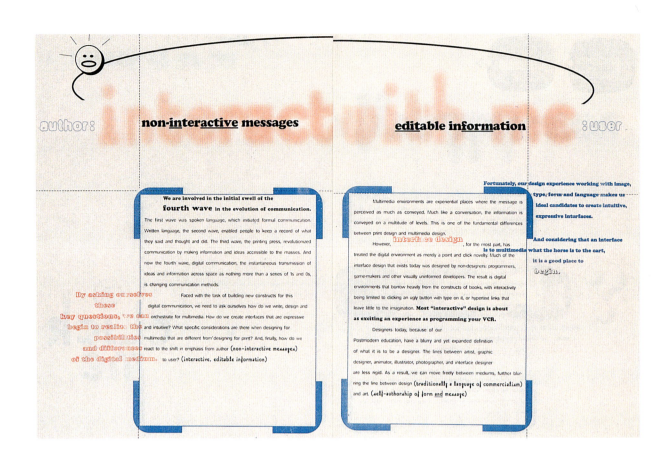

**non-interactive messages**      **editable information** :user

author: interact with me

We are involved in the initial swell of the **fourth wave** in the evolution of communication. The first wave was spoken language, which initiated formal communication. Written language, the second wave, enabled people to keep a record of what they said and thought and did. The third wave, the printing press, revolutionized communication by making information and ideas accessible to the masses. And now the fourth wave, digital communication, the instantaneous transmission of ideas and information across space as nothing more than a series of 1s and 0s, is changing communication methods.

Faced with the task of building new constructs for this digital communication, we need to ask ourselves how do we write, design and orchestrate for multimedia. How do we create interfaces that are expressive and intuitive? What specific considerations are there when designing for multimedia that are different from designing for print? And, finally, how do we react to the shift in emphasis from author (non-interactive messages) to user? (interactive, editable information)

*By asking ourselves these key questions, we can begin to realize the possibilities and differences of the digital medium.*

Multimedia environments are experiential places where the message is perceived as much as conveyed. Much like a conversation, the information is conveyed on a multitude of levels. This is one of the fundamental differences between print design and multimedia design.

However, *interface design*, for the most part, has *is to multimedia* treated the digital environment as merely a point and click novelty. Much of the interface design that exists today was designed by non-designers: programmers, game-makers and other visually uninformed developers. The result is digital environments that borrow heavily from the constructs of books, with interactivity being limited to clicking an ugly button with type on it, or hypertext links that leave little to the imagination. **Most "interactive" design is about as exciting an experience as programming your VCR.**

Designers today, because of our Postmodern education, have a blurry and yet expanded definition of what it is to be a designer. The lines between artist, graphic designer, animator, illustrator, photographer, and interface designer are less rigid. As a result, we can move freely between mediums, further blurring the line between design (traditionally a language of commercialism) and art. (self-authorship of form and message)

*Fortunately, our design experience working with image, type, form and language makes us ideal candidates to create intuitive, expressive interfaces.*

*And considering that an interface is to multimedia what the horse is to the cart, it is a good place to begin.*

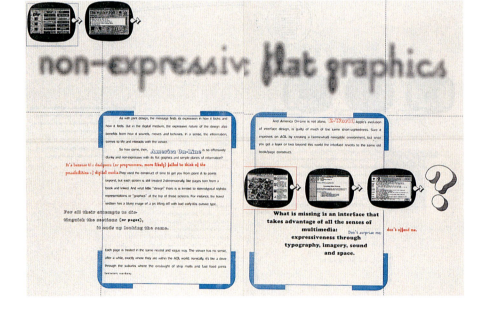

non-expressive flat graphics

As with print design, the message finds its expression in how it looks and how it feels. But in the digital medium, the expressive nature of the design also benefits from how it sounds, moves and behaves. In a sense, the information comes to life and interacts with the viewer.

So how come, then, *America On-line* is so offensively clunky and non-expressive with its flat graphics and simple planes of information?

*It's because the designers (or programmers, more likely) failed to think of the possibilities of digital media.* They used the construct of time to get you from point A to points beyond, but each screen is still treated 2-dimensionally, like pages torn from a book and linked. And what little "design" there is limited to stereotypical stylistic representations or "graphics" at the top of those screens. For instance, the travel section has a blurry image of a jet lifting off with bad early-60s cursive type.

*For all their attempts to distinguish the sections (or pages), it ends up looking the same.*

Each page is treated in the same neutral and vague way. The viewer has no sense, after a while, exactly where they are within the AOL world. Ironically, it's like a drive through the suburbs where the onslaught of strip malls and fast food joints between nowhere

And America On-Line is not alone, *E-World!* Apple's evolution of interface design, is guilty of much of the same short sightedness. Sure it improves on AOL by creating a (somewhat) navigable environment, but once you get a layer or two beyond this world the interface reverts to the same old book/page construct.

**What is missing is an interface that takes advantage of all the senses of multimedia:** *Don't surprise me:* **expressiveness through typography, imagery, sound and space.** *don't offend me.*

*Print is Dead!* is the research portion of an interactive sound and motion project exploring experimental interface design. It seeks to discover what qualities make for a fluid, intuitive interface, what aspects of existing interfaces should be built on or scrapped, and how navigation through digital spaces can become more customisable and expressive. Deliberately crude and purposefully arcane in appearance, the hand-printed book is intended to have a charm and tactility that most multimedia experiences presently lack.

**Print is Dead! Or so it seems**

Spreads from a thesis project

WRITER/DESIGNER  Richard Shanks
PRINCIPAL TYPEFACES  Cooper Black, Suburban

*California Institute of the Arts*
*USA, 1995*

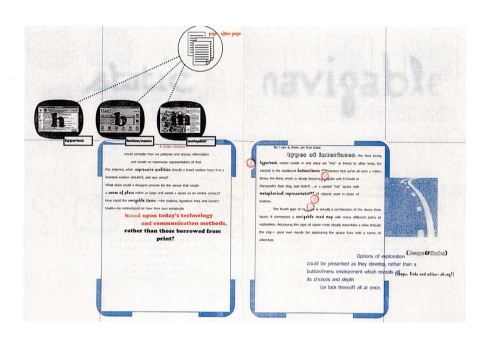

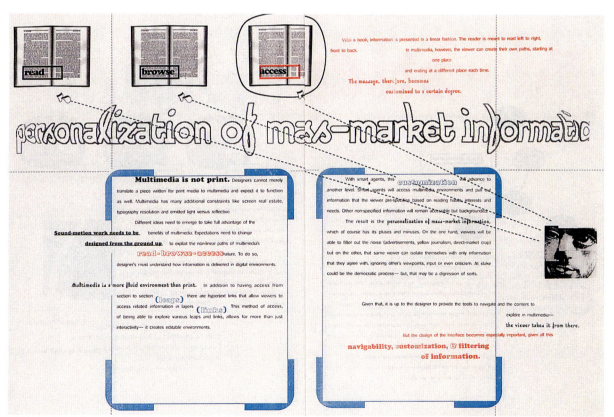

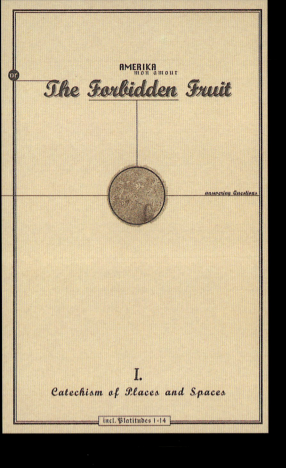

AMERIKA
mon amour

# The Forbidden Fruit

*answering Questions*

**I.**

*Catechism of Places and Spaces*

incl. Platitudes 1-14

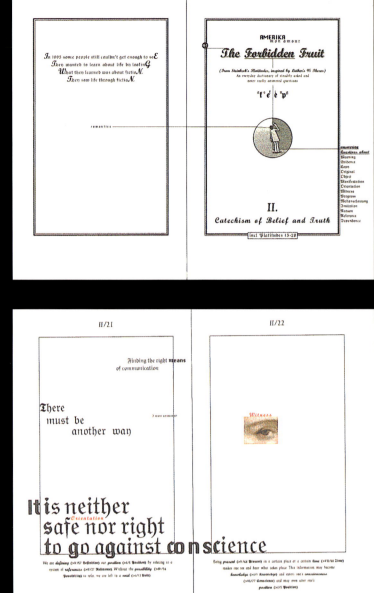

In 1995 some people still couldn't get enough to see
Then wanted to learn about life in losing
What then learned was about fiction.
Then saw life through fiction.

romantics

AMERIKA
mon amour

# The Forbidden Fruit

(from Steinbeck's Platitudes, inspired by Luther's 95 Theses)
An everyday dictionary of steadily asked and
never really answered questions

"t' e' e "p"

answering
Questions about
Meaning
Evidence
Copy
Original
Object
Manifestation
Orientation
Witness
Progress
Weltanschauung
Imitation
Reason
Reference
Dependence

**II.**

*Catechism of Belief and Truth*

incl. Platitudes 15-28

II/21       II/22

Finding the right **means**
of communication

There
must be
another way

Witness

It is neither
*Orientation*
safe nor right
to go against conscience

We are defining (>V/V Definition) our position (>I/1 Position) by relating to a
system of references (>II/27 Reference). Without the possibility (>IV/56
Possibility) to refer, we are left in a void (>I/11 Void)

Being present (>V/68 Present) in a certain place at a certain time (>VII/88 Time)
makes one see and hear what takes place. This information may become
knowledge (>I/3 Knowledge) and enters one's consciousness
(>VI/77 Conscience) and may even alter one's
position (>I/1 Position)

III/35       III/36

Confusion

Ein Zeichen sind wir, deutungslos
A sign we are, without meaning
Schmerzlos sind wir und haben fast
without pain we are and have nearly lost
Die Sprache in der Fremde verloren
our language in foreign lands

Nature

What is unnatural to a being (>V/69 Being) which is able to reinvent its nature?
The artificial becomes our second nature which distances (>IV/44 Distance)
us from our nature as a sign of human progress
(>II/23 Progress)

Being perplexed by the signs of our worldly (>VI/72 Reality) is to reason (>II/16
Reason) to become worried, since it won't take too long until we either
understand (>VI/77 Understanding) their messages
(>I/4 Message), or accept them as new
values (>V/62 Value)

I
Can't
Believe
It's
Not
Better
Yet

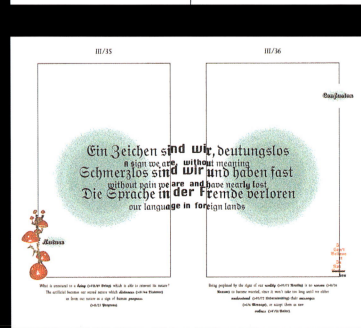

**Amerika Mon Amour or the Forbidden Fruit**

Cover and spreads from a thesis project

WRITER/DESIGNER   Carolyn Steinbeck

PRINCIPAL TYPEFACES   Wittenberg, Fraktur, Script Bold, Chicago

*Cranbrook Academy of Art*
*USA, 1995*

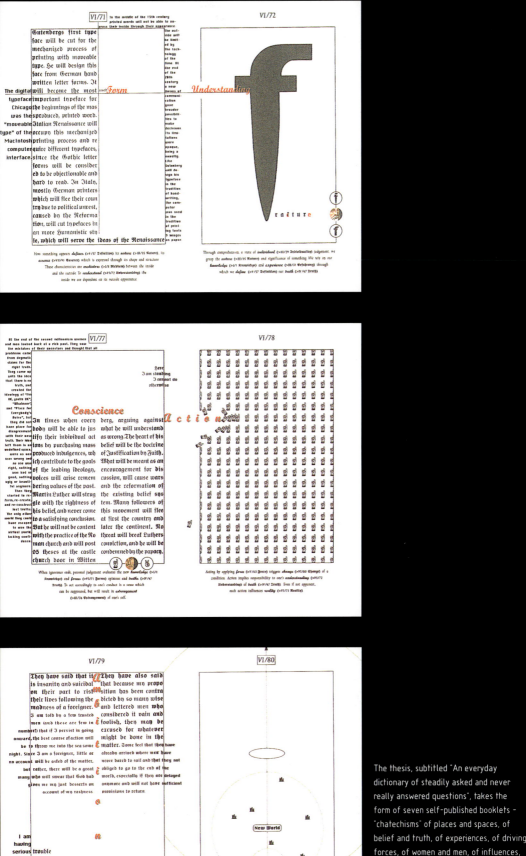

Gutenbergs first type face will be cut for the mechanized process of printing with moveable type. He will design this face from German hand written letter forms. It will become the most important typeface for the beginnings of the mass produced, printed word. Italian Renaissance will occupy this mechanized printing process and re quire different typefaces, since the Gothic letter forms will be consider ed to be objectionable and hard to read. In Italy, mostly German printers which will flee their coun try due to political unrest, caused by the Reforma tion, will cut typefaces in an more Humanistic sty le, which will serve the ideas of the Renaissance

*The digital typeface for Chicago was the "moveable type" of the Macintosh computer interface.*

*Form*  *Understanding*

The out side will be limit ed by the tech nology of the time. At the end of the 20th century a new means of communi cation gave broader possibili ties to make decisions Its limi tations were opaque, being a novelty. Like Gutenberg will de sign his typeface in the tradition of hand writing, the com puter was used in the tradition of print ing texts images on paper

*f  fraktur*

How something appear defines (>7/57 Definition) its nature (>III/15 Nature), its essence (>VII/67 Essence) which is expressed through its shape and structure These characteristics are mediators (>I/8 Medium) between the inside and the outside To understand (>VI/72 Understanding) the inside we are dependent on its outside appearance

Through comprehension, a state of individual (>7/79 Individuality) judgement, we grasp the nature (>III/15 Nature) and significance of something We rely on our knowledge (>I/1 Knowledge) and experience (>III/11 Erfahrung) through which we define (>7/57 Definition) our truth (>IV/47 Truth)

the mistakes of their ancestors and thought that all problems came from dogmatic claims for the right truth. They came up with the idea that there is no truth, and created the ideology of "I'm OK, you're OK", "Whatever" and "Place for Everybody's Rule", but they did not have place for disagreements with their own truth. Their idea left them in an undefined space, were no one was wrong and no one was right, nothing was bad or good, nothing ugly or beauti ful anymore. Then they started to re- form, re-create and re-construct lost truths. The only other world they could be to was the virtual world, lacking confi dence.

Here I am standing I cannot do otherwise

*Conscience*  *Action*

In times when every body will be able to jus tify their individual act ions by purchasing mass produced indulgences, wh ich contribute to the goals of the leading ideology, voices will arise remem bering values of the past. Martin Luther will strug gle with the rightness of his belief, and never come to a satisfying conclusion. But he will not be content with the practice of the Ro man church and will post 95 theses at the castle church door in Witten berg, arguing against what he will understand as wrong. The heart of his belief will be the doctrine of Justification by Faith. What will be meant as an encouragement for dis cussion, will cause wars and the reformation of the existing belief sys tem. Many followers of this movement will flee at first the country and later the continent. No threat will break Luthers conviction, and he will be condemned by the papacy.

When ignorance ends, personal judgement evaluates the new knowledge (>I/1 Knowledge) and forums (>VI/71 forms) opinions and truths (>IV/47 Truth). To act accordingly to one's conduct is a sense which can be suppressed, but will result in estrangement (>III/36 Estrangement) of one's self.

Acting by applying force (>V/63 force) triggers change (>VI/80 Change) of a condition. Action implies responsibility to one's understanding (>VI/72 Understanding) of truth (>IV/47 Truth). Even if not apparent, each action influences reality (>VI/73 Reality)

They have said that it is insanity and suicidal on their part to risk their lives following the madness of a foreigner. I am told by a few trusted men (and these are few in number) that if I persist in going onward, the best course of action will be to throw me into the sea some night. Since I am a foreigner, little or no account will be asked of the matter, but rather, there will be a great many who will swear that God had given me my just desserts on account of my rashness

Then have also said that because my propo sition has been contra dicted by so many wise and lettered men who considered it vain and foolish, then may be excused for whatever might be done in the matter. Some feel that they have already arrived where men have never dared to sail and that they not obliged to go to the end of the world, especially if they are delayed anymore and will not have sufficient provisions to return

I am having serious trouble with the crew

With God's help I shall persevere

New World

World

*Change*

Our imagination (>7/56 Imagination) produces eager ideas which require strong faith (>V/42 faith) in the possibility (>IV/54 Possibility) that they can become reality (>VI/73 Reality) in such a process (>III/42 Process) of making these ideas come true (>IV/47 Truth) one might feel (>III/41 feeling) lonely (>III/42 Loneliness) sometimes.

When our position (>I/9 Position) has become unbearable we have to invest energy (>VII/92 Energy) to move into a new frame of contexts (>V/65 Context) With each step we have to renegotiate our truths (>IV/47 Truth) within the altered order (>VI/76 Order)

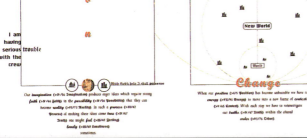

The thesis, subtitled "An everyday dictionary of steadily asked and never really answered questions", takes the form of seven self-published booklets – "chatechisms" of places and spaces, of belief and truth, of experiences, of driving forces, of women and men, of influences, and of conclusions. The booklets frame 95 cross-referenced platitudes – one per page – inspired by the 95 theses arguing against the sale of indulgences nailed to the church door in sixteenth-century Wittenberg by Martin Luther

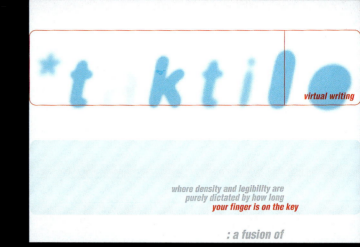

*t ktile

virtual writing

where density and legibility are
purely dictated by how long
**your finger is on the key**

: a fusion of

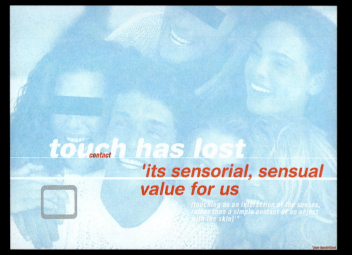

**touch has lost**
_contact_
**'its sensorial, sensual
value for us**

(touching as an interaction of the senses,
rather than a simple contact of an object
with the skin)'*

*jean baudrillard

what we currently create
is language that only
exists in a non-visual
digital space, visible only
on the simulated void of
the screen

*monitor*

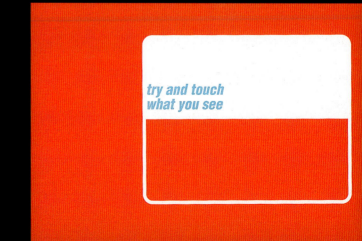

**try and touch
what you see**

**Taktile**

Wall panels for a typeface project

*WRITER/DESIGNER* / Ben Tibbs
*PROGRAMMING ASSISTANCE* / Tony Side
*PRINCIPAL TYPEFACES* / Taktile, Helvetica

*Royal College of Art*
*Great Britain, 1995*

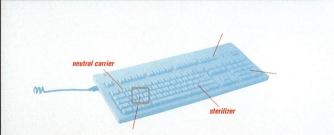

neutral carrier

sterilizer

**literacy will become learning to type on a keyboard**

Digital technology and the keyboard have
had a profound effect on the physical nature
of writing. The emotional directness of mark-
making on a surface has been reduced to the
uniform pressing of a key. Taktile is an
attempt to restore the physicality of writing
by combining the tangible and the digital: the
longer your finger rests on a key, the more
impact it will make on the character's density
and legibility.

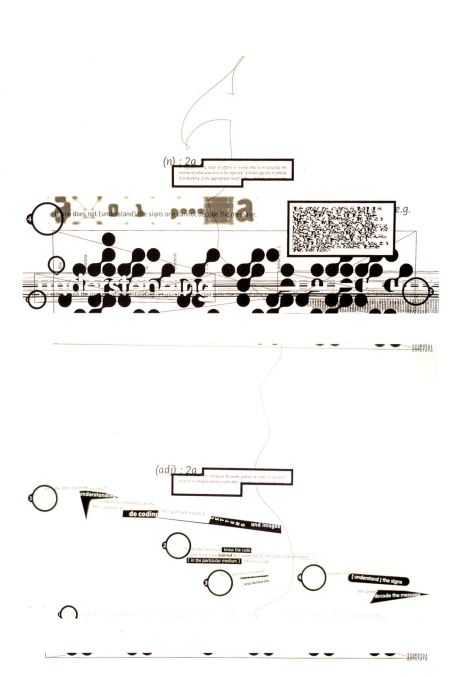

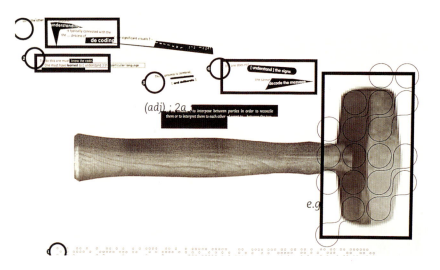

Irony
Mediate

Broadsheets from "Lexicon" project
DESIGNER | Weston Bingham
PRINCIPAL TYPEFACES | Caecilia, VAG Rounded, Rotis Sans, State, Dr No

California Institute of the Arts
USA, 1994

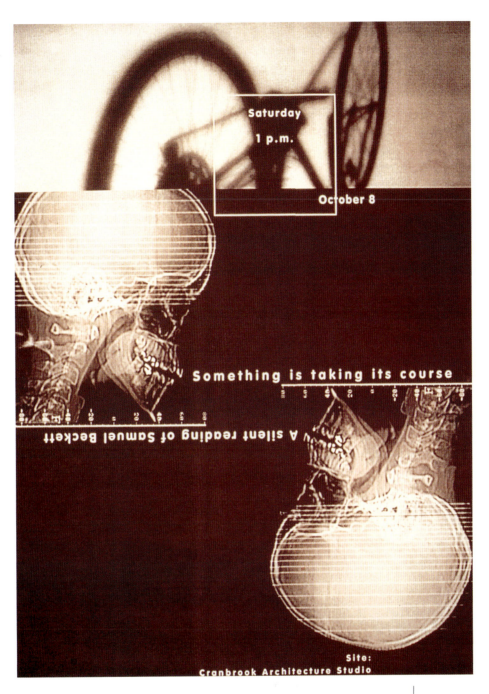

Saturday
1 p.m.

October 8

Something is taking its course

A silent reading of Samuel Beckett

Site:
Cranbrook Architecture Studio

**Beckett #1**

Poster for a performance based
on Samuel Beckett's *Endgame*
Jeremy Francis Mende, Jeff Talbot
DESIGNERS / VAG Rounded
PRINCIPAL TYPEFACE / Jeff Talbot
CLIENT /
Cranbrook Academy of Art
USA, 1995

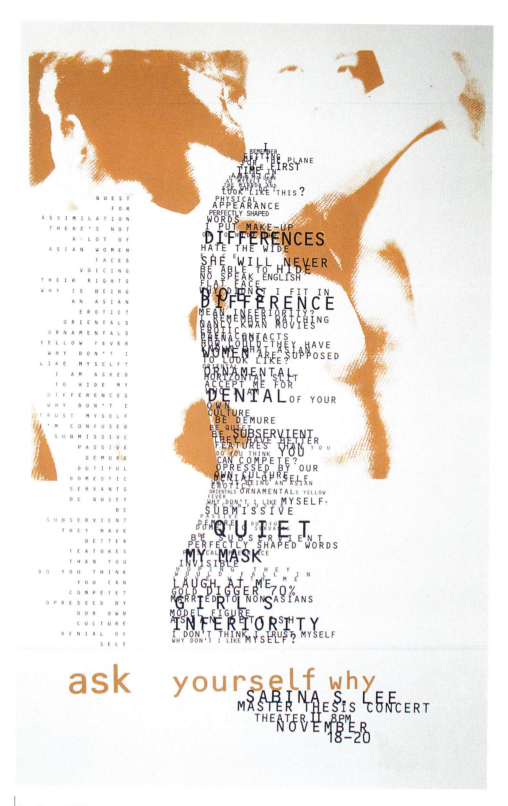

**Ask Yourself Why**

Concert poster

DESIGNER | Michael Worthington
PRINCIPAL TYPEFACE | Letter Gothic
CLIENT | Dance School

*California Institute of the Arts*
*USA, 1993*

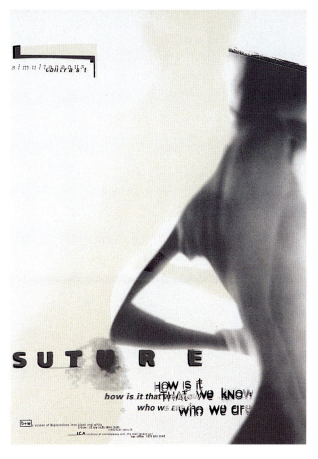

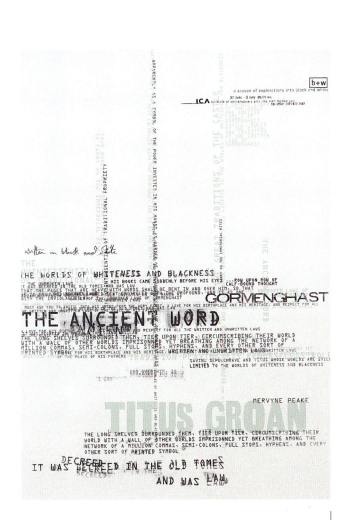

Suture

|  | Poster project |
| DESIGNER | Vivienne Cherry |
| PHOTOGRAPHER | Annelise Howard Phillips |
| PRINCIPAL TYPEFACES | Custom-made for the project |

*Royal College of Art*
*Great Britain, 1995*

**Titus Groan**

Poster project

|  | |
| DESIGNER | Vivienne Cherry |
| PRINCIPAL TYPEFACES | Custom-made for the project |

*Royal College of Art*
*Great Britain, 1995*

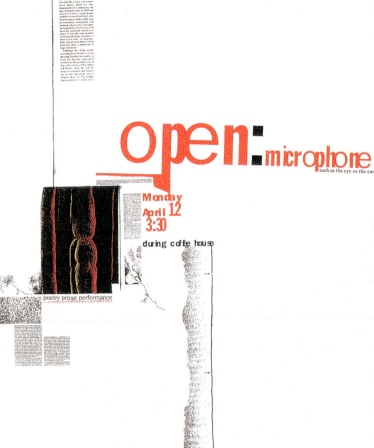

Open Microphone: A Smudge

Poster announcing an open reading on campus
Brian Schorn
Trade Gothic, Snell Roundhand
Open Microphone Series

DESIGNER
PEFACES
CLIENT

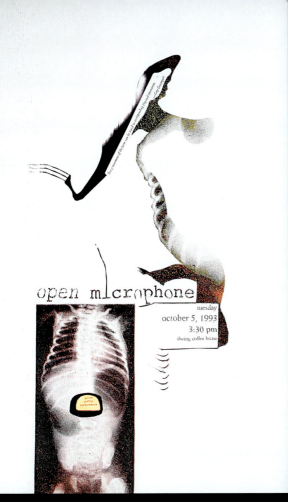

open microphone

tuesday
october 5, 1993
3:30 pm
during coffee house

## Open Microphone: Resonances

Poster announcing an open reading on campus

DESIGNER | Brian Schorn
PRINCIPAL TYPEFACES | Courier, Weiss
CLIENT | Open Microphone Series

*Cranbrook Academy of Art*
*USA, 1993*

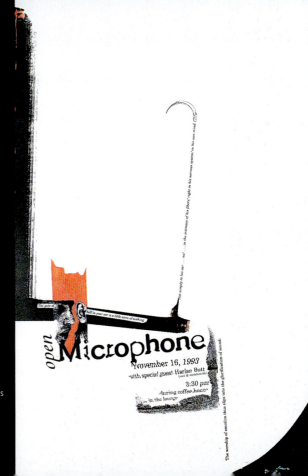

open Microphone

November 16, 1993
with special guest Harlan Butt
(poet & metalsmith)

3:30 pm
during coffee house
in the lounge

## Open Microphone: Gates of Hell

Poster announcing an open reading on campus

DESIGNER | Brian Schorn
PRINCIPAL TYPEFACES | Cochin, Ocraelliot Black, Century Schoolbook
CLIENT | Open Microphone Series

*Cranbrook Academy of Art*
*USA, 1993*

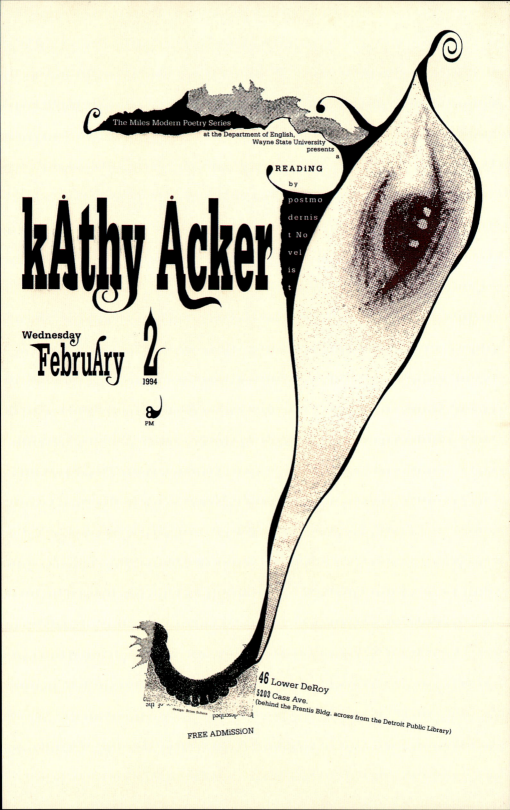

Kathy Acker: Postmodern Novelist

Poster announcing a reading
DESIGNER / Brian Schorn
PRINCIPAL TYPEFACE / Serifa

# 105

MINUTES

*of*

**P regnant**

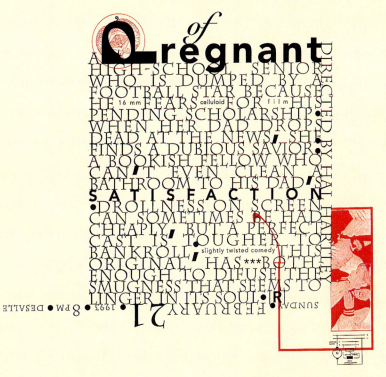

A HIGH-SCHOOL SENIOR WHO IS DUMPED BY A FOOTBALL STAR BECAUSE HE FEARS FOR HIS PENDING SCHOLARSHIP WHEN HER DAD DROPS DEAD AT THE NEWS, SHE FINDS A DUBIOUS SAVIOR, A BOOKISH FELLOW WHO CAN'T EVEN CLEAN A BATHROOM TO HIS DAD'S **S A T I S F A C T I O N** DROLLNESS ON SCREEN CAN SOMETIMES BE HAD CHEAPLY, BUT A PERFECT CAST IS TOUGHER TO BANKROLL; THIS ORIGINAL HAS **★★★** BOTH ENOUGH TO DIFUSE THE SMUGNESS THAT SEEMS TO LINGER IN ITS SOUL. **R**

DIRECTED BY HAL HARTLEY

16 mm    celluloid    film

slightly twisted comedy

SUNDAY • FEBRUARY 21 • 1993 • 8 PM • DESALLE

**Trust (105 Minutes)**

Film poster
DESIGNER  Brian Schorn
PRINCIPAL TYPEFACES  Charlemagne, Avenir
CLIENT  Sunday Night Film Series

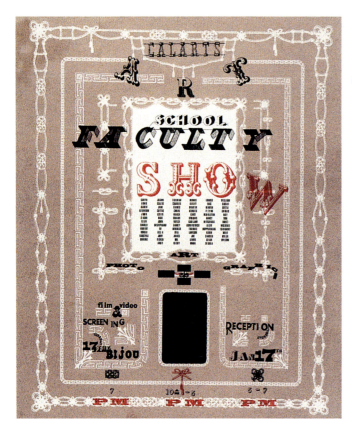

**Faculty Show**

Poster
DESIGNER | Michael Worthington
PRINCIPAL TYPEFACES | Wood Type, Dead History, Compacta

*California Institute of the Arts*
*USA, 1995*

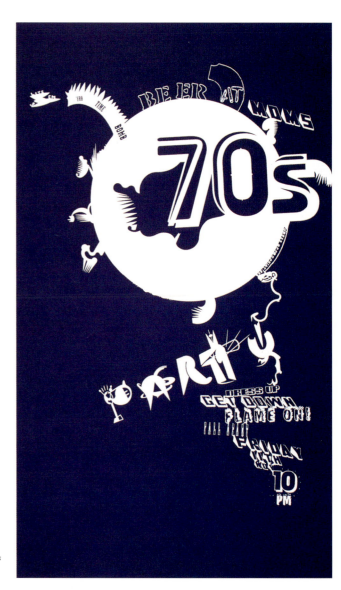

**70s Party**

Poster
DESIGNER | Michael Worthington
PRINCIPAL TYPEFACES | Fellaparts, Wedgie
CLIENT | Student Council

*California Institute of the Arts*
*USA, 1994*

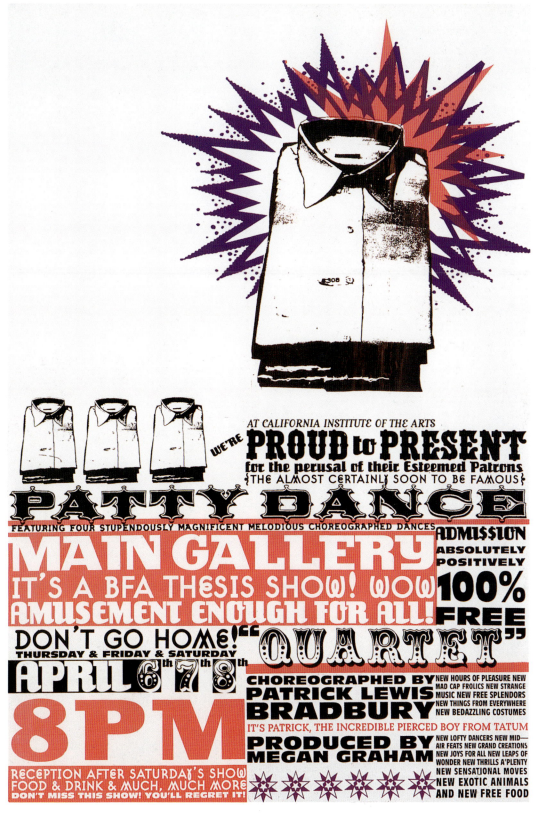

AT CALIFORNIA INSTITUTE OF THE ARTS

WE'RE **PROUD to PRESENT**

for the perusal of their Esteemed Patrons

THE ALMOST CERTAINLY SOON TO BE FAMOUS

# PATTY DANCE

FEATURING FOUR STUPENDOUSLY MAGNIFICENT MELODIOUS CHOREOGRAPHED DANCES

## MAIN GALLERY

IT'S A BFA THESIS SHOW! WOW

AMUSEMENT ENOUGH FOR ALL!

DON'T GO HOME! "QUARTET"

THURSDAY & FRIDAY & SATURDAY

APRIL 6th 7th 8th

# 8PM

RECEPTION AFTER SATURDAY'S SHOW
FOOD & DRINK & MUCH, MUCH MORE
DON'T MISS THIS SHOW! YOU'LL REGRET IT!

ADMISSION
ABSOLUTELY
POSITIVELY
**100%**
**FREE**

CHOREOGRAPHED BY
PATRICK LEWIS
BRADBURY

NEW HOURS OF PLEASURE NEW
MAD CAP FROLICS NEW STRANGE
MUSIC NEW FREE SPLENDORS
NEW THINGS FROM EVERYWHERE
NEW BEDAZZLING COSTUMES

IT'S PATRICK, THE INCREDIBLE PIERCED BOY FROM TATUM

PRODUCED BY
MEGAN GRAHAM

NEW LOFTY DANCERS NEW MID—
AIR FEATS NEW GRAND CREATIONS
NEW JOYS FOR ALL NEW LEAPS OF
WONDER NEW THRILLS A'PLENTY
NEW SENSATIONAL MOVES
**NEW EXOTIC ANIMALS**
**AND NEW FREE FOOD**

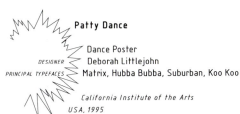

**Patty Dance**

Dance Poster
Deborah Littlejohn

*DESIGNER*
*PRINCIPAL TYPEFACES* Matrix, Hubba Bubba, Suburban, Koo Koo

*California Institute of the Arts*
*USA, 1995*

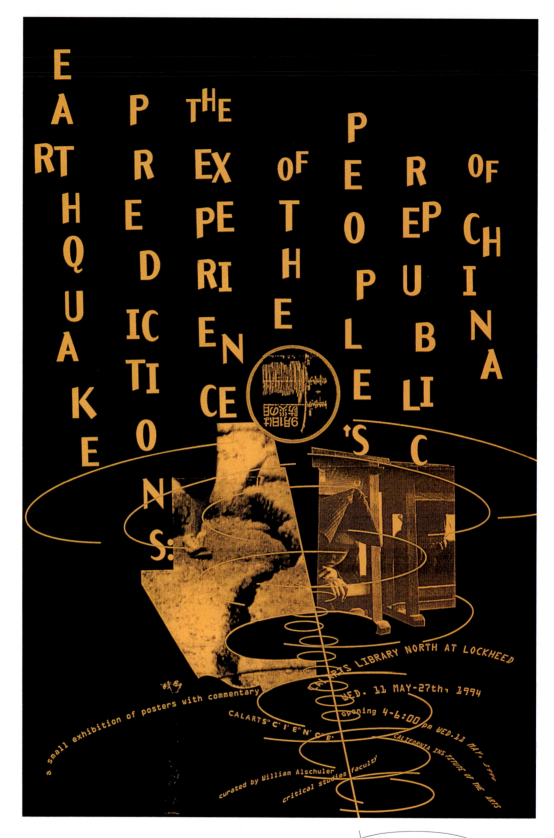

Earthquake Predictions

Exhibition poster
DESIGNER \ Deborah Littlejohn
PRINCIPAL TYPEFACES \ Barry Sans, OCRA
CLIENT \ Critical Studies Department

*California Institute of the Arts*
*USA, 1994*

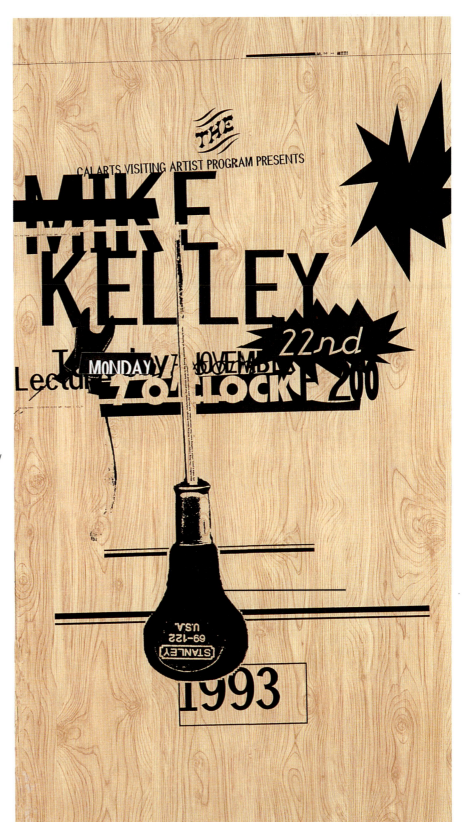

CALARTS VISITING ARTIST PROGRAM PRESENTS

THE

MIKE KELLEY

22nd

MONDAY

Lecture 7 O'CLOCK 200

1993

STANLEY
69-122
U.S.A.

**Mike Kelley**

Poster announcing a lecture
DESIGNERS Deborah Littlejohn, Shawn McKinney
PRINCIPAL TYPEFACE Arbitrary Sans
CLIENT Visiting Artist Program

*California Institute of the Arts*
*USA, 1993*

The designers scanned in many elements
and dragged them together to create a
succession of alternative designs. Believing
the poster to be finished, they pulled back
to discover that the scattered typographic
matter on the pasteboard more closely
reflected the artist's attitude than their
careful composition.

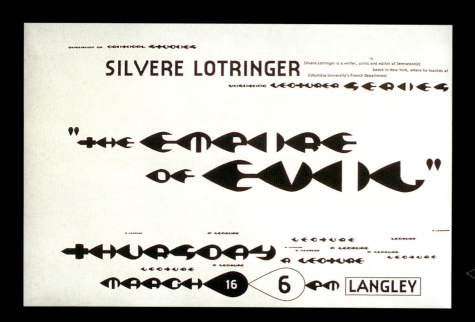

Silvere Lotringer

Poster announcing a lecture
DESIGNER  Geoff McFetridge
PRINCIPAL TYPEFACES  Tear, Citizen
CLIENT  Visiting Artist Program

*California Institute of the Arts*
*USA, 1995*

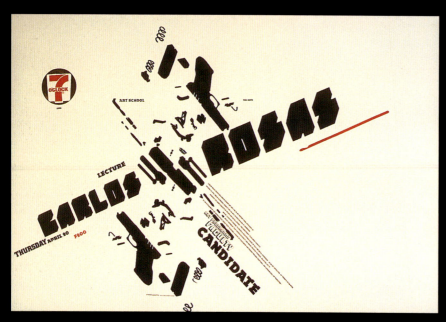

Carlos Rosas

Poster announcing a lecture
DESIGNERS  Geoff McFetridge, Kevin Lyons
PRINCIPAL TYPEFACES  Shaft, Dynamo, Bell Gothic
CLIENT  Visiting Artist Program

*California Institute of the Arts*
*USA, 1994-95*

Sissy Space

Poster for an evening of gay cabaret
DESIGNER Michael Worthington
PRINCIPAL TYPEFACES Sissy, Killer Klown, Dominatrix, Koo Koo Fatboy, Suburban

California Institute of the Arts

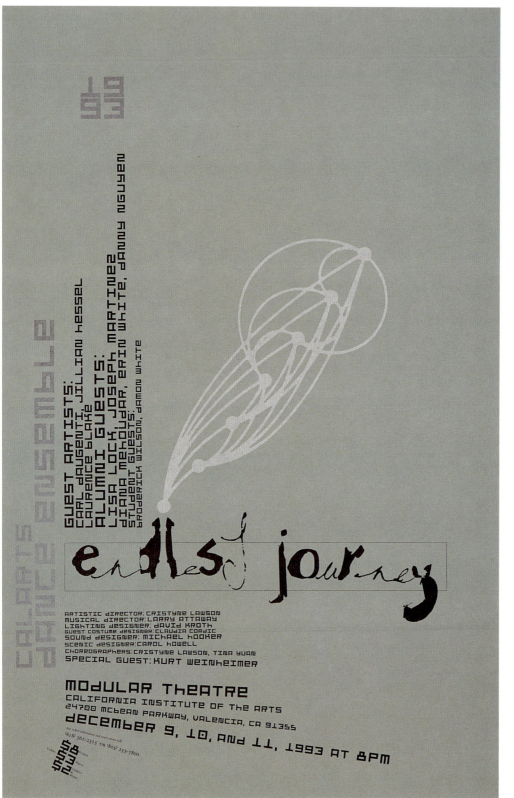

CALARTS DANCE ENSEMBLE

1993

GUEST ARTISTS:
CARL DAUGENTI, JILLIAN KESSEL
LAURENCE BLAKE
ALUMNI GUESTS:
LISA LOCK, JOSEPH MARTINEZ
DIANA MEHOUDAR, ERIN WHITE, DANNY NGUYEN
STUDENT GUESTS:
BRODERICK WILSON, DAMON WHITE

endles journey

ARTISTIC DIRECTOR: CRISTYNE LAWSON
MUSICAL DIRECTOR: LARRY ATTAWAY
LIGHTING DESIGNER: DAVID KROTH
GUEST COSTUME DESIGNER: CLAUDIA CORDIC
SOUND DESIGNER: MICHAEL HOOKER
SCENIC DESIGNER: CAROL HOWELL
CHOREOGRAPHERS: CRISTYNE LAWSON, TINA YUAN
SPECIAL GUEST: KURT WEINHEIMER

MODULAR THEATRE
CALIFORNIA INSTITUTE OF THE ARTS
24700 MCBEAN PARKWAY, VALENCIA, CA 91355
DECEMBER 9, 10, AND 11, 1993 AT 8PM

The structure of the design is
related to the general nature
of dance and to the specific
choreography of *Endless Journey*
(further referenced by the diagram
of infinity) in which dancers flowed
in and out of a trench in the stage.
The Gridlock type designed by Austin
Putman masses together to form the
"audience" for the more animated Eugenius
"dancers" designed by Worthington himself.

Endless Journey

Dance poster
DESIGNER | Michael Worthington
PRINCIPAL TYPEFACES | Gridlock, Eugenius
CLIENT | Dance School

*California Institute of the Arts*
*USA, 1993*

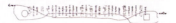

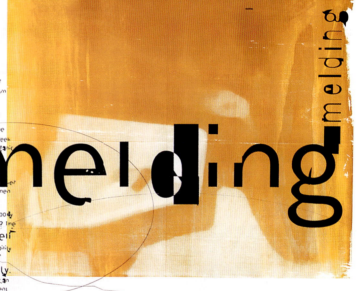

humanachine

The cyborg or the cyborg of cybernetic organism cybernetic organism implies that the implies that the conscious conscious mind steers the mind steers the meaning of the Greek meaning of the Greek cybernetes our organic cybernetes our organic life. Organic life. Organic life energy ceases to energy ceases to initiate our mental initiate our mental gestures. Can we ever gesture? Can we ever be fully present when be fully present when we live through a we live through a surrogate body surrogate body standing in for us? The standing in for us? The stand-in self stand-in self lacks the vulnerability lacks the vulnerability and fragility of our and fragility of our primary identity primary identity. The stand-in self can the stand-in self can never fully represent never fully represent us. The more we us. The more we mistake the mistake the cyberbodies cyberbodies for ourselves, the for ourselves, the more the machine more the machine twists ourselves into twists ourselves into prostheses the prostheses we are melding we are melding.

melding of human and machine

**Melding: Humanachine**

Poster project on the theme of cyberspace

DESIGNER Margo Johnson

PRINCIPAL TYPEFACES Hybrid digital typefaces

*California Institute of the Arts*
*USA, 1993*

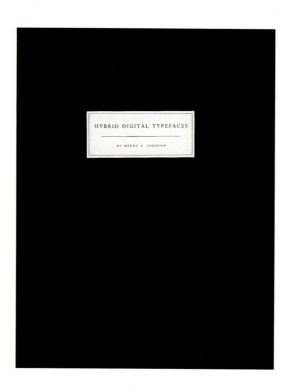

**Type Is Meant To Be Read There Can Be No Deviation From That One Elemental Truth.**

Frankfrank Volume II no.2

Franlin Volume II no.3

## Hybrid Digital Typefaces

Cover and pages from a thesis project book

DESIGNER | Margo Johnson
PRINCIPAL TYPEFACES | Hybrid digital typefaces

*California Institute of the Arts*
*USA, 1993*

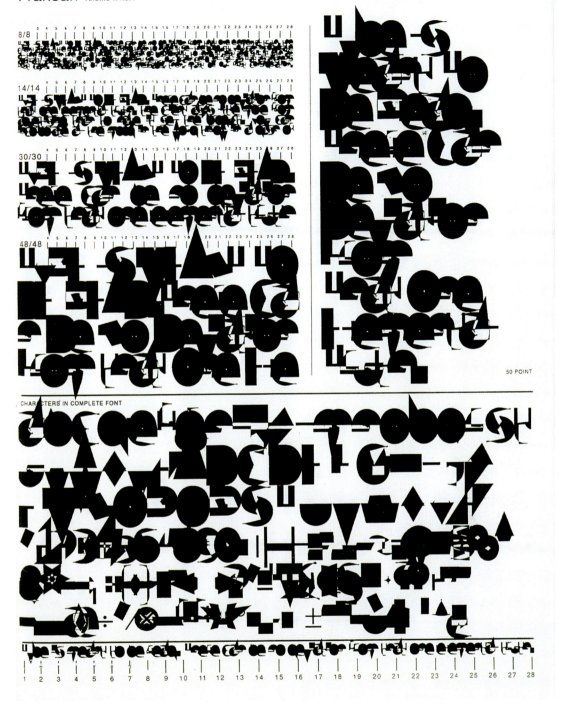

8/8

14/14

30/30

48/48

50 POINT

CHARACTERS IN COMPLETE FONT

1 2 3 4 5 6 7 8 9 10 11 12 13 14 15 16 17 18 19 20 21 22 23 24 25 26 27 28

By applying a numerical matrix to three existing typefaces – Cooper Black, Franklin Gothic, Kuenstler Script – Johnson discovered she could produce random and unexpected letterforms. Three series of 20 new fonts were generated, each named and ordered according to the matrix. A traditional type specimen book, with an introduction and diagrams, showcases the 60 hybrid typefaces and gives the project an air of technological parody.

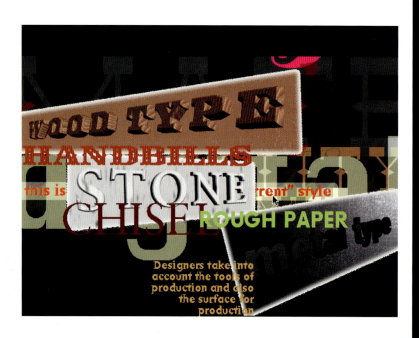

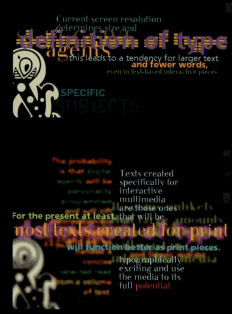

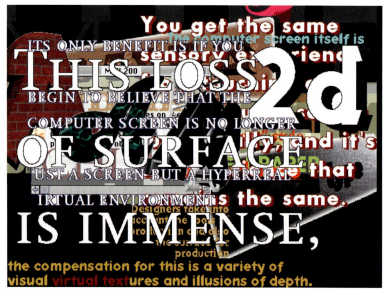

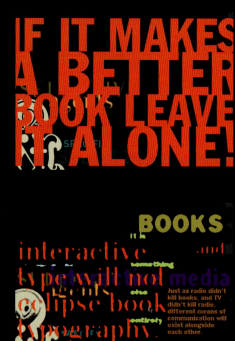

Michael Worthington's thesis, included
on California Institute of the Arts'
25th Anniversary CD-ROM, explores the
possibilities for type in the interactive
medium and asks why it is so often
neglected in design for the screen.
Mostly typographic in content, the
piece offers a fluid illustration of its
own arguments that takes the viewer
on a sound-and-motion journey into
typography's near future.

# "BOOKS

## interactive

.....d

# Digital Luddites

Just as radio didn't
kill books, and TV
didn't kill radio,
different means of
communication will
exist alongside
each other.

fear the book
will be replaced by the

## "push button

## literacy of givens"

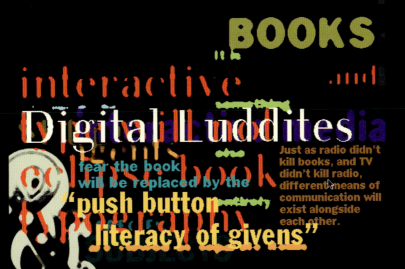

Race, gender and other physical
attributes are irrelevent on the
net, the interface becomes the
only-face and also the only-body.

## where information is
## accepted rather than
## challenged.

Contrary to this is the fact that perhaps
users on the internet are due to
readier to enter into dialogue "techno
anonymity."

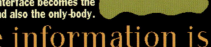

"push button
and debate,

literacy of givens"

**Hypertype**

Screen-based thesis project
*WRITER/DESIGNER* | Michael Worthington

*California Institute of the Arts*
*USA, 1995*

**Andy Altmann** *23, 24, 25, 28, 29, 40, 102, 104, 105*
Born in 1962, Andy Altmann graduated with a BA from St. Martin's School of Art, London in 1985 and received an MA from the Royal College of Art in 1987. He formed Why Not Associates with David Ellis and Howard Greenhalgh immediately after college. The company has worked with a variety of clients from both the private and public sectors, including Next Directory, the Royal Mail, Hull City Council and the Royal Academy.

**Caryn Aono** *176*
Born in Chicago in 1959, Caryn Aono took a Bachelor of Science in graphic design from Illinois State University in 1981. She received an MFA in graphic design from Cranbrook Academy of Art in 1985. Since 1988, she has been art director of California Institute of the Arts' Public Affairs Office and she is also on the faculty of the graphic design programme. Her work has been included in the American Center for Design's 100 Show.

**Chris Ashworth** *64, 65, 76, 77, 138, 139*
Born in Leeds in 1969, Chris Ashworth studied for an HND in graphic design at York College of Arts and Technology, graduating in 1990. In the same year, he set up Orange, which concentrated on youth-related projects. In 1995, he joined Neil Fletcher and Amanda Sissons to form the design team Substance. Clients include MTV and Ray Gun Publishing.

**Phil Baines** *134, 135*
Born in Kendal, Westmorland in 1958, Phil Baines graduated with a BA from St Martin's School of Art, London in 1985 and an MA from the Royal College of Art in 1987. In 1990, he took up a residency at the Crafts Council and, since 1991, he has taught graphic design at Central Saint Martins. His letterpress typography has appeared in several exhibitions, including "British Design: New Traditions" at the Boymans van Beuningen Museum, Rotterdam in 1989.

**Jonathan Barnbrook** *72, 73, 74, 75, 78, 94, 95*
Born in 1966, Jonathan Barnbrook graduated with a BA from Central Saint Martins College of Art & Design, London in 1988 and an MA from the Royal College of Art in 1990. After art school he began working in London as a freelance. He directs typography and live-action commercials through Tony Kaye Films. His typefaces Mason and Exocet are released by Emigre Fonts. In 1996, he launched his own type foundry, Virus.

**Richard Bates** *84*
With partner Allen Hori, Richard Bates is co-principal of the design group Bates Hori. His work has been exhibited internationally in the 1990 touring exhibition "Cranbrook Design: The New Discourse" and at the Design Museum, London and the GGG Gallery, Tokyo. He has received recognition in the *I.D. Annual Design Review* and the American Center for Design's 100 Show.

**Weston Bingham** *200*
Born in 1968, Weston Bingham completed a BFA at the Pratt Institute in Brooklyn. After professional experience with Chermayeff & Geismar in New York, he began graduate studies at California Institute of the Arts.

**Andrew Blauvelt** *150, 151*
Born in 1964, Andrew Blauvelt received a BFA from Herron School of Art and an MFA from Cranbrook Academy of Art. He teaches at North Carolina State University and in 1995 occupied the interim chair of graphic design at Cranbrook. As a designer, he works for cultural and educational clients. In 1990, his work was exhibited in the touring exhibition "Cranbrook Design: the New Discourse" and he has received recognition in the *I.D. Annual Design Review*. He edited the *Visible Language* series "New Perspectives: Critical Histories of Graphic Design" and writes for *Emigre* and *Eye*.

**Frédéric Bortolotti** *120, 121*
Born in 1965, Frédéric Bortolotti studied at the Ecole Nationale des Arts Appliques and the Ecole Nationale des Beaux-Art in Paris. With his design studio vertmiroir, he has worked on projects for the Centre Pompidou, the Institut du Monde Arabe and has created corporate identities for private clients including Cofinoga. Bortolotti is founder of the Bulldozer project and publishes his own work under the name The Red Dozer.

**Anne Burdick** *109, 112, 113, 151*
Born in 1962, Anne Burdick graduated with an MFA from California Institute of the Arts. From 1995-96, she was assistant professor of graphic design at North Carolina State University. As well as teaching and maintaining her own practice, she has written widely about design. In 1995, she guest edited and produced *Emigre* nos. 35 and 36, "Mouthpiece: Clamor over Writing and Design".

**Raul Cabra** *80*
Born in Bogota, Columbia in 1964, Raul Cabra attended the School of Architecture in Caracas, Venezuela. He went on to study graphic design at California College of Arts and Crafts in San Francisco, graduating with a BFA in 1988. Cabra has worked as a senior designer at Tenazas Design in San Francisco on corporate and non-profit communication projects. In 1992, he became co-principal, with Martin Venezky, of the design group Diseño. In 1995, his work was included in the American Center for Design's 100 Show.

**David Carson** *12, 52, 53, 54, 55, 56, 57, 137*
Born in Corpus Christi, Texas, David Carson began his career as an art director/designer at *Transworld Skateboarding* magazine in 1983. He was art director of *Beach Culture* magazine from 1989-91 and art director of *Raygun* from 1992-95. He now divides his time between studios in New York and California. He has worked on commercials for Coca-Cola, Sega and other clients. *The End of Print: The Graphic Design of David Carson* was published in 1995. He is art director of *Speak* magazine.

**Martin Carty** *186, 187*
Born in 1968, Martin Carty completed a BA in graphic design at Central Saint Martins College of Art & Design, London in 1992 and an MA at the Royal College of Art in 1995. He has freelanced for Theatre de Complicite, *i-D* magazine and other clients. He is a partner with Ben Tibbs in the design team Automatic.

**Vivienne Cherry** *184, 185, 203*
Born in Derby in 1970, Vivienne Cherry graduated with a BA in graphic design from Brighton Polytechnic in 1992. A year later, after working as a designer at Mitchell Beazley publishers, she began an MA in graphic design at the Royal College of Art. Since 1995, she has worked as a freelance.

**Scott Clum** *9, 58, 59*
Born in 1964, Scott Clum studied at the Munson Williams Proctor Institute of Fine Art. He has been principal of Ride Design, based in Silverton, Oregon, since 1989. He is design director of *Bikini* magazine and, in 1991, launched his own magazine, *Blur*. His work has been recognised by the American Center for Design's 100 Show and by the Type Directors Club of New York.

**Denise Gonzales Crisp** *112*
Born in 1955, Denise Gonzales Crisp worked professionally for seven years before entering the graduate programme in graphic design at California Institute of the Arts. She has taught typography at Art Center College of Design and Otis College of Art and Design.

**Richard Curren** *20, 21*
Born in San Francisco in 1969, Richard Curren received a BFA from the University of Houston, Texas in 1993. He worked for the Houston Museum of Natural Science, designing computer-animated interactive kiosks. In 1994, he joined Jager Di Paola Kemp Design.

**Zsolt Czakó** *8, 142*
Born in Pécs, Hungary in 1965, Zsolt Czakó studied photography and graphic design at the Hungarian Academy of Applied Arts, Budapest from 1989-93, and undertook postgraduate studies in typography from 1993-94. In 1993, he was a co-founder of the creative workshop ART 'i csók, which undertakes projects for national and international clients. He exhibits regularly and, in 1994, was an organiser and participant in "New Typography", held in Pécs.

**Michael Davies** *62, 63*
Born in 1970, Michael Davies graduated from Kingston University with a BA in graphic design in 1993. Since then, he has worked at Lippa Pearce and as a designer at The Body Shop.

**Barry Deck** *136, 137, 144*
Born in Mount Peasant, Iowa in 1962, Barry Deck graduated with a BFA from Northern Illinois University in 1986 and an MFA from California Institute of the Arts in 1989. He has designed a number of well-known and widely distributed typefaces, including Template Gothic. He has worked for Viacom and Atlantic Records, designing for both print and screen.

**Barbara De Wilde** *46*
Working at Alfred A. Knopf in New York, Barbara De Wilde concentrates on the design of books and literature.

**Mark Diaper** *62, 63*
Born in 1967, Mark Diaper studied at Middlesex Polytechnic, graduating with a BA in graphic design. He has worked at Newell & Sorrell and Lippa Pearce for IBM, Decca, Waterstones and The Terence Higgins Trust.

**Joan Dobkin** *153*
After graduating with a BFA from Rhode Island School of Design and an MFA from the School of the Art Institute of Chicago, Joan Dobkin's main interest lay in painting and drawing. She later began a freelance career in design and completed an MFA at Cranbrook Academy of Art. She is assistant professor of graphic design at Ohio University and also maintains a freelance practice.

**Elliott Peter Earls** *60, 61, 172, 173, 174, 175*
Born in 1965, Elliott Peter Earls studied for an MFA at Cranbrook Academy of Art before gaining professional experience at De Harak and Poulin Associates and Elektra Records in New York. Through his company the Apollo Program, based in Greenwich, Connecticut, he releases typefaces and CD-ROMs. He has worked for Master Card International, Sony Records, the Voyager Company and *Plazm*.

**Birgit Eggers** *63*
Born in 1968, Birgit Eggers was educated at the F. H. Hamburg, graduating in 1993. Since then, she has worked as a freelance, first in London and from 1995 in Amsterdam. Her clients include the publishers Hamlyn.

**David Ellis** *23, 24, 25, 28, 29, 40, 102, 104, 105*
Born in 1962, David Ellis graduated with a BA from St. Martin's School of Art, London in 1985 and received an MA from the Royal College of Art in 1987. He formed Why Not Associates with Andy Altmann and Howard Greenhalgh immediately after college. The company has worked with a variety of clients from both the private and public sectors, including Next Directory, the Royal Mail, Hull City Council and the Royal Academy.

**Stephen Farrell** *96, 179, 180, 181*
Born in 1968, Stephen Farrell gained a Bachelor of Science degree in industrial design from Ohio State University. He is a proponent of visual/verbal integration, which he explores in contributions to the literary and arts journal *Private Arts*. He is a full-time faculty member in the graphic design/digital imaging department of Ray College of Design in Chicago. His fonts are distributed by [T-26].

**Andrea Fella** *176*
Born in 1969, Andrea Fella studied design and twentieth-century culture at the University of Michigan. She worked for the Los Angeles-based firm ReVerb for four years. In 1995, she became associate art director of *I.D.* magazine.

**Edward Fella** 15, 106, 162, 163, 164, 165
Born in Detroit, Michigan in 1938, Edward Fella practised commercial art and design for many years before entering Cranbrook Academy of Art in 1985. Since graduating with an MFA, he has worked for a number of cultural clients and currently teaches on the graphic design programme at California Institute of the Arts.

**Detlef Fiedler** 101, 114, 115, 116, 117
Born in 1955, Detlef Fiedler is a member of the Berlin design group Cyan. The group view themselves as avant-garde in the traditional sense. Designing books, posters and magazines, they have so far worked exclusively for clients in the cultural sector.

**Neil Fletcher** 64, 65, 139
Born in 1969, Neil Fletcher studied graphic design at Hook College of Art and Technology from 1987-89. In 1991, he established Pd-p, working for Sheffield University Union of Students and other clients. In 1995, he joined Chris Ashworth and Amanda Sissons to form the design team Substance. Clients include MTV and Ray Gun Publishing.

**Barbara Glauber** 122, 123, 160, 161
Born in Buffalo, New York in 1962, Barbara Glauber received an MFA from California Institute of the Arts. She teaches at the Cooper Union, New York and is a critic on the graphic design programme at Yale University. She has a New York-based design studio and concentrates on publication design and information graphics for educational and cultural clients. In 1993, she curated the exhibition "Lift and Separate: Graphic Design and the Quote Unquote Vernacular" at the Cooper Union.

**Heike Grebin** 100
Born in Rostock in 1959, Heike Grebin studied architecture at the Hochschule für Architektur und Bauwesen in Weimar and went on to work as an architect for four years. In the late 1980s, she worked as a typographer for a children's book publisher and in 1990 she joined Grappa, the Berlin design group. Grappa are committed to working on low budgets for cultural institutions and many of their clients are based in East Berlin's historic centre.

**April Greiman** 18, 19
Born in 1948, April Greiman graduated with a BFA from Kansas City Art Institute in 1970 and pursued graduate studies at the Design School in Basel from 1970-71. Her Los Angeles-based practice, known for its pioneering use of technology, is involved with interactive and multimedia projects, as well as graphic, motion and environmental design. A former director of the visual communications programme at California Institute of the Arts, she serves as graduate adviser for Art Center College of Design, Pasadena and is an instructor at the Southern California Institute of Architecture. A one-woman exhibition was staged at the Arc en Rêve Centre d'Architecture, Bordeaux, France in 1994 and subsequently toured.

**Julian Harriman-Dickinson** 86
Born in 1972, Julian Harriman-Dickinson studied graphic design, graduating with a BA. He has worked for Lowe Howard-Spink as a designer/typographer. He won a D&AD gold award while still a student.

**Daniela Haufe** 101, 114, 115, 116, 117
Born in 1966, Daniela Haufe is a member of the Berlin design group Cyan. The group view themselves as avant-garde in the traditional sense. Designing books, posters and magazines, they have so far worked exclusively for clients in the cultural sector.

**Andrew Henderson** 26, 27
Born in New York in 1967, Andrew Henderson graduated from Minneapolis College of Art and Design in 1995. He assisted Jan Jancourt on the redesign of the Utne Reader and is the magazine's associate art director.

**Allen Hori** 33, 177
With partner Richard Bates, Allen Hori is co-principal of the design group Bates Hori. His work has been exhibited internationally in the 1990 touring exhibition "Cranbrook Design: The New Discourse" and at the Design Museum, London and the GGG Gallery, Tokyo. He has received recognition in the I.D. Annual Design Review and the American Center for Design's 100 Show.

**Karl Hyde** 140, 141
Born in England in 1957, Karl Hyde graduated from art school with a BA in sculpture, installation and video. In 1980, he formed the rock group Freur with John Warwicker and Richard Smith. With Smith and Darren Emerson, he launched Underworld. He is a member of the design collective Tomato.

**Jan Jancourt** 26, 27, 150
Born in Minnesota in 1957, Jan Jancourt studied for a Bachelor of Science in design at Bemidji State Univeristy from 1977-81. He completed an MFA at Cranbrook Academy of Art in 1985. He was an intern at Studio Dumbar and, since 1986, has been associate professor at Minneapolis College of Art and Design, while pursuing a freelance career with projects for the Walker Art Center and other clients. His work was exhibited in "Holland in Form: Dutch Design 1945-87" at the Stedelijk Museum and in the 1990 touring exhibition, "Cranbrook Design: The New Discourse".

**Damian Jaques** 124, 125
Born in 1965, Damian Jaques completed a BA in fine art at Portsmouth Polytechnic in 1988, and an MA in print-making at Wimbledon School of Art in 1991.

**Alicia Johnson** 53
Born in 1960, Alicia Johnson studied at Hutchins School, a liberal arts programme at the UC Sonoma. She is president and co-director of Johnson & Wolverton, based in Portland, Oregon. The company's clients include Amnesty International, The Democratic National Committee, the AVIA Group International and Ray Gun Publishing.

**Andrew Johnson** 89, 103
Born in Essex in 1968, Andrew Johnson was educated at Brighton Polytechnic, graduating with a BA in 1990, and at the Royal College of Art, graduating with an MA in 1992. As a freelance, his clients have included the Institute of Contemporary Arts, the London Ecology Centre and RTZ Corporation. He has collaborated with Nick Oates on theatre publicity material. In 1995, he became art director of Blueprint magazine.

**Margo Johnson** 108, 188, 215, 216, 217
Born in Toledo, Ohio in 1964, Margo Johnson followed a BFA from the University of Michigan with an MFA at California Institute of the Arts. Since graduating in 1993, she has worked in Los Angeles in a variety of media for clients in the music industry and television. She teaches design and typography at Otis College of Art and Design. Her Hybrid Digital Typefaces project was included in the American Center for Design's 100 Show.

**Jason Kedgley** 49
Born in 1969, Jason Kedgley gained a BA in graphic design from the London College of Printing and an MA from Central Saint Martins College of Art & Design. He is a member of the design collective Tomato.

**Jeffery Keedy** 108, 122, 183, 188, 189
Born in Battle Creek, Michigan in 1957, Jeffery Keedy gained a BFA in graphic design and photography at Western Michigan University in 1981. After a period of professional experience in Boston and Honolulu, he studied for an MFA at Cranbrook Academy of Art, graduating in 1985. He moved to Los Angeles to teach at California Institute of the Arts and was director of its graphic design programme from 1991-95. A polemical post-modernist in his writings, he is a regular contributor to design publications such as Emigre and Eye. In 1991, his typeface Keedy Sans was released by Emigre Fonts. In 1996, he launched a number of new faces through his type foundry, Cipher.

**Chip Kidd** 47
Born in 1964, Chip Kidd was educated at Pennsylvania State University, graduating with a BA in graphic design in 1986. Since then, he has worked as a book jacket designer at Alfred A. Knopf in New York. His designs have been included in the American Center for Design's 100 Show for five years running. In addition to coverage in the design press, his work has been featured in Time magazine and The New York Times.

**Somi Kim** 66, 67, 156, 157, 160, 161, 176
Born in 1962, Somi Kim gained a BA from Harvard University in 1984 and an MFA from California Institute of the Arts in 1989. In 1990, she was a founding partner of ReVerb, a Los Angeles-based design firm whose clients range from grass-roots community centres to corporations, museums and foundations. She is a graduate adviser for Art Center College of Design, Pasadena and a visiting lecturer at Cranbrook Academy of Art and other schools.

**Doug Kisor** 154, 155
Born in Mason, Michigan in 1949, Doug Kisor has been working in design education since he completed an MFA in graphic design at Michigan University in 1984. He is director of the graphic design studies programme at Eastern Michigan University. His work has been included in the AIGA Annual and the American Center for Design's 100 Show. He is working with the Graphic Design Education Association to develop international exchange programmes and has co-developed the Rotterdam-based de Program, which hosts a group of international participants, who work with leading practitioners, theorists and educators.

**Jacques Koeweiden** 128, 129
Born in 1957, Jacques Koeweiden studied at the Royal Academy of Art and Design in Den Bosch from 1978-83. In 1985, he became art director of Vinyl magazine and in 1986 he formed Koeweiden Postma with Paul Postma. The company works for international corporate and cultural clients, including Chiat/Day, Glaxo, the Hogeschule of Amsterdam, the Royal Dutch PTT, UNICEF and Nike. They received a gold award in the 1993 Typography International Awards and were featured in the "Dutch Design" exhibition at the Design Museum, London in 1991.

**Susan Lally** 126
After completing a BFA in painting at the University of Illinois in 1983, Susan Lally went on to graduate studies in graphic design at Cranbrook Academy of Art. She has worked as a freelance designer with various design groups in Chicago and designs for a variety of media with Zun Design. Her work was included in the 1990 touring exhibition "Cranbrook Design: the New Discourse" and she has received recognition in the American Center for Design's 100 Show and How magazine's International Annual of Design.

**Susan LaPorte** 92, 169
Born in 1965, Susan LaPorte received a BFA from the University of Illinois, Chicago and an MFA from California Institute of the Arts. In the early 1990s, she worked as an intern at CalArts and the Walker Art Center. Since 1993, she has been assistant professor of graphic design at Eastern Michigan University. Her typefaces were used in the first five issues of Raygun and have also appeared in Emigre. She was included in the American Center for Design's 100 Show in 1993 and 1995.

**George LaRou** 123, 169, 170, 171
Born in Maine, George LaRou received an MFA from California Institute of the Arts in 1990. He taught for four years at Eastern Michigan University and is an associate professor at Maine College of Art. His work has been featured in the American Center for Design's 100 Show in 1994 and 1995, and in the exhibition "Lift and Separate" at the Cooper Union, New York in 1993.

**Dominic Lippa** *62*

Born in 1962, Dominic Lippa studied graphic design at London College of Printing from 1981-84. He worked at Smith & Milton, Michael Thierens and Newell & Sorrell, before setting up Lippa Pearce Design with Harry Pearce and Giles Calver in 1990. He was art director of *Baseline* for five years. Clients include the Royal Mail, Boots the Chemist and Waitrose. He is on the executive committee of London's Typographic Circle and has judged the RSA Student Awards for three years.

**Deborah Littlejohn** *209, 210, 211*

Born in Raleigh, North Carolina in 1966, Deborah Littlejohn graduated with a BFA in design from Western Carolina University in 1992. She completed an MFA at California Institute of the Arts in 1994. She has worked for ReVerb in Los Angeles and led an Internet workshop at CalArts. She is a designer in the Walker Art Center's design department.

**Whitney Lowe** *66, 67, 156, 157, 176*

Born in 1958, Whitney Lowe was educated at California Polytechnic State University and Art Center College of Design, Pasadena, graduating in 1982. He worked for Knoll International and Anthon Beeke's studio in Amsterdam before, in 1990, becoming a founding partner of ReVerb, a Los Angeles-based design firm whose clients range from grass-roots community centres to corporations, museums and foundations.

**Kevin Lyons** *212*

Born in 1969, Kevin Lyons graduated from Rhode Island School of Design with a BFA in film in 1988. He recently completed an MFA at California Institute of the Arts.

**Seònaid MacKay** *184, 185*

Born in 1970, Seònaid MacKay studied graphic design at Glasgow School of Art, graduating with a BA in 1993, and at the Royal College of Art, graduating with an MA in 1995. She is a designer/film-maker and has exhibited at the Edinburgh Film Festival and Cherbourgh Film Festival. She works for Simple Productions, a graphic and moving-image production company.

**P. Scott Makela** *30, 31, 32, 78, 79, 97, 145*

Born in St. Paul, Minnesota in 1960, P. Scott Makela took a degree in political science before completing a BFA in visual communication at Minneapolis College of Art and Design in 1984. From 1989-91, he studied for an MFA in graphic design at Cranbrook Academy of Art. His first business venture was Makela + Knickelbine Design in Los Angeles. Words and Pictures for Business and Culture, his current venture, is a "multi-aspect" company dealing with advanced design technologies. Clients include Warner Brothers Records, Nike and PBS. He worked as a consultant on the 1990 touring exhibition "Cranbrook Design: The New Discourse". In 1996, he was appointed joint chair (with Laurie Haycock Makela) of the graphic design programme at Cranbrook Academy of Art.

**Geoff McFetridge** *7, 212*

Born in 1971, Geoff McFetridge worked as a freelance designer for snowboard and skateboard companies between studies at Alberta College of Art in Calgary, Canada and California Institute of the Arts. He completed his MFA in 1995.

**Shawn McKinney** *189, 211*

Born in 1960, Shawn McKinney majored in liberal arts/English at Tulane University, graduating with a BA in 1982. He started at the Texan design firm of Fuller, Dyal and Stamper as a copywriter, leaving four years later as a senior level graphic designer. He completed an MFA in graphic design at California Institute of the Arts in 1992. In 1995, he became a lecturer in computer graphic design at Wanganui Regional Community Polytechnic in New Zealand.

**Jeremy Francis Mende** *192, 193, 201*

After gaining a first degree in psychology at UCLA in 1991, Jeremy Francis Mende worked as an art director on various magazines. In 1995, he completed an MFA in graphic design at Cranbrook Academy of Art. He was an intern at Studio Dumbar in 1994.

**Rebeca Méndez** *152, 158, 159*

Born in 1962, Rebeca Méndez graduated from Art Center College of Design, Pasadena in 1984. She worked for several design firms in Los Angeles before rejoining the college as its designer in 1989. She is now its design director, a post that involves both teaching and practice. She was awarded designer of the year in both 1991 and 1992 by The Council for the Advancement and Support of Education and her work has appeared in the American Center for Design's 100 Show and the *I.D.*'s *Annual Design Review*. Her designs are included in the permanent collections of the Library of Congress, the Cooper-Hewitt, National Design Museum and the Getty Center.

**Jennifer Moody** *98*

Born in 1965, Jennifer Moody graduated from Western Michigan University with a BFA and went on to complete an MFA at California Institute of the Arts in 1993. She worked in Chicago as a designer at Cagney & McDowell and ABC-TV. In 1993, she took a position in CalArts' Office of Public Affairs. Her work has been selected for the American Center for Design's 100 Show. She is a partner with Gail Swanlund in the Los Angeles design firm Nice.

**James Moore** *66, 67*

Born in 1971, James Moore graduated from California Institute of the Arts with a BFA in 1993. He works as a designer at the Los Angeles-based design firm ReVerb.

**Patrick Morrissey** *24, 25, 28, 29, 104, 105*

Born in 1972, Patrick Morrissey studied graphic design at the London College of Printing, graduating with a BA in 1994. He freelances for Why Not Associates in London.

**Roelof Mulder** *132, 133*

After studying fine art at the Arnhem Institute for the Arts, Roelof Mulder founded a gallery, released an artist's book, *Speed is what we need*, and exhibited paintings and sculptures internationally. He became involved in interior and fashion design in the early 1990s and began to work full time as a graphic designer in 1992. His clients include the Dutch Red Cross and the Stedelijk Museum, Amsterdam. He won the Rotterdam Design Prize in 1993. Since 1994, he has taught graphic design at the Arnhem Institute and, in 1995, he became an editor and designer of the Dutch architectural quarterly *Forum*.

**Robert Nakata** *10, 41, 42, 43, 44, 45*

Born in Toronto in 1960, Robert Nakata attended the Ontario College of Art from 1979-83. After working as a designer in Canada for two years, he completed an MFA at Cranbrook Academy of Art in 1985. He has worked for design firms in the United States and the Netherlands, including McCoy & McCoy in Michigan and Studio Dumbar in the Hague. He is now with Wieden & Kennedy in Amsterdam. His work was included in the 1990 touring show "Cranbrook Design: The New Discourse" and more recently in "Displaced Voices", a two-person show with Allen Hori at DDD Gallery, Osaka, Japan.

**Lisa Nugent** *66, 67, 143, 156, 157*

Born in 1955, Lisa Nugent was educated at California State University, Long Beach and California Institute of the Arts, graduating with an MFA in 1988. In 1990, she was a founding partner of ReVerb, a Los Angeles-based design firm whose clients range from grass-roots community centres to corporations, museums and foundations. From 1990-94, she taught experimental design and computer typography at Otis College of Art and Design. In 1993, she was a juror for the Type Directors Club of New York awards.

**Nick Oates** *89*

Born in 1968, Nick Oates was educated at Central Saint Martins College of Art & Design, London, graduating with a BA in 1990, and at the Royal College of Art, graduating with an MA in 1992. As a student, he was an intern at Hard Werken Design in the Netherlands. He has worked as a freelance designer in London for Diesel Jeans, Paul Smith and other clients and has collaborated with Andrew Johnson on theatre publicity material.

**Susan Parr** *176*

Born in 1959, Susan Parr was educated at Pacific NW College of Art and Parsons School of Design, graduating with a BFA in 1986. For four years she had her own graphic design studio. In 1990, she was a founding partner of ReVerb, a Los Angeles-based design firm whose clients range from grass-roots community centres to corporations, museums and foundations.

**John Plunkett** *15, 16, 34, 35, 36, 37*

After graduating with a degree in communication design from California Institute of the Arts in 1977, John Plunkett worked with Colin Forbes and Dan Friedman at Pentagram in New York. With partner Barbara Kuhr, he is responsible for the look and feel of both *Wired* magazine and *HotWired*, the first Web-based publication on the Internet. Plunkett + Kuhr's design office is based in Park City, Utah and clients include Carnegie Hall Museum and the Sundance Film Festival. In 1995, *Wired* won the National Magazine Award for design from the American Society of Magazine Editors.

**Paul Postma** *128, 129*

Born in 1958, Paul Postma studied at the Royal Academy of Art and Design in Den Bosch from 1979-84. He worked at Samenwerkende Ontwerpers in Amsterdam and went on to become art director of *Vinyl* magazine from 1985-86. In 1986, he formed Koeweiden Postma with Jacques Koeweiden. The company works for international corporate and cultural clients, including Chiat/Day, Glaxo, the Hogeschule of Amsterdam, the Royal Dutch PTT, UNICEF and Nike. They received a gold award in the 1993 Typography International Awards and were featured in the "Dutch Design" exhibition at the Design Museum, London in 1991.

**Chris Priest** *40*

Born in 1967, Chris Priest graduated from Central Saint Martins College of Art & Design, London with a BA in graphic design in 1989. He worked for Why Not Associates for several years and, in 1995, teamed up with Jo Wright to form the London-based Studio Barbara.

**Pam Racs** *82*

Born in 1964, Pam Racs was educated in graphic design at Art Center College of Design, Pasadena. Since 1994, she has been a designer at Johnson & Wolverton.

**Paul Sahre** *88, 93*

Born in 1964, Paul Sahre was educated at Kent State University, where he completed a BFA in 1987 and an MFA in 1990. From 1992-93, he worked as senior designer at Rutka Weadock, and he is now creative director of GKV Design. He maintains a freelance practice, offering his services free to the non-profit Fells Point Corner Theatre. His work was been recognised by the American Center for Design's 100 Show.

**Katie Salen** *118, 119*

Born in 1967, Katie Salen was educated at the University of Texas at Austin, graduating with a BFA, and at Rhode Island School of Design, graduating with an MFA in graphic design. She was assistant professor of design at the Virginia Commonwealth University and, from 1995, assistant professor in the department of art and art history at the University of Texas. She maintains a freelance practice, designing mainly for non-profit clients. Since 1993, she has been editor and designer of the design journal *Zed*. Her work has been recognised by the American Center for Design's 100 Show.